Functionalism and Indian English Fiction

From Cradle to Grave

Sunitha Srinivas. C.

ATLANTIC
PUBLISHERS & DISTRIBUTORS (P) LTD

Published by
ATLANTIC
PUBLISHERS & DISTRIBUTORS (P) LTD
7/22, Ansari Road, Darya Ganj,
New Delhi-110002
Phones : +91-11-40775252, 23273880, 23275880, 23280451
Fax : +91-11-23285873
Web : www.atlanticbooks.com
E-mail : orders@atlanticbooks.com

Branch Office
5, Nallathambi Street, Wallajah Road,
Chennai-600002
Phones : +91-44-64611085, 32413319
E-mail : chennai@atlanticbooks.com

ISBN 978-81-269-1412-8

Printed in India at Nice Printing Press, A-33/3A, Site-IV, Industrial Area, Sahibabad, Ghaziabad, U.P.

Acknowledgements

I express my immense gratitude to Dr. N. Ramachandran Nair, Professor and Head (Retd.), Department of English, University of Calicut, for his invaluable guidance. My thanks are due to the late Dr. R. Vishwanathan, Professor (Retd.), Department of English, University of Calicut, Mr. Gregory, Department of Anthropology, Kannur University, Palayad, Dr. M.N. Karassery, Department of Malayalam, University of Calicut, and Dr. P. Narayanan, Department of Sanskrit, University of Calicut, for their valuable help and suggestions.

I also wish to put on record my sense of deep gratitude to my parents who have been of help, in one way or the other, in the completion of this book.

Sunitha Srinivas. C.

Preface

Man has created a world of unseen entities and forces analogous to the world perceived by the human senses. Various rituals, ceremonies, and offerings are carried out to placate or thank these superior powers in whose existence human beings believe. These rites and rituals sometimes help to provide meaning and explanation to meaningless and inexplicable phenomena. They play an important role in human life, sociologically as well as psychologically. Being born and brought up in a particular social group, one is recognized as a part of that particular group or community and becomes an integral part of its accepted framework. The social groups have their rituals and ceremonies which contribute towards group cohesion. Rituals act as a bond which holds the multitude together and if the bond is effaced, these multitudes fall into confusion. Apart from allaying fear in the human mind, rituals are also a means of imposing order. They reveal the human desire for order. Psychologically, these rites give confidence in the face of uncertainties, difficulties, and the real and imaginary dangers with which man is surrounded. Most rituals have myths associated with them, thus enabling one to have a better understanding of the ritual performed.

From time immemorial, myths, legends, and religious practices have shaped the Indian mind and imagination. The powerful hold of traditional values, rituals, and attitudes on the psyche of the people of India cannot be overlooked. One finds an infinite variety of religious beliefs and practices in the country. Despite the developments in science, and the tendency towards the dissolution of the old values and their replacement with new ones, rituals and ceremonies find relevance in the modern world. Literature reflects the society in which it originates and cannot be divorced from it. Indicating this reciprocity are the depictions in Indian English fiction. Religious rituals and ceremonies which are an integral part of Indian life and society find expression in creative works as well. Indian English novelists present characters and situations rooted in the Indian ethos. They adopt different ways to present the Indian customs, rituals, and practices. The rituals serve different functions—sociological, psychological, literary, political—in the creative works in which they are portrayed. This book brings out the functional significance of rituals and ceremonies associated with the different phases of human life, in some of the works of Indian English fiction. U.R. Anantha Murthy's *Samskara*, Kamala Markandaya's *Nectar in a Sieve* and *Two Virgins*, Kavery Nambisan's *Scent of Pepper*, Vaikom Muhammad Basheer's *Childhood Friend*, and Manohar Malgonkar's *Princes* and *A Bend in the Ganges* show the functional import of the rites in the first phase of human life. Works like *The Scent of Pepper* by Kavery Nambisan, *Nectar in a Sieve* and *A Handful of Rice* by Kamala Markandaya, *Gauri* by Mulk Raj Anand, *Cry, the Peacock* and *Fasting, Feasting* by Anita Desai, *The Bachelor of Arts*, *The Painter of Signs*, *Grandmother's Tale*, and *The Vendor of Sweets* by R.K. Narayan, and *The Princes* by Manohar Malgonkar reveal the functionalism at play in marriage and its accompanying customs and ceremonies. The functional importance of the funeral rites, which mark the final phase of human life, is seen in R.K. Narayan's *English Teacher* and *Waiting for the Mahatma*, Kamala Markandaya's *Nowhere Man* and *Coffer Dams*, Kavery Nambisan's *Scent of Pepper*, Rohinton Mistry's *Such a Long Journey*, Arundhati Roy's *The God of Small Things*, U.R. Anantha Murthy's *Samskara*, and Mulk Raj Anand's *Lament on the Death of a Master of Arts*. The significance of festivals and the ceremonies related to them are observable in works like *Samskara*, *The Scent of Pepper*, *A Handful of Rice, Nectar in a Sieve*, *Kanthapura*, *The Dark Room*, *The Guide*, and *The Man-Eater of Malgudi*.

A detailed analysis of some of the literary works in Indian English fiction will help to understand the various functions that the rites and rituals depicted in them perform. An effort has been made here to present in book form this study which will be of use to the students and teachers of Indian English fiction besides the upcoming scholars focusing on this area. It attempts to bring out the functional—social, psychological, and literary—importance of the rituals in some of the works of Indian English fiction. It tries to explore the role of rituals and ceremonies in social life as well as the functioning of human personality. The endeavour has been carried out to assist a better understanding of the part played by religion in shaping the life and culture of India.

Sunitha Srinivas. C.

Contents

Introduction

The Indian novel in English has shown a capacity to accommodate a wide range of concerns. The social, religious, and political life of the Indian masses finds expression in literary works. The customs, rituals, and ceremonies associated with different religious, cultural, and ethnic groups, so characteristic of Indian society, have been effectively portrayed by many creative writers. They give the reader a picturesque glimpse of the rituals and practices followed by man. The diverse rituals play a significant role in Indian life and culture. They also form an essential part of the literary works in which they find a place. This book attempts to make a detailed study of the functional importance of the customs and rituals found in some of the works in Indian English fiction.

The Indian creative writer draws his material from the situations of the Indian environment and Indian reality. The Indian myths, legends, and the religious and cultural heritage have shaped the mind and imagination of the people in the country. This influence is so deeply engraved that it finds unconscious expression in literary works. The analysis undertaken here not only focuses on the rites and rituals which are common to different religious communities but also those which do not find a parallel anywhere. One is also able to trace the gradual process by which certain practices are given up in favour of others, or have been modified with the passage of time. While some novelists concentrate on the common rituals and practices, others focus on those which are unknown to many, unique to a particular religion, place, or group of people. The socio-cultural and socio-political relevance of rituals is also traceable in literary works. Rituals form a part of the life and culture of the social groups in Indian society. Their sociological and psychological relevance is stressed by most anthropologists. This book throws light on some of the rituals which mark the transition in human life from one phase to another, and highlights their significance in the works in which they appear. The rituals associated with the different stages of human life (like the birth rites, initiation rites, marriage rites, and death rites) as well as the ceremonies related to festivals contribute towards strengthening social bonds, and thus towards social solidarity. Divided into six chapters, it brings forth the function of rituals in human life and literature.

The introductory chapter focuses on functionalism and fiction. Birth rites and initiation rites mark the early stage of an individual's life. The rites vary in their degree of elaborateness from one culture to another. As the group loses some members through death, it acquires new members by birth, and their initiation into the status of men and women. It thus ensures the continuity of possession by the society. The second chapter analyses Kavery Nambisan's *Scent of Pepper*, Kamala Markandaya's *Nectar in a Sieve* and *Two Virgins*, U.R. Anantha Murthy's *Samskara*, Vaikom Muhammad Basheer's *Childhood Friend*, and Manohar Malgonkar's *Princes* and *A Bend in the Ganges*. Ceremonies associated with marriage too hold a significant place in human life. Marriage involves a readjustment of the social structure whereby the woman's relationship with her family is greatly modified. The analysis deals with some of the customs and practices which have become a part of marriages in India. Some of the customs related to widowhood are also depicted in Indian English fiction. Works studied in the third chapter are R.K. Narayan's *Bachelor of Arts*, *Grandmother's Tale*, *Vendor of Sweets*, and *Painter of Signs*, Mulk Raj Anand's *Gauri*, Kamala Markandaya's *Nectar in a Sieve* and *A Handful of Rice*, Anita Desai's *Cry, the Peacock* and *Fasting, Feasting*, Manohar Malgonkar's *Princes*, and Kavery Nambisan's *Scent of Pepper*. The remarkable variation in customs with regard to death is found in many creative works. The different mourning practices announce the death which has taken place. The rites ensure the deceased his rightful position in the world of the dead, and ease the human mind's fear of the dead spirit wreaking havoc if not attended to properly. Besides enabling a proper disposal of the dead body, the rites also make smooth the changes caused by the death. Works like *Lament on the Death of a Master of Arts* (Mulk Raj Anand), *The English Teacher*, *Waiting for the Mahatma* (R.K. Narayan), *The Coffer Dams*, *The Nowhere Man* (Kamala Markandaya), *Samskara* (U.R. Anantha Murthy), *The Scent of Pepper* (Kavery Nambisan), *Such a Long Journey* (Rohinton Mistry), and *The God of Small Things* (Arundhati Roy) contain references to these rites (chapter four). The various festivals observed in the country reflect the inherent feelings of a nation with a long cherished historical and rich cultural background. The festivals give order to human life. The book also deals with some of the festivals and ceremonies found in India. Literary works acquaint one with the festivals celebrated among different social groups. The fifth chapter tries to trace their importance in R.K. Narayan's *Dark Room*, *Guide*, and *Man-Eater of Malgudi*, Raja Rao's *Kanthapura*, Kamala Markandaya's *A Handful of Rice* and *Nectar in a Sieve*, Kavery Nambisan's *Scent of Pepper*, and U.R. Anantha Murthy's *Samskara*. Numerous forces of nature are worshipped by those who believe in the power of these forces and their influence on the people. Festivals cover such operations as ploughing, sowing, and harvesting; like the *rites de passage* at critical junctures in the life of the individual from cradle to grave, is the seasonal drama at seed-time and harvest. Seasonal rites follow the general ritual pattern which aims at securing the well-being of the community as well as the individual. Myths help when rites and ceremonies demand justification. They are at times adapted by creative writers to suit contemporary life and society. The psychological validity of myths is relevant even when viewed against the contemporary background.

The hold of rites and rituals on the Indian psyche is seen in most of the novels in Indian English. The linguistic means adopted by the novelists to convey a life filled with customs and practices vary. The creative writer in Indian English fiction adopts different methods to convey the Indian sensibility.

Most of these works lay bare the Indian life and society. A sparing use of native words, language registers, etc. often help to create the local ambience. The sociological, psychological, literary, as well as political significance of the rituals and ceremonies in human life and literature is seen here. The study makes known their relevance in the country's life and literature. It enables one to have a feel of the various rituals and ceremonies prevalent in Indian society from times immemorial. A portrayal of Indian life in Indian English fiction will be complete only with a reference to the rites and rituals practised by the people in the country.

This work will be of use to postgraduates, research scholars, and can be used as reference material by students of literature.

Sunitha Srinivas. C.

1

Functionalism and Fiction

Religion has been a source of peace, harmony, and acrimony all over the world. Everywhere human imagination is tied up with certain customs, rituals and practices which it finds difficult to evade. In all ages, men have hoped that by proper performance of religious observances they would obtain some specific benefit. It has as its basis the belief that these practices ensure health, long life, material well-being, growth of crops and the like. Despite the universal character of the rituals, there are differences which mark them off from each other. While many of the beliefs share a common ground, there are others that possess certain traits which make them different and unique. These traits serve to enhance their meaning and purpose.

Multifarious beliefs and modes of worship prevail in India. Some of these beliefs and practices have an indeterminate origin. In spite of being a multi-religious nation, different religious groups in the country live together and follow their rituals and ceremonies. The earliest objects of worship were the forces of Nature, and religion was in essence polytheistic. Later on came the personified gods like Brahma, Vishnu, and Shiva. While the polytheistic nature remained unchanged, people came to believe in a single God, and considered the various personified gods, goddesses, and animistic objects of worship as incarnations of this single God (the Supreme Power). In due course, many reforms were made and protests held against ritualism and orthodoxy. Primitive features of religion were gradually rejected in favour of more refined ones. Assimilation, acculturation, and amalgamation have accompanied the growth of most of the religions in the country. The people of a particular religious community sometimes follow practices which have their origin in other religion or religious groups. The Hindus in the country adhere to many practices which originate from other religions. The *mehndi* ceremony (painting of the hands and feet with henna) held during Muslim marriages is an instance. This festive occasion of Muslim origin, signifying the strength of love between a couple, is now prevalent among other religious groups too. Most of the religions in India have imbibed many beliefs and practices from the religions it came into contact with. Though some of these rituals are now on the wane, most of the religions in the country have tried to incorporate within themselves the alien forms of worship they have come into contact with.

Religious rites are rules prescribing the way men should conduct themselves in relationship to sacred objects. They form an important part of religion. These rites and rituals help to objectify the human feeling of devotion to a higher power. Some tend to relegate it to the obscure world of superstition, disregarding its communicative nature. Rituals are not mere repetitive acts. The term does not refer to something performed just for preserving a custom without anyone knowing why. They have inherent meanings which serve to enhance their significance. In the hands of hypocrites, these rites and rituals are reduced to a mere show of devotion.

The various rituals are performed to please and placate the powers (in whose effectiveness people believe) above man. It thus becomes sacred to its practitioners. A ritual is sacred even if the participants do not carry it out with full reverence. There are simple rituals that take less than a minute to perform as well as more elaborate ones that take several days or more for performance. Rituals mark the basic and irreversible turning points in human life like birth, growing to maturity, marriage, and eventually death. Rituals of birth and naming, rituals marking the attainment of adulthood, weddings, funerals, and festivals are found in every part of the world. Anthropologists have found rites and rituals even in societies which do not possess an institutionalized religion. Rituals often convey a sense of continuity and changelessness. They are sometimes misused by those motivated by avarice and are misunderstood by the naive. According to circumstances, one and the same rite may serve two different functions. Arnold van Gennep points this out when he says, "The same rite, remaining absolutely the same, can change its meaning depending on the position it is given in a ceremony or on whether it is part of one ceremony or another" (Staal 128).

Religious symbols are also indexes of human emotion. They objectify the abstract, and give access to emotional states that resist expression in language. Rituals evoke the emotional responses of fear, joy, hate etc. Hence one has to take into account the process of emotional evocation too. Rituals are ambiguous in their function and meaning. The meaning of a particular gesture in a rite may derive from its position in the sequence or from the context in which the rite takes place. Man often obeys rituals slavishly. This may be due to the fear of public opinion and supernatural punishment, or through a pervading group sentiment. The reason for performing a specific ritual or ceremony is usually the desire for a particular fruit or effect. While certain rites are obligatory, some others are optional. Rituals effect a transition from the realm of the profane to that of the sacred.

Anthropologists have put forward various approaches to the study of religion. Rituals and ceremonies which is a part of religion also come under their purview. Anthropologists like Emile Durkheim, Malinowsky, and Radcliffe-Brown have stressed the functional and psychological importance of religion. They have long perceived that people's religious beliefs and their social organizations are closely interrelated—that religious beliefs validate and regulate social relations. According to them religious rites help to reinforce collective sentiments and bring about social integration. Religion is considered a social phenomenon, necessary for the maintenance of the social order. Rituals which are the handmaid of religion help to express and impress those sentiments of group adherence on which the orderly life of the social organism depends for its survival. These are the customary ways of thinking and acting to which each individual member of the society feels compelled to conform. Anthropologists consider these rites and rituals as essential to the subsistence of society. They all agree in characterizing rituals as a social entity that is functional in the sense that it contributes to the sustenance of social stability and equilibrium.

Literary works reflect the society and the people from which it originates. Indian English fiction is no exception to this. The novelist's subject being man-in-society, the subject matter must also consist of those customs, beliefs, and practices which are a part of man's life. Creative writers voice their protest against orthodoxy and conservatism through the literary media. They try to expose the hypocrisy, and pretensions of an orthodox, tradition-bound society and its members. Novelists like R.K. Narayan adopt an ironic tone to depict these hypocrites who profess to be religious minded. Rituals and ceremonies are found in literary works like *Samskara* (U.R. Anantha Murthy), *The Scent of Pepper* (Kavery Nambisan), and *The God of Small Things* (Arundhati Roy). Narratives like *Kanthapura* (Raja Rao) stress the importance of festivals and ceremonies in bringing the people together. These works highlight the functional import of rites and rituals in Indian English fiction.

According to the functionalist approach, the present functioning and meaning of things do not necessarily have much to do with their origin. Their contemporary meaning and significance may thus have little to do with the shape and form which link them, however remotely, with the past. Every custom or institution, however strange or bizarre, serves some purpose to the anthropologists who support the functionalist's view. Hence, often exotic rituals that made no sense, except as echoes of past glories, fell into their natural place as part of the actual life. The rituals and practices are not aimless eccentricities, but function logically and coherently. Rituals are religious practices that attempt to gain access to the supernatural. The term is also applied to any form of repeated, formalized human activity. Anthropologists point out that societies require collective observances to create unity and consensus. Recognizing the stunning power of rites, religious and political authorities strive to create, manipulate and regulate them. Since there exists the critical distinction between the profane and the sacred, rituals can be said to function as rules of conduct that guide the behaviour of men and women in the presence of the sacred. They provide a powerful way in which the social order is unified.

Each society has its own customs and practices which are felt as binding by its members. The priest officiates on behalf of the whole group. The public rites and collective concerns may also dramatize private psychological conflicts. If rituals were simply public performances that were no longer meaningful in terms of individual psychic experience, they would not have continued to exist. Anthropologists have traced a variety of reasons, like the desire for salvation, immortality, and social order, for human adherence to rituals and practices. Rituals are central to the religious process. They are considered the symbolic representation of what people believe. The various rites and rituals give expression to certain human sentiments and thus serve to keep these sentiments alive. This in turn by their influence on the individual makes possible an orderly social life. The functionalists emphasize the social function of rituals. Rituals are regarded as an expression of the unity of the society and their function is to maintain the social order by reaffirming and strengthening the sentiments on which the social solidarity and therefore the social order itself depend. Durkheim points out this close relation between society and religion. According to him religion reflects the social order. Those who perform collective public rituals do so because they share certain highly valued interests. The absence of a person in the proceedings of a ritual is significant, for it represents a gesture of disrespect—an indication that the missing guest is outside the bounds of current togetherness. Hence people often choose the most widely publicized rituals to stage dramatic walk outs. Hatred or malice in the participants automatically nullifies the mystical efficacy of their ritual communion. Direct acts of physical aggression committed in a sacred context are considered all the more scandalous. Anthropologists see the principal function of communal rituals to be the expression or reaffirmation of sentiments of collective loyalty. People assemble to show and reinforce their existing sense of identity and cohesion. They come together to perform solemn rites at the tombs of their ancestors, for it is believed that paying respect to one's ancestors ensures the general well-being and success. Rituals are sometimes employed to sanctify the establishment. As in the ancient world, in some contemporary societies the office of divine kingship exists. Here the sacred aura of regal legitimacy is such that the health of the king and the prosperity of his people are believed to be entwined. The group nature of religious devotion has thus always been emphasized. It is considered to be one of the most profoundly unifying forces of society. Collective worship draws people together in common devotion and increases the unity and sense of purpose of the communicants.

A consideration of religious rituals should also take into account the inner state of the participants. Along with the social aspect, the individual psyche is also imperative. The psychological and anthropological explanations are to be viewed as mutually reinforcing. Rites and rituals help to allay the fear and tension caused by the unknown. It is not possible to concentrate on religion as a social phenomenon and overemphasize group or social solidarity, for, the society need not always express individual psychic concerns. Many of the ceremonials have a psychological function besides the social one. Hence along with the society in which man lives, his psyche should also be taken into consideration. The expected satisfaction of our needs motivate the performance of religious rituals, which according to belief promise redemption from suffering. Though religious rituals may not be efficacious for the elimination of poverty, the restoration of health, the bringing of rain, and the like, the belief that it does achieve these ends serve the important psychological function of reducing hopelessness. The painful drives (like fear of destruction) and a host of other primitive fears, which threaten to overpower the weak and the defenseless if they become too overwhelming, result in schizophrenic and paranoid breakdowns. Through the performance of certain religious actions, rituals and ceremonies help to reduce fear by making the sacred manifest in ordinary objects. They serve a therapeutic purpose and carry individuals and groups through potentially dangerous or disruptive situations. Rituals become a means of coping with fear and uncertainty. Repressed experiences and impulses that lie dormant in the unconscious may become a source of serious psychological problems. These pressures should be relieved through a harmless mechanism. Man often turns to religion as a source of explanation and relief in times of psychologically disturbing situations.

Birth rites play a significant role in human life. Rituals serve different purposes and possess meanings which enhance their position. Birth rites make the new-born a part of the human world. These rites, performed at the birth of a child, are carried out to wash away the "old life" and to incorporate the child into the ordinary day-to-day life which man leads on earth. The child is symbolically believed to emerge as a "new" being after these rituals are performed at birth. Sometimes a new name is adopted as a symbol of this new life. The old is thus effaced, and one starts life afresh. The various rites of passage function to provide a smooth passage from one social role to another. The individual acquires "new" knowledge and is accepted as a member of the society into which he is born. He assumes responsibilities from which so far he has been kept away. Initiation ceremonies are held to prevent future harm, illness or weakness. These rites symbolically remove the initiate from the status of a child and confer upon him the new position of adulthood. Sometimes a part of the human body is even sacrificed during these rites to secure the safety of the rest of the body. Anthropologists have traced three phases in these rites of transition. The three phases were first identified by Arnold van Gennep who coined the term rites de passage, and thought it to be a universal phenomenon which accompanies transition of any kind among human beings. The three phases (found in initiation rites) are separation from the old state, transition, and reincorporation into the new. These rites often take the metaphoric form of death and rebirth. The neophyte symbolically dies when separated from the old identity, is reborn, and finally reincorporated into the new state.

Rituals long antedate the development of institutionalized religion with priests and their followings. They are composed of symbolic acts which possess meaning. Ceremonials demarcate, emphasize, affirm, solemnize, and also smoothen critical changes in social relations. A powerful instrument for change as well as the continuance of status quo, they make use of many concrete symbols which often reflect belief systems, the nature of the participants, and their community. While it sociologically serves as a binding force (contributing towards social integration), psychologically it helps the human mind to shed fear and achieve a sense of stability. Socially and psychologically it holds an important place in human life.

Collective worship "draws people together in common devotion and increases the unity and sense of purpose of the communicants" (Murphy 195). In India, religion plays an important role in individual and social life. The different religious groups in the country have their rituals and ceremonies. Most of the people here strictly adhere to their beliefs and practices. Literature being a reflection of life, mirrors the customs, beliefs, and practices of the people in the country. The works written in Indian languages are deeply rooted in Indian culture and therefore reflect a particular sensibility which makes their translation into English or other languages difficult. Indian English novelists have incorporated Indian myths, rituals, and ceremonies into their literary works to create an Indian atmosphere and feeling. This is often done at the risk on the part of the Indian writer of being charged as catering to a western audience. Since religion occupies a pivotal position in social and individual life, a realistic description of Indian life includes references to the rituals, beliefs, and practices prevalent in the country. Indian English writers have always made use of religious symbols in their works. Attempts are made through creative texts to expose the hypocrisy of

Indian orthodoxy. While some writers make only a passing reference to rituals and ceremonies in their works, others focus entirely on the religious life of their characters. A number of rituals, ceremonies, and festivals are found in Indian English fiction. These works depict not only the pious and the orthodox but also the hypocrite and the heretic.

Ritual is a very important aspect of Hindu religion. These rituals range from the daily puja to the very elaborate rites connected with various stages of human life. The different objects of veneration and worship in a particular community may appear very startling to those not familiar with their religion. Most of these rituals in the country are performed by the Brahmins. Amongst others it is carried out by an officiating priest. Most of the elaborate and complex rituals bring out the central element of power of gods and Nature. Many of the social groups have their own rituals and ceremonies which are evident in works of fiction. Kavery Nambisan's *The Scent of Pepper* depicts the practices and customs found among the Kaleyandas (a group of people who live in the Coorg region). The novelist mentions some of the religious rituals which are unique to them here. In a note to the reader Kavery Nambisan points out that the inhabitants of this region "have many cultural traits and religious rituals with no counterparts elsewhere in India" (*The Scent of Pepper*, xiii). Some of these rituals and ceremonies may appear bizarre to those who are not familiar with the Kodava customs and practices. The Kaleyandas have their distinctive wedding ceremonies, funeral rites, and naming ceremonies. Along with the story of the Rao Bahadur, who presides over an extended family, the Kodava rituals and ceremonies which are central to their life have been etched here. While one gets a glimpse of the Parsi life in Rohinton Mistry's *Such a Long Journey*, the Muslim life is vividly depicted in Vaikom Muhammad Basheer's *Childhood Friend*. This not only helps to familiarize the readers with the rituals and practices of a particular community, but also to have a better insight into their life and culture.

Rites and rituals mark every stage of human life. There are birth rites, initiation rites, marriage ceremonies, and funeral rites amongst most social groups. They serve to demarcate one phase of life from the other, and set the seal of public recognition and approval on such significant turning points in human life as birth, naming, puberty, marriage, and death. The three phases traced by anthropologists are found in the initiation rituals depicted in Indian English narratives (like *Samskara*). While portraying the Muslim life in South India, Vaikom Muhammad Basheer refers to the initiation rites among the Muslim community living there. The author describes the circumcision rite among Muslim boys, and the 'ear-piercing' ceremony among the Muslim girls in his *Childhood Friend*. These rites function as rites of transition. To mark the transition in a socially and psychologically appropriate manner, the novice is separated from his old position. He enters a transitory limbo, and finally gains his new position in the adult society. In the modern world, the change in status is often accomplished by schooling, while in primitive society it was marked by the scarring rituals performed on the neophyte. A commonly traced symbolism in these transition rites is that of death and rebirth. It follows the birth-death-rebirth pattern found in the vegetative world. Psychologists like Freud have given psychological interpretations to these rites. According to them initiation rites like circumcision present a symbolic castration of the son. Drawing from Freud's theory of Oedipus Complex, psychologists point out how the rites help to sever the mother-son relationship at birth and initiate the child into a world of men. The pattern of rejection-initiation-return is found in some of the works of Kamala Markandaya (*Nectar in a Sieve*). Some of the novelists also portray how the conservative adapt themselves to the changing attitudes and values of the world around them. A society bound by tradition, customs and prejudices gradually gives way to a new one with different ideas and attitudes. The people are often forced to accept the sweeping changes, sometimes quietly and sometimes under protest. Customs, rituals, and ceremonies fill the lives of the orthodox and the conservative.

Ceremonies and rituals are said to safeguard the people against dangerous influences in life. During these ceremonies various malign forces are propitiated and offerings made to appease them. The person is thus insulated against the dangers feared. Deliverance from danger is often ascribed to some beneficent spirit and the water with which the person is purified of that danger takes on the character of "holy". The imposition of restrictions and taboos, found all over the world, is presented in literature too. The psychological force behind some of the rituals and ceremonies has been hinted at in some of the Indian English novels. Creative writers like Anita Desai concentrate on the psychological development and inner conflicts and tensions of the characters they portray in their works. Myths drawn from the Indian cultural tradition are also employed by novelists to bring home their point. They are retold to suit the contemporary society (Mulk Raj Anand's *Gauri*) or used as a structural parallel by the creative writer (R.K. Narayan's *Man-Eater of Malgudi*). Religious concepts and actions often provide meaning to human existence. Mishaps like epidemics and drought which affect an entire nation are attributed to the wrath of gods or the ancestral spirits. People turn to rites and rituals to avoid danger, sickness and other misfortunes. Creative writers raise their voice against orthodoxy, conservatism, and religious oppression through their creations. These works become a powerful medium of voicing their dissent, and in bringing about drastic social changes.

The creative writers of Indian English fiction have to seek the aid of a foreign language to convey the ceremonies and festivals of Indian origin. As Raja Rao observes, one has to convey "in a language that is not one's own the spirit that is one's own" (*Kanthapura*, "Foreword", 5), for, English is the language of "our intellectual make-up" (5) but not "our emotional make up" (5). The tempo of the life must be "infused into our English expression..." (5). Indianness is often conveyed through the use of images and symbols. Novels like *Kanthapura* convey a "distinctive Indian sensibility" (Narasimhaiah, *Fiction and the Reading Public*, 78). Though

Indian English novelists at times use English equivalents for Indian ways of expression, they mostly keep the Indian terms in original for typically Indian items of food, dress, rituals, and festivals in an attempt to recreate the Indian ethos. A translation would not bring the rich connotation embedded in them. Consequently words like *puja*, *arati*, *tali*, Diwali, Dussera, Navaratri etc. have entered the fictive world. At times italicization of these Indian words is resorted to (in Kavery Nambisan and Kamala Markandaya).

Since people are born everywhere, grow to maturity, marry, and eventually die, universally one finds birth and naming rituals, rituals marking the attainment of adulthood, wedding ceremonies, and funeral rites. They are imaginatively employed in creative works. The close tie between society and religion cannot be overlooked. Communal rituals help to reaffirm the sentiment of collective loyalty. Besides following their familiar, native practices and beliefs, people may come to accept or even reject the customs and practices alien to them. This is evident in a number of literary texts. Rites and rituals have an important place in Indian life and society and are inextricably entwined with human life. They exercise a tremendous influence in this multi-religious nation.

2

The Neophyte

Human behaviour is in a large measure influenced by the values bequeathed by religion. The feelings and strivings of man conform not only to the conditions in which he lives, but also to tradition, customs, and practices. Particular customs take root in each community and become part of its way of life. Gradually it is handed down from generation to generation, and serves as a base for the development of a more refined culture.

Despite very strong individual differences, the members of a particular society share common beliefs, values, and attitudes which constitute their culture. Their shared beliefs and values are often replaced or modified with time. People commonly consider their own practices and attitudes as correct, and look upon those who do not share them as inferior. A person's customs and ideas may appear bizarre or barbaric to another. Even the most ordinary custom may seem absurd when viewed from the perspective of a foreign culture. The best instance is found among the Hindus in India, who consider the European custom of eating meat as disgusting for, in their culture the cow is a sacred animal not to be slaughtered for food. Certain people find as barbaric the ceremonies which initiate adolescent boys and girls into adulthood. They wonder why a person willingly endures hardship merely to be accepted as an adult.

The practices which accompany a given system of belief are invariably objectified in ceremonial observances, and ritual actions. These accompanying set of ritual actions, sacrifices, prayers, and other observances play an important role not only in the lives of people, but also in the works in which they are portrayed. They help to reinforce one's belief and also to enhance the solidarity of social life. Psychologically, rituals provide reassurance and help the individual to secure mental and physical stability. They are often reduced to a mere repetition of certain words and movements, the significance of which we do not know. Under such circumstances religion loses its sanctity and becomes a mere emulation of rituals, rhythmic hand clapping, group singing, body movements, and syncopated drumbeats.

Rituals and ceremonies form an integral part of Indian life. Much of the population in the country believes in rituals and practices which are of primitive origin. The different religious groups in the country follow different rituals and celebrate various festivals. The worship of gods and goddesses, accompanied by intricate rituals, and sacrifices, often stretch over a number of days. Each religion, in this multi-religious nation, has its own rites and rituals, its own history of origin, and its own concepts, which not only characterize it, but also define and represent it. The different religions share as well as differ in their rites and ceremonies.

A portrayal of Indian life in Indian English fiction will be complete only with a reference to the rites and rituals practised by the people in the country. Various festivals, ceremonies, and rituals associated with them, have found their way into novels and short stories. The interaction between the world of human beings and that of gods, or other supernatural elements can be found in many works. Select novels, originally written in various Indian languages are now being translated, thus enabling readers to get acquainted with the rituals, practices and way of life of those living in other parts of the country. These rites and rituals, which lie deep in the Indian psyche, have influenced creative writers even when the medium of expression is not their regional language. Indian life being inextricably related to them, the ceremonies find expression in creative writing.

Many Indian writers have portrayed rituals and ceremonies in their works. Novels like *Samskara*, *The Scent of Pepper*, *The Dark Room*, and *Kanthapura* are loaded with details of rituals and festivals. Some of these rituals and ceremonies find their meaning in myths. The Indian collection of myths has also provided material to the novelists. R.K. Narayan has made use of the Bhasmasura myth in *The Man-Eater of Malgudi*, while Mulk Raj Anand has used the Hindu myth in *Gauri*. These often become methods used by the novelist to come to terms with his cultural past. A serious preoccupation with myths and ceremonies is hence seen in many novels. Myths have been used for exploring certain areas of human psychology. The frequent references in the novels to local gods and presiding deities, like Goddess Kenchamma and Talakamma, serve to affirm people's faith in the benevolence of the gods they worship. Religion thus dominates Indian life. It is as important to the Bengalis in Bhabani Bhattacharya's *A Goddess Named Gold*, as it is to the Punjabis in Khushwant Singh's *Train to Pakistan*.

Rituals represent the dynamic aspect of religion. Though, with developments in science and technology, focus has shifted from religion to science and reason, when reason fails to provide help, man turns to the mysterious and the inexplicable. Rituals, beliefs, and superstitions thus continue to have their hold on man. This book assesses the functional importance of rites and rituals in some of the works of Indian English fiction. Apart from the psychological importance of rituals and ceremonies, are the effects some of them have on the social structure.

Religion with its rituals and practices, influences individuals from birth to death. It makes its presence felt in different ways, at different stages of their lives. Individuals growing up in a particular culture will almost invariably come to believe in the various aspects of that culture and practise its customs. Certain rituals and ceremonies mark the early stage of an individual's life. Apart from the ceremonies associated with birth, which sometimes the parents have to undergo, there are 'name-giving' ceremonies, puberty rites, and initiation rites.

These rites differ not only from society to society but also on the basis of sex.

Among many groups, even before the child is born the mother has to undergo certain elaborate ceremonies. The woman is often isolated just before giving birth, and she returns to society only on taking the purificatory bath after giving birth. In some societies it is the husband who has to undergo these rituals. As soon as the woman feels the birth pangs, her husband puts on some of her clothes and retires into a dark room. The mother of a newly born child often lives entirely apart for a whole month or more. The period of her seclusion varies from society to society. During this period, which may extend from five weeks to a year, the woman is considered unclean and often has to remain in a separate hut. This period of seclusion being over, she has her purificatory bath and rejoins her group. In societies where the husband takes to his bed for some days after the birth of the first child, the woman goes about her daily household chores. This is done to avert evil influence.

The Tiya women of Malabar have to undergo elaborate ceremonies with the object of pacifying the evil spirits which may disturb her at the time of delivery. A pattern is drawn on the ground beneath a structure made of plantain-stems, around which the woman walks and throws into it a burning wick. Singing and dancing continue far into the night and at the conclusion of the ceremony rice is thrown over her and animal sacrifices are often made (Hutchinson 440). The Hindu Nair women also go through ceremonies during the various months of confinement.

The 'naming-ceremony' among many groups is an occasion for inviting friends and relatives. A feast is often given after the initial rituals and ceremonies are over. Among many tribes, the name being a universal mark of identity is changed at puberty. The number of days after which the name is given varies from society to society. Sometimes the new-born child is given a double name—one kept secret and the other which is used on ordinary occasions. Among the Hindus the senior male member of the family repeats the child's name in its ear three times. They also have a 'rice-giving' ceremony, when the child is given rice for the first time. This usually takes place in the sixth month after the child is born. Among the Brahmins, as soon as the child is six months old he or she is weaned. The child is fed on solids for the first time. An auspicious day and time is chosen. A *homam* in honour of the nine planets is made, arati is performed, and offerings are made to the household gods. Guests are invited and a feast is held. In some social groups the child has its name given before birth, while among some others the name of the child never transpires, it is known only to the father and the astrologer. The father whispers it in the child's ear and at puberty the child receives a new name. The change in name thus symbolises the change in status—the transition from childhood to adulthood—the child has undergone. In certain tribes the parents change their names at the birth of their first child. The Brahmins have their *nama-karma* ceremony at which the child is given its name.

All societies demarcate birth in some ritual fashion. The Christians practise the ceremony of baptism. The child is thus incorporated into the body of the church. The ceremony includes the sprinkling of water on the baby's head. Baptism became "the essential rite in establishing a child's social identity. It publicly confirmed his parentage, incorporated him into the Christian community, gave him surrogate "spiritual" parents, and expanded his range of potential patrons. Most important of it all, it gave him or her name, that marker by which individuals identify themselves throughout life" (Muir 22).

The various gods and goddesses are often propitiated to avoid evil influences on the new-born. Offerings of milk, rice, turmeric powder etc. are made to appease them. This is said to prevent the evil influences from wreaking havoc in the form of fever, chickenpox, measles, and other ailments. Goddess Shasthi, who looks after the welfare of children and protects them from harm is worshipped by many. The desire for a male child made it necessary to take extra precautions to save the child from baneful influences. The Matrikas, it was believed, mostly singled out male babies because males were more precious than females and, by hurting them they could hurt the family more. Hence the new-born male child is often dressed in girl's clothes and made to wear bangles and kohl to simulate feminity.

Among the savage tribes the birth of the first child seals the marriage alliance. The birth of a child is taken as a natural sign of the completion of the marriage tie. It psychologically binds the pair together in the joy that a new life is born into the world. The birth of the first child leads among many groups to a renewal of marriage. The pair remains separate until a second marriage ceremony takes place.

The passing of childhood and the entry into adulthood is marked by initiation rites. Initiation rites are usually supervised by the adults of a culture. The adolescents undergoing initiation may range from ten to twenty years of age. These rites mark the passage of an individual from the social status of a child to that of an adult. It thus emphasizes his transition from childhood to adulthood. The public nature of the ceremony often assists him in assuming a new identity. Initiation prepares the boys and girls for the responsibilities in later life and also for contact with each other. Instructions in future duties are often imparted. These boys and girls are given instruction in customs which are supposedly known only to adults. Arnold van Gennep traces three phases in these rites of passage. They begin with the rites of separation which displace the individual from his or her previous status as a child. This is followed by the rites of transition, which temporarily suspend the subject between his or her old and new state, and the rites of aggregation or incorporation which brings the person into the embrace of the new community. The pattern of birth-death-rebirth found in the vegetative world can be found in the rituals by which children undergo symbolic death before being reborn as adults.

The initiation ceremonies divest a person of his status as a child in the domestic domain and invest him with a social status. Male children pass out of the possession of the parents into the direct possession of the horde. This is symbolically expressed in the initiation rites. These rites are said to ensure the continuity of possession by the society. As the group loses some members by death, it acquires new members by the birth of children and their initiation into the status of men and women. Among certain groups of people when a girl reaches puberty the rights over her are transferred from her father and his horde to her husband, while in the case of a boy he is transferred from his position of dependence on his father to that of an adult member of the horde.

Initiation rites vary in their degree of elaboration from one culture to another. The initiate is first removed from society for a certain period and is later taken back into the group in his new status. Often each sex is tabooed to the other. These individuals are given instructions in their responsibilities as adult males and females. This is also accompanied by certain ritual observances which function to endow their assigned activities with an aura of sanctity. The person is thus formally received into the community of adults. As a part of these initiation rites, the person concerned has to often undergo restraint, privation, and even pain. The permanent deformation of the person by means of cutting, boring the nose or ears, knocking out the teeth may also take place. Sometimes these initiation rites involve branding, to remove the sins one may have committed. The orthodox often submit themselves to a repetition thereof at irregular intervals. Its purpose is thus similar to the Christian practice of confession. Sometimes the initiate receives a name, has a 'god-father' and the initiation is mainly done by the sponsors. The boy must personally take the vows as soon as he is old enough. The 'ear-piercing' ceremony among the Hindus and the Muslims is also a form of initiatory rite.

During initiation ceremonies the initiate may be whipped. This is done not with the intention of torture. It is considered as a rite of exorcism to take off the bad influences and to make future events propitious. Among the Thonga, a South American tribe the boys undergo a three month hazing ordeal. Circumcision is performed. They are isolated from all for several months and have to undergo tests of endurance and manliness. This severe initiation, in which the boy is often exposed to beatings, is considered necessary to signal the child's passing into adulthood and to establish clearly the male role for the young boy. The boy is from now on treated like a man. A.M. Vergiat in his *Les Rites Secrets des Primitifs de L' Oubangui* traces the colour symbolism in the various rites among the Manja (Banton 56). According to him black is the colour of death and impurity. The warriors smear themselves with soot when they leave for war and the people in mourning stay dirty. They do not wash themselves. White is the colour of rebirth. It protects them from illness. The initiated boys, at the end of the rites, paint themselves white. They are new men. The relatives of the dead also paint themselves white, for white purifies. Red is a symbol of life, joy and health. Vergiat points out that "the natives rub themselves with red for dancing and those who are sick pass it frequently over their bodies" (Banton 57).

The ceremonies associated with puberty are a recognition in some fashion or other of the child's new status of adulthood. Puberty is often a complex ritual-filled period during which the young girl is immersed in the process of identification with her role in society. The entire community may take part in the ceremonies. Many societies have formal customs and rituals marking the period of adolescence and preparing the child for the adult role. Sometimes great attention is paid to the magical education of children. Tattooing may also take place at the puberty ceremonies. In certain societies the ceremony includes a redistribution of all the property. Sometimes the puberty rites for boys and girls may be socially celebrated in the same tribe in identical ways. For both—the boy and the girl—it marks their entry into a new status. In the case of girls who continue to reside in their homes after marriage the puberty rites represent an announcement of the girls changed status. As a part of the puberty rite the girl goes through a period of ceremonial seclusion. She is confined to a room, or a hut specially made for this occasion. Betel leaves, arecanuts, and pots filled with water are sometimes placed around the girl. Among some groups offerings are also made. At the end of the period of pollution the hut made for this purpose is set on fire and the girl is taken back into her group after a purificatory bath. Certain tribes consider these ceremonies performed at puberty as marriage rites.

When a Hindu maiden reaches maturity she is kept in a dark room for four days and is forbidden to see the sun. She is regarded as unclean and no one may touch her. Her diet is restricted to boiled rice, milk, sugar, curd, and tamarind without salt. On the fifth day she has her purificatory bath. The mat and other things in the room in which she had been secluded are thrown away. The Rarhi Brahmans of Bengal compel a girl at puberty to live alone, and do not allow her to see the face of any male. She is kept in a dark room for three days and has to undergo certain penances. Fish and sweetmeats are forbidden. She must live on rice and ghee. Among the Tiyas of Malabar a girl is thought to be polluted for four days. She is secluded and kept in a room festooned with garlands of coconut leaves. She sleeps on a grass mat of a particular kind. Another girl keeps her company and sleeps with her. But she may not touch any other person, tree or plant, or see the sky. Her diet is strictly vegetarian, without salt, tamarind, or chillies. She is also armed against evil spirits with a knife which is placed on the mat or carried on her person.

The precautions taken to isolate the girl are for her own safety as well as for the safety of others. About the reason for the seclusion of girls at puberty James Frazer writes:

> The motive for the restraints so commonly imposed on girls at puberty is the deeply ingrained dread which primitive man universally entertains of menstruous blood. He fears it at all times but especially on its first appearance; hence the restrictions under which women lie at their first menstruation are usually more stringent than those which they have to observe at any subsequent recurrence of the mysterious flow. (790)

The object of secluding the woman is hence to neutralize the dangerous influence. Her very touch it is believed, turned wine to vinegar, blighted crops, killed seedlings, drove bees from their hives, rusted iron and brass. "In short, the girl is viewed as charged with a powerful force which, if not kept within bounds may prove destructive both to herself and to all with whom she comes in contact. To repress this force within the limits necessary for safety of all concerned is the object of the taboos in question" (794-95).

The initiate often has to undertake fasts, to prevent evil influences. Many food items are tabooed. This taboo is later taken off ceremonially. The food women have touched are often tabooed to boys, for feminine weakness could be transmitted by eating them. Introduction to the forbidden food is thus a regular part of the ceremonies which end initiation among some social groups. Amongst certain social groups, as part of the initiation rites, the mothers stand in a line facing their sons, and sprinkle each other with water. This signifies that the boys are no longer under their mother's control. A long period of post-partum sex taboo is said to make the child dependent on the mother and engender father-son rivalry. These initiation rites serve to prevent this rivalry.

Some of the initiation rites like the *upanayana* ceremony, 'ear-piercing' ceremony, and circumcision are found in novels like, *Samskara* and *Bharathipura* (U.R. Anantha Murthy), and *The Serpent and the Rope* (Raja Rao). Investiture with the sacred thread is essential in the case of a Brahmin boy. This cord, called *punul* in Tamil, is worn from the left shoulder falling on to the right hip. It is spun by persons of the same caste, to avoid the possibility of its being defiled by passing through "unclean" hands. The ceremony is called *upanayana*. It is an introduction to knowledge. After the priest fixes the auspicious day, the invitations are sent to friends and relatives. The neophyte has to undergo certain *purificatory* ceremonies and it is only on the second day that the investiture takes place. The boy then receives the *mantrams* from his father. The ceremony ends only on the fourth day. The "new" brahmin now takes his place amongst the elders of the caste. After a brahmin is invested he is expected to keep the anniversary every year. This period from the ceremony of *upanayana* until marriage is looked upon as a time of study, trial, of subordination, and of initiation into the rules and regulations of caste. This is the time to learn to read and write, to commit the Vedas and *mantrams* to memory. Now he has to take the greatest pain to conform to the rules and customs of his caste. From the time he receives the cord he obtains the right to read the Vedas, to perform sacrifice, and also to give or receive alms. An initiation rite common among the Muslims is circumcision. Novelists like Vaikom Mohammed Basheer and Salman Rushdie have referred to it in their works.

Apart from these initiation rites, there are also those rites which initiate individuals into their hereditary occupation or profession. In some societies these rites are performed as soon as the child is born, while among others it takes place at a later stage in the individual's life. Initiation rites mark the beginning of a new life of responsibility. The person has to undergo tests of endurance, fasting, and purification. With this he enters a new phase in his life.

Since the Vedic age people have performed religious rituals and ceremonies. Every religious rite was looked upon as sure to produce desirable results. These rituals and customs continue to exert a strong influence on the Indian masses. One cannot ignore the tremendous sway of tradition and belief on the millions who surge towards pilgrim centres and perform numerous rituals. Most of the rituals are carried out to propitiate or conciliate the "powers superior to man which are believed to direct and control the course of nature and of human life" (Frazer 65). Religion, with its rituals and practices, forms an indispensable part of Indian life. Being a multi-religious nation, each religious group in the country has its own beliefs and rituals.

Literature, which is considered "an expression of society" (George 5), cannot ignore the hold of religion on the minds of the people. The Indian psyche retains a respect for the supernatural and the mystical concepts that often defy rational explanation. Rituals and ceremonies which form an integral part of Indian life have found their way into creative works by Indian writers. The Indian novelist has "to operate in a tradition-bound society where neither a man's profession nor his marriage [is] his personal affair. His life [is] mapped out by his family or his community or his caste" (Mukherjee, *Realism and Reality*, 7). A writer's views and attitudes, which condition his work, are thus the result of a number of influences which operate upon him. Religion, its beliefs, rituals, and practices, form a recurrent motif in many of the works in Indian English fiction. The works in regional languages too help to familiarize one with the life, customs, and manners of the people inhabiting a particular region. The portrayal of these beliefs and rituals help to create the Indian ethos.

Human existence from cradle to grave is in a state of flux. This has called forth a series of rites of passage in human life. Various rites are carried out during pregnancy and after birth to mark the birth of the child. Rituals are performed during the naming of a child, its first solid food, its first outing, first hair cut, earlobe piercing etc. These are carried out in the initial phase of human life. Religious observances like the 'naming' ceremony are performed after the birth of a child. The child is usually given a name (among the Brahmins) after the eleventh or twelfth day of its birth. It is similar to the ceremony of baptism amongst the Christians. Guests are invited and feasts held to mark the occasion. The transition from the state of childhood to that of adulthood is marked by the initiation rites. This marks the separation from childhood and the person's entry into manhood or womanhood. It enables the person (the initiate) to move smoothly from one role to another. This change in status is often a period of anxiety and uncertainty for the subject of the change and for all around. The shift brings with it a corresponding change in his role in life. These rites are social events which "transform" the individual and give him a new identity. The three phases of these rites—separation, transition, and reincorporation—are considered universal. The ceremonies connected with initiation are performed by the initiated members of a community. Tradition is thus sanctified and transmuted from generation to generation. This ensures that traditional knowledge is not lost and traditional social relations are maintained. Even death rites function as rites of transition, for it initiates the deceased into the world of the dead as a spirit and reincorporates the living to their life on earth. The stages of the life cycle in man are marked off by biological crisis. But the biological changes are considered just a physical manifestation of the child's metamorphosis. The changes are often taken as a spiritual phenomenon which has to do with not just the boy or the girl but his or her family, tribe and even the celestial bodies up in the sky. Puberty rites are performed to mark the passage from one stage of life to another in which one has to learn and enact the social roles in one's life. The child is usually secluded ceremonially in a small enclosure and elaborate ceremonies are performed. The rites include rites of separation, rites of transition, and rites of incorporation. The individual is ritually removed from society, is isolated for a period, and finally reincorporated back into society in his new status as an adult. Each sex is tabooed to the other, for it is against the dangers of sexual contact that the process is directed. Taboos are imposed but they are gradually taken off with the new responsibilities the child takes on himself. The significance of puberty rites, as expressed in primitive thought, arises from the notion that at initiation the individual dies and is born again. The primitive tribal rituals of initiation became sophisticated with time. The concept of birth-death-rebirth, associated with these rites, is derived from the observation of plant life. The period of seclusion, the age of the initiate, ceremonies, all differ from country to country, and from community to community.

Novelists like Kamala Markandaya and Kavery Nambisan have referred to some of the birth rites in their works. *Nectar in a Sieve* and *The Scent of Pepper* highlight the significance of similar rites in these novels as well as in the lives of the people portrayed in them. Vaikom Muhammad Basheer's *Childhood Friend* throws light on the Muslim initiation ceremony of circumcision performed on boys and the 'ear-piercing' ceremony among girls. Manohar Malgonkar's *The Princes* and *A Bend in the Ganges* follow the process of initiation that the protagonists undergo. U.R. Anantha Murthy's *Samskara* and Kamala Markandaya's *Two Virgins* trace the transformation of its characters as well as structurally share the three phases of the *rites de passage*.

All societies demarcate birth in some ritual fashion. Customs associated with birth form a part of the traditional life in Coorg. The Kodava women have to undergo elaborate customs prior to the birth of a child. Kavery Nambisan's *The Scent of Pepper* refers to various Kodava customs the pregnant women have to undergo even before the child is born. An authentic depiction of the life, customs, and practices of the people of Kodagu is found here. Their life, filled with "weddings, funerals, naming ceremonies and house-warming pujas" (9), is portrayed in detail. Kavery Nambisan refers to Nanji's (Baliyanna's wife) first confinement and some of the Kodava customs at the outset. According to custom, Nanji leaves for her father's house for her first confinement in the seventh month. It temporarily frees her from the busy life at her husband's house. A detailed description of the Kodava custom "to overfeed pregnant women" (11) is given:

> Tradition demanded that pregnant Kodava women eat eggs laid by red hens, two ladles of ghee a day and rotis with wild honey, in addition to a lehyam made of jaggery, sesame seeds, cashewnuts, almonds and sunflower seeds in the morning and a cleansing paste of garlic, asafoetida, cinnamon and pepper at night. They drank coffee with cloves and cardamom, and milk boiled with saffron, until they passed perfumed urine, perspired perfumed sweat, wept perfumed tears and breathed perfumed breath and their skins gave off such pungent smells that passers-by could feel their nostrils twitch when they came within five hundred yards of a pregnant woman. (11-12)

The Kodavas treat their women (be it a widow or a pregnant woman) with love and respect. Their culture is beautifully etched in the novel. The pregnant women lead a life of excesses. The novelist humorously comments on the Kodava custom:

> That wasn't mindless pampering but a wise tradition, because more often than not women succumbed to puerperal sickness. Only the tough survived, and they were so tough that they lived through ten or twelve

> confinements until menopause rescued them from the hazards of fertility and they pulled on, often outliving more delicate husbands. (11)

In contrast to this treatment among the Kodavas is the one meted out to Nanji by her stepmother. Nanji is subjected to a meagre diet by her. This results in the death of the new-born child, and Nanji's return to her husband's house after the obligatory forty-five days in bed. The situation makes her decide to handle future pregnancies without her stepmother's help. It is significant that the story opens with a marriage, refers to Nanji's confinement and then to the Rao Bahadur's death. These rites connected with the crucial stages of human life recur in the novel. It marks the beginning and end of different generations. Nanji is portrayed as a woman of strength, with none of the feminine weaknesses. In keeping with it is her act of defying the irrelevant Kodava customs. The novel also refers to Mallige's (Nanji's daughter-in-law) confinement. The experiences with her stepmother during her first pregnancy makes Nanji take care of Mallige later on. Despite the differences between them, Nanji nurses her daughter-in-law thus disregarding custom. The descriptions toss much light on the relationship between the two. Customs associated with birth form a part of almost every culture. The descriptions of the Kodava customs not only give a glimpse of the Kodava culture and life, but also hint at the relationship between Nanji and Mallige.

The 'naming' ceremony amongst most social groups is an occasion for rejoicing. The number of days after which the name is given varies from society to society. On an auspicious day the child is given its name. A feast is given after the initial ceremonies. Some of the customs and observances associated with birth are found in Kamala Markandaya's *Nectar in a Sieve*. An entirely different handling and portrayal of birth rites is seen here. The work deals with the life of Nathan and Rukmani in a village. The birth of a daughter, named Irawaddy (Ira), fills the couple with disappointment. It refers to the inferior status accorded to a girl child. The celebrations which follow the birth of a son seven years after Ira's birth is a sharp contrast to the reactions which the birth of a daughter triggers. A feast is held on the tenth day after the birth of the child and the whole village is invited to it. Rukmani's friends come to help her with the work. Describing the occasion Rukmani says, "When all was ready we spread the leaves under the gaudy marriage pandal Nathan had borrowed for the occasion and ate and drank for long, merry hours" (21). For Nathan and her, the feast is an expression of their happiness and pride at having a male heir. The celebration becomes one of the rare moments of happiness and plenty in their life which is otherwise filled with poverty and misery. Though the novelist does not refer to any rituals associated with the occasion one finds how the feast held by the family becomes a means for the people to join and celebrate. The novel also refers to the 'naming' ceremony of Ira's illegitimate child. The birth of a child "too fair" (117) arouses much interest, and people gather to see the albino child. To put an end to the long line of callers Nathan decides to hold the child's 'naming' ceremony. A short description of this ceremony—"It is the custom to have a ceremony on the tenth day from birth: this is the custom, and I [Rukmani] had followed it for all my children" (119)—is provided in the novel. Rukmani describes the festive occasion as she recollects it. Friends and neighbours arrive with gifts. The child is named Sacrabani. It is noteworthy that Ira remains unperturbed by the commotion created by her child. There is much discussion on the child's peculiar looks. Selvam, Ira's brother, comes to her rescue declaring it to be "Just a matter of colouring" (121) or "lack of it" (121). The incident throws light on the close relationship between Ira and Selvam. Towards the end of the novel, it is Selvam who looks after the lone Ira and her son. Selvam's easy attitude towards her son brings Ira closer to him. Here too one does not find a description of the rituals and ceremonies. The ceremony is in sharp contrast to that held at the birth of Nathan and Rukmani's first son. There is no description of the feast or preparations at Ira's child's 'naming' ceremony, and focus is laid on the albino child and the family's attempt to make it a part of the society in which they live. The child continues to be left out due to his albinism. The people as well as the children refuse to accept him into their company except as a hanger-on. The absence of his father at the 'naming' ceremony is also significant and contributes to the child's status as an outcast. M.K. Naik considers the rural life in the novel as "contrived" (Dhawan, *Commonwealth Fiction*, 212) due to the novelist's description of "the public naming ceremony of Ira's child which is born in sin" (Dhawan 212). Though it is difficult to concur that the rural life here is contrived, one is sure to agree with M.K. Naik that a village which permits a 'naming' ceremony for an illegitimate child "exists only in the expatriate imagination of [the] creator" (Dhawan 212). Such ceremonies are a part of the traditional Indian village life, but "no traditional Indian village will allow so permissive a code of sexual morality" (Dhawan 212). The ceremony described is an attempt made by the family to legitimize an illegitimate child in a traditional and orthodox Indian village. A reference (through Rukmani and Ira) is also made to the socio-religious forces which create problems of acceptability and respectability for a childless woman. The inter-cultural forces as well as the novelist's personal, social, and religious heritage have a bearing on her works.

The Scent of Pepper refers to the 'naming' ceremony (of Subbu's son and that of his friend Govinda) celebrated among the Kodavas. It reveals the financial disparity between the two families. While Govinda belongs to a poor family which has to toil hard in life, Subbu belongs to an affluent Kodava family. The account of the ceremony throws light on this:

> At Govinda's, the rites were simple: a temple puja was performed by the grandfather.... The grandmother applied a large black dot of coal mixed in ghee on the baby's forehead and named him Vishnu, and served a lunch of rice, sambar, palya and payasam to the dozen guests who sat in the temple courtyard. (200)

In contrast to this is the Kodava ceremony to which a large number of guests are invited:

> The Kodava ritual was elaborate: Mallige insisted that every family they knew in Athur be invited and...the Kaliyanda and the Kademada clan. The guests admired

> the infant, thrust rupee coins into his hands and ate chicken *palav*, pork and *paputtoo*, mutton fry and egg curry.... (200-01)

Subbu's son is named Thimmaya which is anglicized by Mallige to Timmy. Subbu, who did not like this anglicization, called his son Thimmu, while Nanji referred to him as "that boy" (201). The narrative indicates this difference in temperament between Mallige and her husband's family. Mallige's actions support this, for she shows only contempt for the Kodava ways. While Subbu is at one with the Kodava culture, Mallige, with her preference for sophistication, finds herself more at ease in the city. The novel repeatedly refers to some of the rituals and practices, connoting their relevance in the Kodava life. Besides bringing into the light the Kodava customs and rituals, the novel is also an illustration of how these practices form an integral part of the Kodava life and culture described in it.

Apart from the rites associated with birth, novelists also refer to initiation rites in their creative works. It is true of Indian English fiction too. These rites which involve a number of phases make the neophyte a member of his community. Creative writers often describe the life and culture of their own community in their works. Vaikom Muhammad Basheer's *Childhood Friend* presents a picture of the life and customs of the Muslims. The novelist criticizes the obsolete Muslim customs and provides an account of the old beliefs and traditions prevalent among his community. As Basheer himself admits, one of his ideas in writing *Childhood Friend* is "to project the glory of the bygone days of Islam and at the same time to point out the failure of present day Muslims to adjust to the modern life because of this mythical past" (Basheer, Introduction X). Like many other novelists Basheer too sets his characters in a world he is familiar with. The story revolves around Majid and Suhra, the two childhood friends, and their affectionate relationship from childhood to youth. Islam preserves the ancient custom of circumcision. The removal of the foreskin of the penis is often considered the male emulation of uterine bleeding and thus of female fertility. It is one of the first of the trials to which the boy is exposed on the road to manhood and a marker of his liberation from the world of women. Circumcision is also considered as the sacrifice of a portion of the organ to ensure the well-being of the rest. This involves the concept of renunciation in sacrifices to propitiate or gain God's favour. Corresponding to this Muslim initiation rite is the Hindu initiation rite of *upanayanam* peculiar to the Brahmins who observe it with great solemnity. The *upanayanam* (investiture of the sacred thread) among the Hindus and circumcision among the Muslims are initiation rites for the boys in the community. Various taboos and ritual avoidances are imposed on the initiate. These rites are performed for the boys to "pull" them over to the men's side from a woman's realm into which they are born. Basheer refers to the Muslim ritual of circumcision in his *Childhood Friend*. Majid's circumcision ceremony is described as "an event that enlivened the whole village" (13). The reference to the ceremony is appropriate in the context of the growing up of a Muslim boy narrated here. The ceremony declares Majid's father's affluence:

> It was during the holidays. Majid's circumcision ceremony was an event that enlivened the whole village. There were fireworks and feasting. Majid was brought on the back of an elephant to the sound of a band and by the light of portable gas lamps! Then there was the feasting. More than a thousand people took part. (13)

The ceremony is an expression of Majid's economic status. Suhra's 'ear-piercing' ceremony which is in sharp contrast to this exposes the economic disparity between the two families—that of an areca-nut dealer (Suhra's father) and a timber merchant (Majid's father). The novelist beautifully conveys the anxiety and ignorance of the two children regarding the rites:

> The initiation took place before the feast.... The whole day Majid was afraid. Something will be cut off! What is it? Will he die? He was weak from fright. He felt he would not live through the day. He had no idea what was going to happen. All Muslim men are initiated.

> There is not one who is not. Still.... 'How do they do this initiation?' Majid asked Suhra.

She knew nothing about it!

> All she could do was to console him by saying, 'Whatever it is, you won't die'. (13)

Through the two children's eyes the novelist describes the rites vividly. It throws much light on the Muslim culture. The initiate (Majid) is secluded and taken to a small room. Apart from the barber (Ossan) who carries out the rite there are only a few men (the initiated) in the room:

> In many instances an individual who is ritually unclean is looked upon as a source of danger not only to himself but also to those with whom he comes into contact or to the whole community. He may therefore be more or less excluded for a time or even permanently from participation in the social life of the community. Frequently, if not always, an obligation therefore rests upon the...unclean person, to undertake the necessary process of purification. (Brown 207)

Majid too is isolated and his breaking the taboo (he goes to attend Suhra's 'ear-piercing' ceremony) creates a lot of commotion. As a part of the rite Majid's clothes are removed and he is blindfolded:

> Somewhere in all that confusion he experienced a slight pain on the part of his body where his thighs met. A sensation like the tearing of the dried film of an areca-nut leaf. Just for a moment. Soon everything was over and there was the sprinkling of water. He was left with a blistering, burning feeling. (14)

In a childlike manner Majid describes the rite that has been performed on him:

> In the commotion Majid took a look.... It was not exactly like dipping your finger into a bottle of red ink, but rather like having a circle of ink at the end of the finger from the mouth of the bottle without actually touching the ink.... Just a faint sign of bleeding.... (14)

After Majid is healed he is taken to the mosque. He is bathed and dressed when his period of seclusion ends. The novel describes it as a "great occasion" (15). The initiate at this point rejoins his society. A person who is taboo is usually restored to his normal condition by rituals of purification:

> A ritual prohibition is a rule of behaviour which is associated with a belief that an infraction will result in an undesirable change in the ritual status of the person who fails to keep the rule. This change of ritual status is conceived in many different ways in different societies, but everywhere there is the idea that it invokes the likelihood of some minor or major misfortune which will befall the person concerned. (Brown 134-35)

Psychoanalysts interpret male genital mutilation as a symbolic expression of male envy of woman's reproductive powers. It is believed that men, in incising the penis, are symbolically creating an analogus of menstrual blood and female genitals. The male-female dichotomy is stressed in these customs and practices. These rites are considered necessary by most social groups. A girl grows up in a world of bearing and raising while a son grows up in a domestic world of women, and hence must be removed from that world to enter a world of men, one full of competition, strife, and danger. A boy once initiated is no longer a mere spectator but an important participant and responsible for maintaining traditions. Gradually domestic and economic responsibilities increase (as in Majid's case) and the newly initiated moves towards a full participation in the sacred and the secular life. The male child passes out of the possession of his parents into the direct possession of his horde at initiation. The social group thus gains some new members as it loses some through death. These rites and ceremonies signal the child's passing into adulthood and help to establish clearly the male role for the young boy. Freud calls the period of the onset of puberty "genital stage" (Whitman 56), which is "characterized by less concern for immediate self-satisfaction and more concern for others. The person, no longer pleasure-oriented, has become reality-oriented and ready for a fully socialized adult life" (Whitman

56-57). As Malinowsky points out these rites also ensure the continuity of tradition:

> [Similar initiation rites were considered] a ritual and dramatic expression of the supreme power and value of tradition in primitive societies; they also serve to impress this power and value upon the minds of each generation, and they are at the same time an extremely efficient means of transmitting tribal lore, of insuring continuity in tradition and of maintaining tribal cohesion. (Staal 131)

In *Childhood Friend* Basheer also draws some of the loveliest and indelible pictures of a young Muslim girl's transition into a "new" world. Suhra's 'ear-piercing' ceremony takes place ten or twelve days after Majid's circumcision. Like Majid, Suhra is ignorant of the rites and is filled with anxiety. Unlike at Majid's, there were "no great celebrations or crowds to be seen. Majid thought it was because they were not rich. If they had been rich, there would have been drums and fireworks and feasting" (15). The two events proclaim the economic position of the two families. Suhra's ears are pierced:

> Her face was flushed and her eyes were red. Both ears were pierced from top to bottom and tied with black thread. The right ear had eleven holes and the left one ten. Majid knew that when the ears healed, the threads would be taken out and silver *halqats* inserted instead. Then later on, for her marriage, gold ones would take the place of the silver ones. (15)

Majid goes to attend the ceremony in spite of the pain he has to bear, thus breaking the seclusion imposed on him. He wonders whether the 'ear-piercing' will hurt her, and despite the "pain of a thousand wounds...[which] seemed to go right to his very heart..." (15), he reaches Suhra's house without anyone seeing him and asks her, "'Did it hurt very much?'" (15). The two ceremonies throw light on the Suhra-Majid relationship. The incident reveals their love and concern for each other. Through a more socially aware Majid, Basheer criticizes these customs later on in the novel. The novelist points out the socio-economic dimension of these ceremonies which force Majid to face reality and take up a job after many years of wandering. The new awareness makes Majid criticize and even condemn these customs as "stupid customs" (39). Majid has to find husbands as well as make money for the gold ornaments and dowry for his two sisters. Between the two of them his sisters had forty-two holes in their ears. This makes Majid criticize the practice and say, "Umma, if only there was none of this 'ear-piercing' and so on! Why only in our community are there these stupid customs—stupid ways of dress and stupid ornaments...!" (39). Realizing the uselessness of rebelling against the accepted practices of society he himself says:

> Why blame them? They did these things according to the custom of their generation. They did not consider whether these things were necessary or not. To diverge even the slightest bit from the old customs—it was very difficult! But was this realistic in the circumstances? (39)

In Basheer one finds the abundance of humour which underlies implied criticism of outdated marriage customs that have no basis in the teachings of the Prophet. Through Majid, he laughs at the Muslim world and lays bare the evils of society like the dowry system. Amongst some of the social groups 'ear-piercing' forms an essential part of the puberty rites. This rite observed by certain Indian tribes is often explained in terms of fertility magic as "the lobe made in the ear is supposed to have some sympathetic effect in opening the womb and making the child-birth easy" (Bhattacharyya 83). It is considered a form of offering of blood to the deity, similar to the physical mutilation performed by savages. Such rites have a magical or mysterious significance in the outlook of the primitive people.

While some of the creative works in Indian English fiction contain descriptions of initiation rites, works like *The Scent of Pepper* and *Two Virgins* concentrate on the changes—from childhood to adulthood—the characters undergo. Manohar Malgonkar's *The Princes* and *A Bend in the Ganges* also trace the transformation of its protagonists from ignorance to maturity. The hero, in his progress, either emerges victorious or is crushed and defeated in the process of life. The pattern of his moral growth either culminates in his self-realization, or his realization of the inadequacy of his individual dreams and his future in life. *The Scent of Pepper* mentions the gradual initiation of Subbu, Nanji's son, into adulthood. The novel does not refer to any rituals which go with this change and goes on to mention Subbu's realization of his manhood, and enrolment in the school. Dawning of a new awareness in the boy is related in the novel:

> It was during his half-naked days that Subbu observed his manhood with wonder and curiosity. He observed its shape, size, the hooded tip and tiny lipless slit, its colour, personality, its softness and hardness. Sometimes he felt his heartbeat there and wondered if his soul wasn't enshrined in that friendly organ [which he compares to an elephant's trunk]. (36)

Cured of his crippleness, Subbu prefers to lead a life of excitement instead of wasting time in a classroom. He becomes tired of "tame games" (41) like kabaddi and hockey and soon develops a passion for cock-fights and a preference for hand-rolled beedis. Nanji too becomes conscious of the change in Subbu. The gradual metamorphosis in Subbu is traceable in the descriptions provided here:

> Subbu was bored with boys his age and preferred to follow pubescent youths who stalked the village in search of excitement. They joined festival processions, rocked before garish tableaux of gods and climbed hills to visit temples; they wore flowers behind their ears and danced at weddings blocking the bride's path for hours... and they stopped to glut on the wedding feast of pork, palav and payasam. (41-42)

Subbu is also initiated into his father's (Baliyanna's) job as a vet. As a part of this process of growing up is Subbu's attitude towards Clara, and his love for Chinni. The days of aimless wanderings, cock-fights, and smoking slowly come to an end and Subbu moves away from his brothers and playmates. Nanji, finding him "in the process of struggling into manhood" (116), sends him to the Crystal Palace to be with his grandmother, Chambavva. This is similar to the seclusion imposed on the initiate. Subbu returns after six months of disciplined life under Chambavva and gradually takes on a social role. He later joins the Congress, goes to jail, then joins the army, carries out his father's last rites, and finally returns home after a brief spell of city life. Subbu's relationship with his mother contains traces of the Oedipal relationship. Nanji is a dominant figure in his life. Subbu is not able to lead a happy life with his wife, and finally returns to his mother. The strong bond which binds him to her from birth continues till the end of the novel. Various instances in the novel support this:

> As a special gesture, she [Nanji] let him suckle till he was five, until one day she realized he did it for pleasure. Alarmed that she might be harming her son, she stopped suckling him. Subbu reacted with rabid tantrums.... [But] Nanji stayed firm. (32)

> People said Subbu was her favourite. It was true. What could you do when something bigger than yourself pulled you to one child over the rest and you hung on to him with teeth that were stronger than a tiger's teeth, until you knew you had to let go because otherwise he would struggle free and your teeth would maul him? That wasn't what she wanted for her son. (239-40)

Nanji is unable to accept Mallige as Subbu's wife. In Freudian thought the male child must seek identification with society in order to resolve the Oedipal conflict. In societies where long periods of post-partum sex taboos are imposed, it creates dependency on the mother, arouses the sexual desire of the male child for his mother, engenders father-son rivalry and leads to sexual anxiety. Adolescent male initiation ceremonies help to break this dependency on the mother, and resolve the father-son rivalry. As Freud observes, sexual instinct is not completely absent in childhood. The germs of sexual impulses are already present in the new-born child and these continue to develop for a time, but are then overtaken by a process of suppression. The novelist does away with a description of the rites and vividly conveys the slow changes which Subbu undergoes. Such a description is markedly different from the references to the Kodava marriage rituals, death rites, and other ceremonies connected with festivals which abound in the novel. A similar portrayal is also found in *Two Virgins*. The novel deals with Saroja and her sister Lalitha's growing awareness of the adult world. The two react differently to the situations around them. The novel set in an Indian village, presents the process of growing up through the eyes of Saroja, the youngest daughter of Appa and Amma. Saroja is the initiate while Lalitha, the cynosure of all eyes, is already in her adolescence. The novel frequently refers to the transition they undergo. As it progresses, a child's world view gives way to a more mature narrator. Saroja goes through a slow transformation from adolescence to womanhood. The novel traces the awareness of adult sexuality as a part of this process. Jaya and Lalitha, who are older than Saroja, are presented as sexually more informed. But (indicating their different natures) the thought of "it" disturbed Saroja. Though Saroja unconsciously acknowledges her being inferior to Lalitha, she has much the same interest in the new knowledge which is a part of the changes she experiences. Unlike Lalitha, Saroja resists all the temptations which lure and ruin her sister. Saroja is deeply rooted in her culture and lives within its traditional pattern. Thus she appears as a foil to her sister. The two characters are drawn in such a way as to make the transformation and the ending of the novel possible. While Saroja appears more mature at the end of the novel, Lalitha is ruined by the city life and its ways. Lalitha's behaviour when the two are caught in a storm indicates her nature as well as the theme of initiation which runs throughout the plot. Lalitha with her "bold and free" (72) nature stood naked in the rain, "her body spattered and blotched with mud [indicating her later life]" (71) which Saroja "would not have done, not even in the dark..." (71). Lalitha also attempts to impart a new awareness to her sister. This further underlines their different natures. While Lalitha "ran her hands down her body, down the length of it, touching its secret places" (72), describing it as "lovely" (72), Saroja who lets Lalitha's fingers explore her does not feel "wild" (73) sensations as the latter does. Saroja's yearning to attain forbidden knowledge is only a natural concomitant of the initiation procedure. Both the girls slowly leave childhood behind, each having a foretaste of knowledge from different sources. The changes Saroja feels within her can be mapped out clearly. The novel focuses on Lalitha and her actions, but it is through Saroja that the process of growing up and the theme of initiation are dealt. Indicating her sister's role in Saroja's transformation, Saroja herself says, "It seemed...as if her sister was destined to shape the stream of her life" (221). This influence cannot be overlooked. The growth—Saroja's transition and the new awareness she gains—is explicitly stated in the novel. Saroja refers to her uninitiated state which separates her from the rest of her family:

> ...they were initiates, the three [Amma, Appa, and Lalitha] of them. They knew about union, and frenzy, and the ejection and admission of seed in which was shrouded the creation of life: the minute, exact detail of it was kept from her. (222)
>
> The thing that was opaque to her [Saroja] was plain to them [Amma, Appa, and Lalitha] but they were not telling Saroja, who was virgin. (223)

This distinction between the initiated and the uninitiated members of the society is found amongst most social groups. Saroja, impatient and curious, wants to know the secrets into which the initiated (Amma, Appa, and Lalitha) do not let her in. It leaves her outside the ring of their knowledge. A confused Saroja is not sure whether she wanted to be inside or outside their circle of knowledge. *Two Virgins* shows an excessive preoccupation with sexuality (and its awareness) as a part of growing up (and the theme of initiation). The novelist explains the character's development in terms of deep rooted sexual cravings. It not only deals with the theme of initiation into the mysteries of sex but also with a series of other initiations, like the initiation into modernity, city life and western culture which Lalitha and her family experience on leaving their village. Mr. Gupta becomes the instrument of Lalitha's initiation into the world of art as well as the glamorous city life. The novel presents the story of an adolescent growing into a woman (Lalitha) and a child into an adolescent (Saroja). The three stages of initiation rites are found here. It begins with

Saroja's family moving away from the village to the city. The experience in the city makes Saroja emerge more mature and sane, and plays a significant role in her development. The ultimate return of Amma, Appa, and Saroja to the village marks their reintegration into the rural set-up. Lalitha who goes against the dictates of society is left behind. As in *Two Virgins*, the structure of *Nectar in a Sieve* is also based on the archetypal pattern of rejection, initiation, and reintegration. Poverty and the rise of tannery put an end to the agricultural life of Nathan and Rukmani. While their children Selvam and Ira stay back, Rukmani and Nathan are forced to reject their land and move to the city. A traditional agricultural society in the throes of change is depicted here. They are then initiated into city life. City life proves unsuited to them, and it makes their life more miserable. The hardships weigh them down. This separation from the land on which they toil, and to which they are closely linked, leads to Nathan's death. After his death Rukmani returns home, marking a reintegration into the village life. With Rukmani's return, the archetypal pattern is completed.

The customs and traditions of India get ample recognition in Manohar Malgonkar's novels. These offer testimony to his intimate knowledge of Indian life, customs, and familiarity with the cultural traditions of India. Manohar Malgonkar's *The Princes* and *A Bend in the Ganges* deal with the theme of initiation. *The Princes* revolves around an Indian Prince Abhay, the Yuvaraja of Begwad (also the last of the Rulers of Begwad, and the narrator of the story). The historical and personal perspectives fuse in the novel as Abhay's process of initiation progresses. The novel besides being a political one is also a story of initiation. It traces the growth of the hero towards knowledge and self-realization (reminding one of a bildungsroman which records the chronological and intellectual development of the hero). The neophyte has an encounter with the adult world, undergoes experiences that reveal aspects of human life he finds incomprehensible, and finally emerges mature and wise. The different stages of Abhay's initiation are seen here. It is a process which is complicated and during which the hero faces oppositions, ventures into unknown fields. He finally surfaces as a successor to his father, adopting the same old traditional values he had opposed as an adolescent. The hero's point of view undergoes a tremendous change. The development of the protagonist in *The Princes* is also accompanied by the affirmation of traditional values. The problems of growing up are beautifully portrayed. The hero gradually discovers in himself an urge to grow out of his immediate surroundings. His career at Prince's School and college at Jubalpore play a significant role in his development. In this transition from boyhood to adulthood, the three phases of separation, initiation, and reintegration are traceable—Abhay ventures out of his accustomed environment, encounters sex, war, and death, is transformed through a series of rites and revelations, and returns to join the adult group. At the age of eleven, he is initiated in a "ceremony" by his father (Hiroji Maharaja) who repeatedly stresses the need to be a "man" when Abhay weeps over the death of his pet ram, Cannonball—"Men who weep cannot call themselves men" (30), "We are like lions, we do not weep for dead lambs" (31), "It is most important not to squeal, to show hurt. Be a man, my son" (31). At the banquet the cooked ram is a part of the dishes. The Maharaja carves out its eyes and hands it to Abhay to eat. He thrusts them into his mouth praying, "'Make me a Man, O Lord'.... 'Make me a Man'" (33). Abhay's complex process of initiation begins with his seclusion from his mother and childhood associations. Revealing the ignorance of a neophyte are Abhay's words and actions:

> 'Make me a Man', Was this what it involved, the process of becoming a man? I threw away my fork and it fell with a clatter amidst the dishes piled on the main table. I grabbed the other eye [of the cooked ram] firmly with my fingers and thrust it into my mouth, deliberately and defiantly, and once again my father held out the glass of whisky before me. (33)

A more mature Abhay recollects the pangs of growing up and refers to his "childhood as a blur of perpetual bewilderment, of an almost constant awareness of inadequacy, of a desperate striving to make adjustments" (35). Like any other initiate, Abhay too has to adjust himself to the new knowledge he gains. Critics like James. Y. Dayananda have referred to Abhay's initiation:

> Abhay's initiation ceremony shows adult society testing his endurance and indoctrinating him. But it does not carry him firmly into maturity and understanding; it only leads him upto the threshold, leaving him enmeshed in a struggle for certainty and self-discovery. Abhay takes his first tentative step towards maturity under the tutelage of his father. But he still has to go through a variety of experiences, pleasant and unpleasant, to complete his initiation into this select group. (99)

Abhay's initiation progresses with his formal education at school and college. His years at school are accompanied by a breaking away from childhood and learning the ways of maturity. His teachers as well as Kanakchand (his schoolmate) act as his instructors. Through Kanakchand, Abhay comes into contact with poverty in India. Another important influence on him is Mr. Moreton, his English tutor. Abhay himself refers to this:

> I now feel he [Mr. Moreton] may have been the greatest single influence of my early days. He was perhaps the only man in the palace who treated me as an equal, not as a child, but as an adult and for much of the time, not as a prince either, but an ordinary man. He was always interested in what I had to say.... Even though he represented authority, I found myself regarding him more and more as a guide and mentor, even as a companion. (38-39)

The prince's education consists of riding, boxing, music lessons and lessons in wielding a sword. The hero's revolt against his father is also an assertion of his manhood. His father too acknowledges the process of growth in Abhay. Abhay himself recognizes the changes he undergoes:

> That unhappy scene in the room with the fifty-eight dead tigers and the old swords and shields nailed to the walls was like the ending of a phase. For many years

> from that day our [Abhay and his father's] relationship became even more coldly formal than before. (22)
>
> My [Abhay's] problems, I now realize, were by and large the problems of every growing boy; the problems of facing up to the process of stepping into manhood, demanding adjustment in my relationship with my parents and friends, replacing the wide-eyed vision of a boy with the ever narrowing one of a man.
>
> I felt the awkwardness of my years; even in the presence of my mother I seemed to detect new complexes in myself, aware that I was no longer a little boy who could break into her privacy as and when I willed, that there were many things I could not confide in her. (97)

The custom of providing young men with healthy concubines prevailed in Begwad. The Maharaja was presented with his first concubine on his sixteenth birthday. Though Abhay sends his concubine away when he is presented with her, he accepts one later in his life. Abhay is initiated into sex, during his visit to Simla, through Minnie Bradley, the Anglo-Indian girl. His relationship with her makes Abhay aware of "how deep [his] roots went into a Hindu past, and how [Minnie and Abhay] seemed to belong to separate compartments" (185-86). The revelation that his love for Minnie meant nothing to her brings a disillusioning experience. Travels undertaken too play a significant role in his growth. The various experiences in his life—Abhay is made a cadet sergeant, posted at a battalion, sent for action, forced to live under canvas, has to move from place to place and subsist on hard ration—contribute towards his final conversion. Abhay's words and actions serve to emphasize the changes he undergoes during the course of his transformation:

> My impressions of the days in the training camp were overshadowed by an awareness of a total breaking away from my roots. It was almost as though I were a fugitive, leading a new life under a new name, a second-lieutenant Bedar of the Satpura Rifles. (177)

The shift is accompanied by the new knowledge and awareness it brings:

> Until I returned from war service, I used to squirm with shame at the thought of my father's private life. I now realize that, obsessed with the narrowness and naive values of youth, I judged him harshly, as indeed most of his world seems to have judged him. It was the war that helped me to grow up and to broaden my vision, the war and also the sudden explosion of the urges of my body; and then I acquired what I like to think is a civilized tolerance for human frailties, learnt to tear my mind away from the petty and often false loyalties of childhood and youth. (53)

As a part of the process of growing up is his hatred for his father and love for his mother. Abhay's later attitude towards his parents also point to the transition he has slowly undergone:

> And my father's open preference for them [the concubines] was a continued torment to me. Now of course I can understand how even the loveliest of women can make themselves hateful to men; that love, as much as mere sex, is not necessarily concerned with looks, and still less is it concerned with refinement.... (55)

Abhay returns home after two years, shedding illusions, experiencing a new understanding about the world, and with his return he identifies himself more and more with the adult world. He marries Kamala, horsewhips Kanakchand, and finally becomes an image of his father. It is through Abhay's eyes that one sees the events described in the novel, and one notices his developing consciousness. His speech and actions bring out the development of his character. The disparity between Abhay an uninitiated youth (at the opening of the novel), and Abhay the narrator (older) is clearly visible. The conversion becomes complete when Abhay accepts the values upheld by his father. Abhay himself becomes aware of this close resemblance:

> ...I [Abhay] myself went a long way towards sharing his views and values as far as our state was concerned [earlier Abhay had opposed his father's views]. Indeed it

> seems to me that with the passing of the years, I have come to identify myself more and more with those values, with the result that today I feel myself a spokesman for whatever the princely order once stood for.
>
> "Maharaja Abhayraj, proved to be just as much of a reactionary as his father," the Settlements Minister wrote in his memoirs. He was referring to me, of course, instead of feeling resentful, I was elated by the rebuke, proud of being thought like my father. (18)

The themes of Indian independence and of the growing up of a prince are interwoven into the novel. Abhay's growth is skilfully interwoven with the historical theme. The two plots (the public and the personal) run parallel to each other. The initiate (Abhay) has an encounter with the adult world, undergoes experiences that are new, and finally emerges mature—Abhay is "ceremonially" initiated by his father, is taught at school and college, revolts against his father, is introduced into sexual knowledge, learns from war and travels, returns to the adult world, and identifies himself more and more with his father's values. Though the novel does not give a detailed description of any initiation ceremony, it offers the various experiences which initiate Abhay into the world of adults. Numerous experiences carry him towards the final stage. The novelist employs the device of repetition, reversal, and contrast to emphasize the likeness (and the transformation in Abhay) between the hero and his father. The roles of the father and the son are reversed gradually, and the novel celebrates the conservative and traditional values. The influence of tradition on Abhay is clear from his reminiscence of childhood and adolescence. He appears deeply rooted in his princely tradition. The pattern of his life is broken and he moves out on his own. The war enables him to withdraw from his immediate surroundings. This, in a way, inscribes his growth. At the beginning Abhay is portrayed as a foil to his father, but towards the end (after the Maharaja's death) Abhay occupies his father's place. He succeeds briefly to the title of his father, abdicates and becomes a spokesman for his father's values. At the end Abhay is seated in the same tiger-rug room from which he had run out protesting against his father:

> [The] juxtaposition of the two points of view [that of Hiroji Maharaja and Abhay] creates a tension between the two poles of adulthood and youth, thus intensifying the theme of initiation. We get the impression of a complex, growing, and fluid personality as it encounters experience, a personality as it is defined in the interpenetration of its past and present self-awareness. (Dayananda 109)

Like his father, Abhay too has a conventional Hindu marriage, whips Kanakchand (ten years later), and accepts his father's values. He gradually enters the princely fold and accepts its ways, ensuring the victory of tradition. Instances like the public flogging, nights with the concubines, the traditional marriage, his visit to the Jamdar-Khana (the family vault) point this out. The transformation becomes clear when one notices the change in Abhay's attitude. Abhay reveals his own preference for the princely order:

> Episodes in their [Hiroji Maharaja and Abhay] lives like those of marriage and concubinage are rhythmic or parallel in the sense that the form of the episode is the same in each and yet antithetical and offering contrast in the sense that one episode presents us with one kind of reality, one set of values, and the other presents us with a different kind of reality, a different set of values. (Dayananda 116)

Manohar Malgonkar employs reversals and repetitions with different outcomes. They contradict and negate the events which previously occur (as in *The Princes* and *A Bend in the Ganges*). With Abhay's reverting to values and traditions of the old order of his father, the victory of tradition is ensured. The novel clearly traces Abhay's transformation. The personal tragedy of the prince is artistically and deftly combined with the political background described in the novel.

A Bend in the Ganges too contains the theme of initiation. The work depicts the movement, towards self-awareness and knowledge, of Gian Talwar, Debi-dayal, and Shafi Usman (though Debi-dayal and Shafi Usman die before reaching the final stage of transformation). The themes of non-violence and violence exist side by side in the novel. Gian Talwar and Debi-dayal represent these two principles of life. His is a journey from humiliation and cowardice, betrayal and deception to strength and tranquility. The novelist takes Gian through all the stages of development and presents his growth towards moral maturity. Gian comes to Duriabad out of Punjab in pursuit of higher education and is exposed to Gandhi's influence. He resists the attempts of Debi-dayal and Shafi Usman to convert him to the creed of non-violence. Gian is initiated into the higher world of Kerwad House, and also to the one without taste and refinement. The forces of destruction are at work here. It begins with Dada's discovery of the image of Shiva while digging his fields at Piploda. His conversion from the worship of Vishnu, the God of Protection, to the world of Shiva, is a symbolic recognition of the initiation of the process of destruction. The further operations of the destructive element are found in the defeat of the terrorist movement, the breaking up of Sundari's marriage, the disruption of normalcy on the Andamans by the arrival of the Japanese, and finally the outburst of communal frenzy. Manohar Malgonkar does not take Debi-dayal and Shafi Usman through all the stages of development though they too undergo changes in the process. Debi-dayal moves from involvement in national politics and public life to a stage of indifference to politics. It culminates in his withdrawal into domestic life. He embarks on his quest for development as a terrorist, eating with the Hindus, Muslims, and Sikhs alike, flouting the sacred impositions of religion and renouncing its taboos. The initiation into the terrorist group is accompanied by an oath of initiation which is signed in blood. In due course Debi-dayal is transported to the Andamans. On his return to India he is less actively involved in politics. He even assumes a new name, Kaluram, like Gian Talwar. Disillusioned with politics, he gets involved with Mumtaz. Along with his indifference to politics is his withdrawal from public life. He decides to go to Duriabad and assumes a Muslim name, Karim, but gets killed in the communal riots. Shafi Usman's transformation (to violence) is motivated because his father had become a victim of Jallianwala Massacre. Like Debi-dayal he too hates the British. As his religion means nothing to him, he converts to Sikhism. Shafi Usman becomes the leader of a group of Hindus, Muslims, and Sikhs, and renounces vegetarianism. He is gradually transformed into a fanatical hater of Hindus. His actions reveal the change in his outlook. Instead of warning all the Freedom Fighters that their meeting place was going to be raided he warns only Muslim members. The others are hence arrested and put in jail:

> He [Shafi Usman] had changed, almost inevitably, as the whole of India had changed. The fervour of youth had been tempered, its follies rectified.... As far as Shafi was concerned...he had now become convinced there was no possibility of the Hindus and Muslims living together. The days of religious unity...was gone. (294)

On his return to India his life as a Sikh appears absurd to him. Shafi Usman and his friends even enter the Kerwad House, insult and abuse Sundari and her parents during the riots. He destroys the statue of the Hindu gods, but in the scuffle gets killed by Sundari. His initiation thus comes to an end. It is on Gian Talwar's initiation and growth—his growth towards self-knowledge and understanding of the world—that the novel focuses. He is transformed from the impulsive young man who participates in the purificatory ceremony and Gandhi's non-violence to a mature adult who comes to save Sundari and her family during the communal riots at the conclusion. Gian too passes through a series of ordeals to achieve maturity. With his throwing a blazer made of imported English material (in the opening chapter) begins Gian's brief career as a disciple of Gandhi. He goes to college, and there meets Debi-dayal who belongs to a terrorist group dedicated to overthrow the British rule in India. Though he declares himself to be a follower of Gandhi he does not want to get involved in the activities around him. His brother Hari's murder by Vishnu-dutt destroys his heroic picture of the self and there begins a period of doubt. The views on non violence crumble, and nationalism wavers. As he comes into collision with reality, he accuses himself of being a coward. Gian deviates from non-violence, kills Vishnu-dutt and is given a sentence of transportation for life (like Debi-dayal) to the Andamans where he remains confused. There ensues a period of deceit. He hides Sundari's letter to Debi-dayal, acts as a spy for Patrick Mulligan, spies on the other inmates of the prison, and even betrays Debi-dayal. On leaving Andamans, he takes a false name (Maruti Rao) in India, meets Debi-dayal's family and lies about his friendship to him and succeeds in getting a job with a new name (Gian Joshi). The short period of non-violence appears as a cover for his cowardice. Sundari too refers to Gian's moral degradation. The communal riots after partition witness a new Gian, who for the first time accepts reality. He rushes to help Sundari and her parents, thus overcoming his selfishness. The flux in the political scene is accompanied by the transformation in Gian Talwar. Gian himself refers to the change:

> "Since we are talking about my degradation, may I tell you that that is partly the reason why I have come?" Gian said. "To try and prove, if only to myself, that there can be some good in the weakest of human beings...don't you see that I am trying to make up?". (351-52)

A new Gian emerges when Shafi Usman and his friends attack Sundari's house. Gian fights them boldly and saves Sundari. By now he attains self-knowledge and maturity which he lacks at the opening of the novel. Gian alone moves to the final phase of transformation and growth and this progress from "innocence" to "knowledge" is clearly drawn. His experiences (in Konshet, Andaman, and Duriabad) discipline him and develop his character. The novel probes into his state of mind and analyses his progress:

> Malgonkar takes Gian through three stages in his growth toward moral maturity. First, he is unable to distinguish between the heroic dreams of his commitment to Gandhian non-violence and the harsh realities of his own nature and of the politics of India's struggle for freedom. Second, he goes through a period

> of confusion and doubt, of deceit and rationalization, as reality begins to intrude upon the falseness of his private dream world. And finally, he solves his problem when he abandons his search for comfortable justifications and learns to see the world in its true light. (Dayananda 127)

A reversal in the fortunes of both Gian Talwar and Debi-dayal takes place here. Gian murders Vishnu-dutt to avenge his brother's murder while Debi-dayal's fight against the British ends abruptly due to the treachery of his leader Shafi Usman. Both are set in opposition to their previous stand due to the reversal. As G.S. Amur remarks:

> The value that the novel does seek to affirm is the value of love which transcends violence and non-violence—the real and the unreal—and brings about freedom and fulfilment to the individuals. This is the value that Gian, the unheroic hero, and Debi-dayal, the heroic hero, both discover in the act of living out their separate yet strangely involved lives. (104-05)

While *The Princes* reveals a convention-bound traditional world, in *A Bend in the Ganges* a similar atmosphere is revealed through Gian Talwar (whose family closely follows the traditional customs and practices). The skilful use of symbols (like the tiger-rug room in *The Princes*, and the image of Shiva in *A Bend in the Ganges*) acquires a symbolic meaning due to their recurrence. Both, *The Princes* and *A Bend in the Ganges*, trace the slow but sure alteration of their respective heroes which lead to their self-realization. Both his heroes undergo conflicts and crisis, which try them and turn them into fully developed personalities.

The protagonist in *Samskara* too passes through the different phases found in the rites of passage. The Hindu society with its superstitions, outmoded beliefs, caste prejudices and ritualism is exposed by U.R. Anantha Murthy. The story revolves around the death of Naranappa, the "outsider", in an orthodox brahmin *agrahara* named Durvasapura. His death creates commotion in the *agrahara*. Living rebelliously amidst the orthodox brahmins, he antagonized his kin. Thus, "[a]live, Naranappa was an enemy; dead a preventer of meals; as a corpse, a problem, a nuisance" (3). The very title of the novel is significant for it refers not only to the rituals (*samskaras*) attended to by the brahmins but also the refinement (*samskara*) which they have not attained. A Sanskrit word (*samskara*) with manifold meaning is chosen as the title. It means forming well or thoroughly, making perfect, refinement, forming in the mind, conception, idea, faculty of recollection, preparation, making sacred, making pure, a sanctifying or purificatory rite, any rite or ceremony, funeral obsequies etc. The epigraph to the novel points this out. The title thus suggests the transformation Praneshacharya, the spiritual leader of the *agrahara*, experiences and through him the *agrahara* may undergo. Though the novel does not contain any elaborate description of the initiation rite, structurally it shares the three phases of the *rites de passage*. These phases are found in the transformation which Praneshacharya undergoes. The novel, which opens with the death of Naranappa, raises a number of questions and concludes with the transformation of the religious leader. Naranappa had questioned the brahmins of the *agrahara* and uncovered their *samskara* (refinement of spirit). In his attempt to resolve the dilemma of who should perform the dead man's death rite (a *samskara*), the Acharya (Praneshacharya) begins a *samskara* (a transformation) for himself. The conflict here is primarily between the orthodox life led by the brahmins in the *agrahara* which is full of rituals and decadent practices, and the unorthodox or demonic way represented by Naranappa and his followers. The novel without "accepting or rejecting either of the two,...brings out the inadequacies of both when pursued in excess and in isolation from the other" (Gupta, *Journal of Commonwealth Literature* 23). Though Naranappa questioned the secrets of brahminism, he led a life which the other brahmins secretly longed for. As A.K. Ramanujan points out, they find in him their own "inmost unspoken libidinous desires" (Afterword 140), their "mocking anti-self" (Afterword 140). The process which initiates the spiritual leader into a new world is clearly visible here—the world of Naranappa and his friends. In the first part the hero is "ripe and ready" (2) to attain salvation. This is gradually proved wrong. Naranappa's death shatters a calm and routinized life in the *agrahara*. Though Praneshacharya followed rigorous self-denial all his life, he too, like the other brahmins, enjoys the sensuous beauty of the heroines in the poetry he recites and explains to them. The sudden sexual experience with an outcast (Chandri) initiates him into a new world. He thus participates in the condition of his opposite—a life entirely different from his past. Naranappa serves as a scapegoat to the brahmins who find in him their own unspoken desires, and try to exorcize him. He responds to these brahmins with defiant ridicule and withering contempt. In contrast to the impoverished lives of the brahmins is the epicurean life of Naranappa who has rejected the principles and ideals of brahminhood. While seeking an answer to solve the problem, Praneshacharya becomes one with his opposite (Naranappa). The Sanskrit learning and ascetic practices which are a part of his life are thrown aside as he sleeps with a low caste woman. Through crisis he begins to transform himself. Gradually the place of action shifts from a brahmin agrahara to the mind of the protagonist. It is not just compassion but also a "terrible" (47) and "uncontrollable wilfulness" (47) and pride in his knowledge that makes Praneshacharya try to change Naranappa to his orthodox ways. The death upsets his world and raises different questions ultimately leading to his transformation. The Acharya finds himself unable to lead the brahmins who look up to him for a solution. The initial section of the novel shows him as a member of the brahmin community. His relationship with Chandri marks the beginning of his initiation and break from the earlier order. Signifying the change, his awakened senses differentiate between the aridity of the brahmin *agrahara* and the lush nature around him and Chandri. The sight of the dead rat, his bed-ridden wife, and the smell of the rotting body now fill him with disgust. The story moves like a *rite de passage*. It involves the three stages of separation, transition, and reincorporation —the Acharya's flight from his accustomed village, his journey through the world of fairs where he is in a "neither-here-nor-there" (131) state, and the final stage (one finds the Acharya on its threshold) which is not dealt with in the novel. The initiation rites mark the initiate's change in status. Such a change is often accompanied by a change of place, seclusion, and a return (as with Praneshacharya). After his "new experience" (82), Praneshacharya leaves the *agrahara* and moves out of his accustomed circle "leaving everything behind" (91). He thus merges with his opposite through the low caste Chandri who lived with Naranappa before his death. On moving out of his routinized world, the Acharya is initiated into a new world of activity by Putta (a representative of Naranappa's world whom he meets during his wanderings) who accompanies him in his journey away from the *agrahara*. Putta acts as a catalytic agent in the Acharya's process of transformation. Praneshacharya's aloofness gradually disappears and he responds to Putta's company and human affection. The novelist beautifully portrays the psychological turmoil which the protagonist undergoes. The Acharya realizes that he cannot "live outside the contacts of men" (92). Putta takes him to the Melige festival, and thus initiates him into a new world. From a rootless and disembodied state he involves himself in the human world of passion and experience. Praneshacharya finds it difficult to be a part of the world filled with cock-fights and liquor. He feels "the dread of being transformed...to [a] demon" (121). Indicating his shift to another stage, he says, "I have moved to the next stage of soul, leaving the ghostly stage behind" (123). The Acharya loses his former self and assumes an entirely new personality. Praneshacharya breaks the taboos associated with death and moves closer to his anti-self. Like Naranappa, who did not attend his wife's funeral, Praneshacharya does not complete his wife's last rites. He starts behaving like the libertine and even invites Putta to the temple. The novel itself refers to this conflict. Unlike Naranappa, Praneshacharya is unable to shed his fear completely. The dead body rotting and waiting to be cremated looms large in his mind. He despises "the tigerish world of cock-fights" (130-31) into which he will fall on shedding his brahminism. Unable to participate in it he stands outside the "world of ordinary pleasures" (115). The single act (of sleeping with Chandri) removes him from his accustomed world and places him on the road to transformation. Praneshacharya may reject the brahminical world of penance, but may not be able to embrace the world of cruelty. At this stage he belongs neither to the old life (his life in the *agrahara*) nor to a new one as his changeover is incomplete. The Acharya finds himself in an indeterminate stage. The passages referring to his liminal stage show Praneshacharya's awareness of his transformation—"Now my person has lost form, has found no new form..." (98), "Trishanku-state" (109), "a piece of string in the wind, a cloud taking on shapes according to the wind" (109), "...a hovering demon, rootless object in the hustle and noise" (114), and words like "I am neither here, nor there" (115) etc., support this. The experience helps him realize the importance of human interdependence, that his decision involves others (an entire agrahara). The Acharya emerges, at the end, on the threshold of the final phase of reintegration and decides to take on the responsibility of Naranappa's last rites. He chooses to shed his respectability by confessing the truth to the brahmins at Durvasapura. The novel does not describe the effect of his unorthodox ways on the orthodox agrahara and its brahmins and ends inconclusively. Through the transition of the central character, it portrays questions of selfhood. The change that Praneshacharya undergoes (notwithstanding the uncertainty and conflicts within him between the brahminic and demonic) is significant in his life. This initiation into the world of demonic experience is "a transformation which in all probability would change the course of his (Praneshacharya's) future life in significant ways" (Gupta 21). The novel makes one speculate whether Praneshacharya will be able to transform the decaying *agrahara* and its hypocrite brahmins with the new knowledge that he has attained. But, when it "ends" there is little hope that Praneshacharya will succeed in his attempt to liberate himself, and his community from the shackles of outmoded customs and practices.

Though birth and initiation rites are found in some of the creative works, only a few of them provide a detailed account of these rituals and ceremonies associated with the initial phase of human life. These rites are used differently by creative writers. Sometimes a description or short reference to these rituals is made by novelists to throw light on the culture of the community. Besides concentrating on the process of growing up, creative writers also draw upon the three phases of initiation rites which are considered universal and significant. The plots of such works move like a rite de passage. The birth and initiation rites, which mark the initial period of an individual's life, form a part of almost every social group. Some of these works in Indian English fiction also demonstrate how rites and rituals differ on the basis of caste, sex, community, society etc. Rituals mark birth as well as the transition from childhood to adulthood among most social groups in India. Besides being an occasion for the people to come together, birth and initiation ceremonies formally make the child a part of the social group to which he belongs. While the birth rites make the new-born a part of this world, the initiation rites confer on him the status of an adult and with it new responsibilities. The child thus becomes a part of the society and has new roles to perform. Similar rituals and ceremonies are essential as they bring the people together and make smooth the transition for the initiate. As the society loses its members through death, it gains more members through birth and initiation. These rites being significant in human life have found their way into literary works.

While the birth rites make the child a member of society, the initiation rites divest the person of his status as a child in the domestic domain and invest him with a social status. The public nature of the ceremony often assists him in assuming a new identity. The ritual observances which accompany it function to endow the assigned activities with an aura of sanctity. The individual then goes on to perform more significant roles in his life. Novelists have portrayed this transition differently. While some concentrate on the ritualistic aspect, others dwell upon the process of transformation the initiate undergoes. The neophyte thus passes through the different phases before assuming a new identity and entering a new phase in his life. That these rites have a social and psychological impact is evident here.

3

The Nuptial

The wedding remains the greatest social occasion in our life. It is considered as a socially approved, sexual, and economic union between a man and a woman. The rituals and ceremonies associated with marriage make it a sacred tie to be borne till death. A marriage involves a readjustment of the social structure whereby the woman's relation with her family is greatly modified, and she enters into a new relation with her husband. It usually starts with the appointment of a match-maker by the girl's family to seek a suitable boy. When the preliminary negotiations are over, and the dowry settled, there is a formal betrothal, followed by the marriage. Among many communities a marriage procession is taken out on the occasion of the first formal visit of the bridegroom to the bride's house for marriage. After marriage she is brought to her future house. She then visits her parents after a few days.

In India people make all kinds of careful investigation, from horoscope of the bride and the groom to the ancestry of the parents of the couple, when it comes to marriage. While some go in for elaborate marriage ceremonies others are married by civil authorities. Among some groups there is no ceremony and the bride leaves with the groom to his parent's house. Sometimes what is fundamentally the same rite in two different societies may have different purposes. A same ritual may be used by two groups on two different occasions. While among the Hindus it is a widow who is forced to shave her head, among the Kafirs it is the bride who has to shave her head.

Very diverse are the ways of obtaining a wife. Betrothals may be arranged between infants, or relatives may select a bride for the youth. A betrothal is considered as sacred and as binding as a marriage ceremony by some sections of the society. In such societies a girl betrothed in childhood is a widow for life if he, to whom she is betrothed, dies even before she sees him. Usually the negotiations are handled and the marriage arranged by the immediate families or by go-betweens.

A common practice associated with marriage is that of consulting the horoscope. The horoscope holds an important place in a Hindu household and is consulted every now and then. Though referred to on many occasions, it is inevitable when a Hindu wedding is celebrated. It is only when both—of the bride and the groom—the horoscopes match that the marriage takes place. Among the Cingalese, an astrologer has to decide before the marriage whether the horoscopes of the suitor and the girl suit each other. Often when it didn't suit they carried out marriage by proxy. "Once when the bridegroom's horoscope was not suitable, he produced that of his infant brother, which was satisfactory. This child personated the groom and was married to the bride" (Crawley 55).

The reference to the horoscope is found in a number of Indian English novels. In *Grandmother's Tale* the narrator tells us about his grandmother who performs a variety of tasks all through the day, one of which is "studying horoscopes and arranging matrimonial alliances" (1). Letters of offers for marriage come, enclosing horoscopes from parents who have daughters, first for Gopi and later on for his son in *The World of Nagaraj*. In *Reminiscences*, the initial exchange of letters and horoscopes takes place before the marriage. Anita Desai's *Cry, The Peacock* is about a young girl, Maya, who is obsessed with a childhood prophecy of disaster which cannot be averted. Obsessed with death she brings about the death of herself, her husband—Gautam, and her mother-in-law. R.K. Narayan's *The Financial Expert* satirically points out that in the modern world if the astrologer is paid enough he will fix the horoscope the way one wants. In *The Bachelor of Arts*, Chandran's father has no faith in the horoscope, but the Sastrigal asks him, "How are we to know whether two persons brought together will have health, happiness, harmony and long life, if you do not study their horoscopes individually and together?" (78). Health, happiness, harmony, and long life are usually the reasons for which horoscopes are consulted. This serves to ensure that nothing bad befell the couple. But often, sending the horoscope for comparison was a sign that both the parties were not averse to the alliance. On the basis of the horoscope the priest fixes the auspicious date and time for the marriage.

In spite of man's attempt to rationalize everything, astrology continues to influence him. The reason why astrology continues to have such an influence on the Indian psyche lies in the area of psychology. Perhaps, it fulfils our intrinsic craving to know about the future, or our strong desire to believe in something. The feeling of awareness about the future which the horoscope provides mitigates our feeling of helplessness and loneliness.

While some cultures have marriages with elaborate ceremonies, others have no ceremony at all. The proposal of marriage and the arrangements are conducted not by the bride or groom but by friends, or relatives, who thus serve as proxies. The 'bride-seeing' ceremony plays an important role in marriage. The bridegroom and his relatives arrive on a particular day at the bride's residence to "examine" her. In some societies a method of selection is prevalent in which a young man and a maiden retire into the jungle and light a fire. Then the maiden takes up a burning fire-brand and applies it to the man's back. If he cries out from pain, he is rejected otherwise the marriage is carried out (Hutchinson 454). The bridegroom often wins his bride after tests of physical fitness and courage. There is also marriage by capture in which the bride tries to escape and the groom, with her parent's consent, pursues her and brings her back.

In many societies marriage involves economic consideration. The economic transaction may take several forms, the most common being bride price. It is a gift of money or goods given to the bride's kin by the groom or his kin, which gives the groom the right to marry the girl. Thus a compensation to the bride's kin for the loss of her labour. Sometimes the groom works for the bride's family, thus replacing bride price with bride service. Among certain tribes in South Africa, the bride price is handed over to the bride's mother's brother on behalf of the bride for whom it is paid.

After the bride and the groom are decided, preparations are made for festivities in the homes of both the parties. Invitations are sent out in advance to their kinsfolk and friends. Customs related to wedding festivities vary in different regions. The bride is often loaded with all the gold she possesses. The bridal trousseau is also on exhibition at many wedding ceremonies.

To a Hindu, like any other individual, marriage is the most important occasion in his life. It is a subject of endless conversation and of the most prolonged preparations. A pandal or canopy is put up and rituals are performed to ward off any hindrance or misfortune which might occur during the celebration of the marriage. Often the bridegroom is taken to the bride's place in a large procession. Thus it becomes an occasion of social festivity. Mulk Raj Anand refers to such a procession in *Gauri*. It is under the canopy that the priest conducts the marriage ceremony. The bride and the bridegroom are seated on a dais made for this purpose. The women often perform the ceremony of *arati* to ward off evil. At the auspicious moment the bridegroom ties the *tali*, the Hindu sign of marriage corresponding to the wedding ring of the Christians, around the neck of the bride. Among certain groups this wedding-string is passed around to be blessed by the wedding guests. In some castes a chain of black beads or a string stained with turmeric is used instead of a *tali*. The bridegroom may also touch her forehead with *sindur*. To ward off evil influence, a vessel containing turmeric water is kept at certain wedding ceremonies. Among some people it is a custom to interpose a 'screen' or 'curtain' between the bridal couple. At the end of the wedding ceremony the clothes of the bride and the groom are sometimes tied together. Amongst the Hindus, the father gives away his daughter in marriage to the groom by placing her hand in his. In the marriage service among the Christians also, someone is required to stand as the donor of the bride. The father thus bestows his daughter upon the man whom he deems worthy of her. This ceremony is called *kania-dana*. It signifies the renunciation of parental authority over the bride. The bridegroom ties the *tali* accepting her as his wife. The thrice repeated circuit of the newly married couple around the sacred fire is a mutual ratification of the contract they have made with one another, for there is no more solemn engagement than that entered into in the presence of fire, which Hindus look upon as the purest of their gods.

Among the Hindu Nairs the union is publicly established in a ceremony during which the husband ties the gold ornament, *tali*, around the neck of his bride. She lives in a large household, with her family, where she is visited by her husband. This has been dealt with in novels like S. Menon Marath's *The Wound of Spring* and O. Chandu Menon's *Indulekha*. At a Christian wedding ceremony the couple exchange vows and receive the blessings of the priest. After the wedding, the couple, their relatives, and guests retire to the wedding feast. The opulence of these banquets depended on the means of the family. Amongst certain groups the wedding couple is anointed with oil and turmeric. They also worship the guardian spirits. Sometimes, as a part of the marriage ceremony, the groom is stopped at the door of the bride's place by her sister to answer some riddles. Also part of this ceremony is the stealing of the groom's shoes.

There are various social signals which indicate that a marriage is taking place. The marriage procession and the marriage feast are two of them. The actual ceremony is often publicly ratified by the couple eating together. Sometimes rice and flowers are thrown on the couple during the wedding. This is done to propitiate the evil spirits. The scattering of rice on the bride and the groom is done to ensure prosperity and happiness in their life ahead.

Among many religious groups the bride is behind a veil when her husband comes to claim her, and, only by marriage is that veil lifted to him. The ceremony is often called the 'uncovering of the face' or the 'lifting of the veil' (Trumbell 43). This ceremony is seen among the Muslims in India. At the end of a Christian marriage service, the bridegroom lifts the veil of his bride and kisses her. The very word 'nuptial' means the 'veiling' of the bride to receive her husband (Trumbell 43).

Sometimes marriage is conducted by proxy to avoid misfortune. The Brahmins consider marriage with a third woman very unlucky. To avert the misfortune resulting there from, a mock ceremony is performed in the course of which the widower ties a tali on a plant, which is then cut down. The actual marriage is thus the fourth one (Hutchinson 454). A Brahmin marriage is extended over a number of days and involves a number of rituals and ceremonies.

Thus in the East the week of the wedding is one of ceremonies, feasts, processions, noise, show, and parade of wealth.

Even after years of reform, the view that a woman's life is rendered meaningless once her husband dies or deserts her is still the dominant one. As a widow she has to live in seclusion. A widow has to live a life of her own, for an orthodox society isolates her. She has to keep away from all festivals and ceremonies, be it familial or social, for her presence is considered inauspicious. The ancient and barbarous custom of *sati* force the widows to sacrifice themselves. It is considered her duty to throw herself voluntarily on the funeral pyre of her husband. This cruel practice has been abolished to a certain extent in the Indian society.

As soon as her husband dies, *tali*, the wedding-string, which is the sign of marriage is removed from her neck. A widow's bangles are broken, the *kumkum* on her forehead is wiped off and she is dressed in a white sari. But the greatest of all miseries is the forcible shaving of her head. A widow is often forced to submit herself to these cruel practices, which are ensured employing the threat of social excommunication. In *Kanthapura*, Raja Rao portrays a progressive widow through Ratna. Though a widow, she does not dress and live in the conventional style of a widow. She wears bangles, coloured saris, uses ***kumkum*** mark on her forehead, and parts her hair. In the novel she is much criticized for her unconventional ways. The Indian woman is often portrayed as being bound by superstition and conservative traditions. There are works which present human beings caught in the flux of tradition and modernity, bearing the burden of the past and the aspirations of the future. Creative writers often question their society's orthodoxies, and articulate openly their dissent from accepted notions.

The ceremonies connected with marriage vary according to caste, religion, and position in life. The wedding festival often becomes an occasion for establishing one's position and influence "by displaying as much ostentation as possible" (Chaudhuri 41). It is also an occasion to show one's "sense of social obligation and kindness to all without distinction of rank or wealth" (Chaudhuri 41-42). Very often it becomes a competition to establish one's equality with the family into which one is marrying and often an attempt to show one's superiority.

Marriage is the oldest institution in human life. It is as well an important social occasion, which announces to the people around that the young bride and groom are bound in wedlock. The marriage rites and ceremonies give religious and social recognition to the sexual behaviour of the male and the female. Marriage in Indian culture is not only an alliance made by a man and a woman, but also an alliance between two families. To the Hindus, marriage is not merely an arrangement for a man and a woman to live together. To them the *vivaha* or the marriage ritual is one of the sixteen *samskaras* (sacraments). While marriage is a religious rite, it is also an occasion for social celebration in which two families are brought together in a close relationship. The relatives and friends on both the sides assemble to participate in the event. Socially it is the announcement of a new relationship. The Hindu marriage is not merely a legal contract but a sacrament which lends a sort of permanency to wedlock. The rituals and ceremonies which accompany it give a special significance to the union which would otherwise be a simple gratification of the sexual instinct:

> Since marriage is a sacred contract made between a man and a woman, society mobilizes all its forces, legal as well as moral and social, to cement the union stable. It has to be solemnized at sacred seasons, auspicious days or time. (Joseph 175)

The religious ceremonies performed by the priests are a necessary and important part of the marriage ceremonies. These rituals sanctify the union. Besides giving publicity to the union, they gain the acceptance of society for the newly wed. The Hindu marriage rites stress the permanency of the marriage bond and the co-operation of the husband and the wife. The important ceremonies associated with marriage are the betrothal (*nischitartha*), the handing over the bride (*kanyadanam*), the mutual firm clasping of hands between the bride and the groom (*panigrahanam*) and the seven meaningful steps (*saptapadi*) which the couple take around the sacred fire. These solemnize the tie and ensure abundant food, wealth, vitality, and all round happiness. The various rituals and vows ensure mutual harmony, happiness, continued compatibility, prosperity, and marital success. The couple prays for progeny, long life, and well-being. These religious *samskaras* have the sanctity and approval of society. The different forms of marriage are different ways of obtaining a wife. There are the pre-marriage rites, the principal marriage rites, and the post-marriage rites. The indissolubility of the tie is an essential principle firmly established among the Hindus. The moment the marriage knot is tied, after the enjoined marriage rites are performed, they become partners for life. The tie is broken only by the death of one. With marriage, the female child passes out of the possession of her parents and out of the possession of her horde into the possession of her husband. This transfer sometimes involves compensation in the form of bride price or bride wealth. The husband and the wife are considered one, and the ceremonies observed by the husband without the co-operation of the wife do not yield the desired result. Hence an orthodox Hindu performs all ceremonies in the company of his wife. The marriage rites and ceremonies, along with the *mantras* recited "bind" the husband and the wife together. Apart from the marriage feast (in which the partaking of food indicates oneness), the marriage procession which announces the marriage brings the people together. Music is sometimes played to signal the beginning or end of a ritual. It is supposed to scare away the undesirable invisible beings from the marriage pandal and the premises. The presence of *Agni* (the sacred fire) contributes to the inviolable sanctity of the marriage rites. The bridegroom marries his bride in the presence of *Agni*, the god of fire, and various other *devas* whose presence is invoked and who are supposed to be present at the time when the marriage ceremonies take place. The marriage tie is solemnized in the presence of the divine. It is believed to purify the bride and animate her with the activity of procreation. A marriage usually involves a readjustment of the social structure whereby the bride's relationship with her family is greatly modified. She enters a new and close relationship with her husband. Before the marriage, the girl's family members are outsiders for him, as he is an outsider for them. It constitutes a social disjunction which is not destroyed by marriage. The social conjunction results from the continuance, though in altered form, of the wife's relation to her family, their continued interest in her and her children. Two separate and distinct social groups, families or lineages, are brought together through the union of a man and a woman. The religious ceremonies performed by the priest aim not merely at averting spiritual dangers, but also at the success of the union. From time immemorial certain rites and ceremonies have been associated with the institution of marriage. These rites often differ from society to society, and even in different epochs. The various ritualistic formalities which accompany a marriage sanctify the union.

The marriage ceremony involves a number of stages, beginning with the selection of the bride and the groom. In orthodox societies this is done by the elders. An auspicious date is fixed, and sometimes a betrothal takes place. The horoscope and the dowry are two important customs associated with the preliminary formalities. The parents exchange the horoscope of the bride and the groom. An astrologer is consulted to decide the match. It is only after a lot of initial discussions that the marriage is approved and celebrated. A number of works in Indian English fiction contain reference to this *samskara*. Raja Rao, R.K. Narayan, and Mulk Raj Anand have depicted these ceremonies in their works. These rites are portrayed in different ways. While Raja Rao concentrates on the philosophical and spiritual aspect of marriage (*The Serpent and the Rope* presents a ritualistic and symbolic union of Ramaswamy and Savitri), R.K. Narayan's works expose the tradition-bound conservative society of Malgudi. Novelists like Lalithambika Antharjanam (*Agnisaakshi*), K.B. Sreedevi (*Yajnam*), and Rajam Krishnan (*Lamps in the Whirlpool*) expose the tragic plight of women caught in an orthodox and conservative set-up. Most of the Indian novels refer to the customs and practices closely associated with the Indian culture, each novelist depicting them in his own way. R.K. Narayan's *Bachelor of Arts*, *Vendor of Sweets*, *Painter of Signs*, and *Grandmother's Tale*, Mulk Raj Anand's *Gauri*, Kamala Markandaya's *Nectar in a Sieve* and *A Handful of Rice*, Anita Desai's *Cry, the Peacock* and *Fasting, Feasting*, Manohar Malgonkar's *The Princes*, and Kavery Nambisan's *The Scent of Pepper* are instances.

The superstitious and the orthodox closely adhere to the age old traditions and customs associated with marriage. In an orthodox society one finds the traditional method of "arranging" marriages after comparing the horoscopes of the bride and the groom, taking into consideration the family, status, caste, relative affluence and future prospects of both the families. These rigid caste prohibitions and difficult astrological hurdles in India are referred to by R.K. Narayan. The role of the matchmaker, who is appointed to find a suitable bride or groom by the respective parties, at the Indian wedding is also important. Indian English novels like *The Bachelor of Arts*, *Gauri*, *Nectar in a Sieve*, and *A Handful of Rice* depict this customary practice. In *The Bachelor of Arts* Ganapathi Sastrigal is appointed to give out that he is acting on his own, while in *Nectar in a Sieve* Old Granny plays a similar role. Ravi's father comes from his village to play the role of a matchmaker as Ravi has no one to do so in the city (*A Handful of Rice*). Ravi mentions the disparate nature of the urban and the rural set-up. A contrast to his present state is provided by his recollection of his village:

> Women came and went, and one always knew which girls had come of age, which young men were looking for brides, and when the time was, there was never any shortage of emissaries, you never had to look for one because they were always there, experienced women who went determinedly back and forth until the marriage was arranged. Yes, there it would have been different, he would have had no problems at all. Ravi sighed for his village, a thing which he did not often do; and was unhappy. (48-49)

While Ravi's father comes and carries out the preliminary negotiations in *A Handful of Rice*, in *Gauri* a barber acts as the go-between. The society's orthodox belief in astrology is humorously presented in *The Bachelor of Arts*. The second part of the novel contains much of the discussions on marriage and the customs and practices associated with it. Chandran has to face the hurdle of rigid customs and useless traditions like matching the horoscope existing in the Hindu society. The difficulty of love marriages in an orthodox Indian society is presented here. Caste, status, and financial position of the two families concerned are taken into consideration. In Chandran's marriage too there is the question of caste, subcaste, dowry, family status, and finally the tallying of horoscopes. Since Malathi (the girl he loves) too is an Iyer there is no difficulty regarding the caste and subcaste. Difficulties arise due to the low status of her family. Her father is only a head clerk while Chandran's father is a retired high ranking government official. The customs and traditional practices shatter the hero's romantic illusions. What happens in Malgudi is typical of the orthodox Hindu society in India. It appears as a microcosm and symbol of India. Chandran's mother is the depository of age old customs and traditions. Being very conservative, she makes a lot of fuss regarding the dowry and the social status of the bride's family. The clash between tradition and modernity, and the two generations (that of Chandran and his parents) is suggested through their differing views. His romantic love for Malathi clashes against his mother's cherished convention, superstition, and fatalism. Through Chandran's mother, as well as characters like Jagan in *The Vendor of Sweets*, Sriram's Granny in *The Waiting for the Mahatma*, and Raju's mother in *The Guide*, R.K. Narayan presents the problems regarding custom in a tradition-bound society. In *The Painter of Signs* the orthodoxy is represented by Raman's aunt who is averse to his alliance with Daisy and vehemently opposes the match. Expressing her dislike, she leaves on a pilgrimage. With regard to customs, one finds the clash between the two generations here too. The old stick to the traditional social values which the younger generation feels have frustrated them in life. Chandran's mother disapproves of the match because of social conventions and rigid caste prohibitions that are to be followed and respected in society. She refuses to disregard the traditional practices and clings to them. A go-between (Ganapathi Sastrigal) is appointed, for according to custom the proposal must come from the bride's side. Chandran is unable to brush aside the considerations of family, status, and dowry and arrange his marriage. The hold of customs and the insistence of the orthodox on "respecting the old customs" (70) is conveyed vividly:

> For his sake they were prepared to compromise to this extent: they were prepared to consider the proposal if it came from the other side. Whatever happened they would not take the initiative in the matter; for they belonged to the bridegroom's side, and according to time honoured practice it was the bride's people who proposed first. Anything done contrary to this would make them the laughing-stock of the community. (70)

The horoscopes are matched to ensure happiness, health and harmony in life. This custom associated with marriage is referred to in a number of works. In spite of man's attempt to rationalize everything, astrology continues to influence him.

The Kodava belief in comparing the horoscope, the auspicious season for marriage, and the inauspicious month of *kakkada* (thirty days when marriages are not held) is found in *The Scent of Pepper*. It forms a significant part of the marriages which take place in Malgudi. *The Bachelor of Arts* humorously mentions the difficult astrological hurdles which Chandran has to overcome to carry out his marriage. Consulting the horoscope is one of the common Hindu practices associated with marriage in India. Novels like *Grandmother's Tale*, *The World of Nagaraj*, and *The Financial Expert* also refer to the custom of consulting the horoscope. Chandran's mother comments on the custom:

> It is the custom. When a girl is ready for marriage her horoscope will be sent in ten directions, and ten different persons will see her and approve or disapprove, or they might be disapproved by the girl herself; and after all only one will marry her. (158)

A traditional Hindu marriage involves a number of preliminary formalities, and Chandran's mother checks his exuberance referring to it, and the chances of the marriage not taking place. The never ending rituals associated with marriage make Chandran's life miserable:

> First, our astrologer must tell us if your [Chandran's] horoscope can be matched with the girl's; and then... their astrologer will say. Let us hope for the best. After that, they must come and invite us to see the girl.... After that they must come and ask us if you like the girl. And the terms of the marriage must be discussed and settled.... (83-84)

That the horoscopes do not tally cause much frustration and despair in him. A clash between custom and reason ensues. The hero initially sweeps aside his mother's orthodox views. Ironically he later submits to his parents' wishes and marries the girl of their choice. Though Chandran's unorthodox views do strike a modern note, soon he shows himself as a conformist submitting to the traditions and customs of his community. The returning of the horoscopes (as they do not match) gives rise to further debates and discussions. The long controversy over the matching of the horoscopes is not only humorous, but also creates a picture of the convention bound society of Malgudi. The vehement quarrel over the superiority of the horoscope provides instances of humour. The different calculations are finally attributed to the difference in the almanacs used. Like Chandran's mother, the novelist himself refers to the fatalistic attitude of the people:

> We believe that marriages are made in heaven and a bride and groom meet, not by accident or design but by the decree of fate, the fitness for a match not to be gauged by letting them go through a period of courtship but by a study of their horoscopes; bride and groom meet and love after marriage rather than before. (Walsh, *R.K. Narayan: A Critical Appreciation* 17)

The irony lies not only in the incompatibility of the horoscope but also in Chandran himself. Though he rebels against the system, he is also conditioned by the selfsame system more than he is aware of it. In the battle between custom and reason, custom and tradition win. The autobiographical element in the novel is significant, for the author himself underwent a similar situation in his life. A reference to his marriage is found in R.K. Narayan's *My Days*:

> My horoscope had the Seventh House occupied by Mars, the Seventh House being the one that indicated matrimonial aspects. The astrological texts plainly stated that Mars in the Seventh House indicated nothing but disaster unless the partner's horoscope also contained the same flaw, a case in which two wrongs make one right. (108)

Unlike Chandran's, a more favourable reading by another expert enables R.K. Narayan's marriage to take place. The role played by the matchmaker, the trust in the horoscope, the discussions on dowry, caste, and status, connected with marriage are also found in R.K. Narayan's *Grandmother's Tale*, *Vendor of Sweets*, and Manohar Malgonkar's *The Princes*. The hold of astrology on the human mind is beautifully portrayed by Anita Desai in *Cry, the Peacock*. The novel explores the turbulent emotional world of the neurotic protagonist Maya. Born into an orthodox family, she is haunted by the disturbing memory of the astrologer who had predicted that she or her husband would die four years after marriage—"Death...to one of you [Maya or her husband Gautama]. When you are married—and you shall be married young" (30), suggests the inevitability of death. The death of Toto, her pet dog, triggers off the memory of death and the albino astrologer who had made the prediction. From the very beginning the novel refers to the "indefinable unease" (12) Maya feels at the back of her mind. The final disaster is hinted at the very onset where Maya is in the fourth year of her married life. There is a repeated reference to the impending doom. The action revolves around the horoscope and the prophecy. Using the device of the interior monologue the novelist presents the "intolerable grapple with thoughts, feelings and emotions" (Iyengar 464) of the protagonist. This inner turmoil is also "reflected in the language, syntax and imagery" (Iyengar 464) of the novel. Because of her failure to establish a fulfilling relationship with her husband, Maya inhabits a world full of morbid fears and turns neurotic. Through a psychologically disturbed female protagonist Anita Desai brings out the impact of astrological predictions on the human mind. The novelist portrays the obsessional thoughts of her hypersensitive character, thus beautifully capturing the psychic states of a woman haunted by the awareness of death. As Maya herself admits, tradition, superstition, and custom were all "alien" (61) to her once. It is the prediction which brings doom in her life. There is a constant to and fro movement between the past (of Maya's life with her father, and brother, and the albino astrologer's prophecy) and the present (her life with Gautama and his family) in her mind. The haunting memory of the horoscope and the prophecy work like a leitmotif. The prophecy leaves such a deep impression on her that even after years of the incident it remains vivid in her mind. To escape from reality Maya seeks refuge in the childhood memories which fill her mind. But her "Hindu" psyche refuses to let go the astrologer's prediction. The prophecy lingers in her unconscious and surfaces in disguised and distorted forms, manifesting her hidden fears.

Various incidents, like the death of Toto, her brother Arjuna's letter, and a typical Indian scene like a temple with a lingam (a Shiva temple), an oil lamp, and a fortune teller examining the hand of a young girl to be married, remind her of the horoscope and the prediction. Anita Desai does not focus on the details of the incidents but concentrates on the impression these objects have on Maya's psyche. The prediction wreaks havoc in Maya's life. She finds it difficult to adopt a fatalistic approach to her problem. Though after the prediction astrology had never been uttered or even mentioned in her presence, the albino astrologer lingers in her mind and casts a shadow on her life. She is consoled with the words, "'we must learn to accept'" (54). These mnemonic words from childhood recur in her mind, but she is unable to accept the disaster foreseen on reading the horoscope. Her father burns her horoscope but does nothing to allay the fear in her. The inevitability of death is suggested from the very beginning and what is left for one to know is who is to die—Maya, or Gautama. The novelist objectifies her (Maya's) mental state through symbols like the dust storm, and the cry of the peacock. The syntax too shares the qualities of her disturbed mind loaded with thoughts of death. Though the astrologer had emphasized the potency of prayer and faith to avert the disaster, Maya is unable to extricate her thoughts from the fear of death and her love for life. Through the recurring memory of the horoscope and the incident, the novelist conveys her protagonist's preoccupied mind. The tensions within Maya give rise to severe headaches which are symptomatic of her desire to elude reality. The albino (white, symbolizing death) astrologer lingers in her mind, and through the world of dreams, nightmares, and fantasies the astrologer's prediction surfaces again and again making an escape from the thoughts impossible. Psychologists like Freud point out the peculiar behaviour of superstitious people:

> [A superstitious person has a tendency to] ascribe to external chance happenings a meaning which will become manifest in real events, and to regard such

> chance happenings as a means of expressing something that is hidden from him in the external world. (257)

Unable to face reality she concludes that even for the fulfilment of the astrologer's prophecy her death is not necessary. It is her desire for self preservation that makes her shift the burden of the prophecy on to Gautama. Maya finally transfers the prediction on to her husband. Psychologists have studied the peculiar behaviour of compulsive neurotics. They elucidate how compulsive neurotics have a certain typical peculiarity with regard to superstition and the possibility of the death of other persons. Their superstitions are often private ones which have a common origin with their neurosis. There exists in Maya nostalgia for childhood in which no marriage or death haunts her mind. The horoscope and its prediction become the primary reason behind Maya killing her husband, and her morbid fears which lead to insanity. The deep attachment to her father and marital incompatibility only aggravate the situation and drive her towards insanity. While the prediction leads to neurosis, marital discord contributes to her neurotic fantasizing. Gautama has only contempt for the rituals and considers them absurd. The novel constantly hints at the difference in their temperament. Expressing their difference in temperament is Gautama's lack of belief in "bogus ceremonies" (14) and "empty rites" (17), and Maya's obsession with an astrological prediction which her husband refuses to take seriously or dwell upon. She finds herself married into a family which "would hoot with derision at the mention of superstition, with pity and scorn for those who allowed their lives to be ruled by them, and ruined by them" (75-76). The subject is rejected by his family as puerile (as Maya's childishness). In an orthodox family like hers such a marriage would never take place. To avoid further problems she is married into a family which does not ponder over horoscopes. The novel clearly indicates that Maya's family is tradition-bound:

> Born of a family of Brahmins that for generations had lived their lives...according to prescribed patterns, had married according to the advice and suitability of their

> horoscopes, had diligently taken up careers that the pundits had chosen for them out of the constellations, had had their children's stars studied and speculated upon before they even spoke their first recognizable words.... (75)

The socio-familial background and upbringing as well as the fatalistic attitude to life create trouble in Maya's life. Since she comes from an orthodox family it is natural for her to be obsessed with her horoscope and astrology:

> ...Maya has enclosed herself in a world of superstitions and is unable to break out of the constraints imposed by the orthodox society, with its belief in horoscopes and future-telling. It is from her Indian background that she has nurtured both a love and fear of the unknown. But in her case it is self destructive and carries negative associations. (Uniyal 158)

The horoscope and the prediction are not Maya's hallucinatory creations as Arjuna's letter too refers to it. The novel is a fascinating psychological study of neurotic fears and anxieties caused by age old superstitions, marital incompatibility and disharmony. Anita Desai here concentrates on the superstitious fears which influence human life. Astrology plays a significant role in an orthodox person's life. In *Cry, the Peacock*, the prediction is carried out by Maya though she transfers it on to her husband. The novelist shows how an obsession with superstitious beliefs leads to disaster and even death. Gautama's death at the end of the novel is reminiscent of the albino astrologer's prediction, and his words that the "stars do not lie" (29). One is thus left with a belief in astrology and the predictions it makes.

Like the horoscope, the 'bride-seeing' ceremony also forms an integral part of any traditional Hindu marriage. The ceremony at which the bridegroom's party comes to "examine" the bride is described in some of the Indian English novels. In *The Bachelor of Arts*, Chandran, brought up in a conservative and convention ridden society is unable to violate the age old customs and traditions. Through the hero the novelist expresses his own preference for the traditional and the conventional. Chandran marries according to his parents' wishes. The horoscopes match and R.K. Narayan provides a short description of the 'bride-seeing' ceremony in which the girl is coaxed to come before the "viewers". A similar, but humorous description of the 'bride-seeing' ceremony is found in *The Vendor of Sweets*. The novel, *The Bachelor of Arts*, depicts the clash between Mali (representing the new values) and his father, Jagan, (representing the old values), and Jagan's final escape from the world of responsibilities. Jagan confronts a new world where marriage has lost its sanctity. The clash between the ancient customs and the modern values become explicit as Jagan tries to make his son adopt the traditional ways of life. The fact that Mali and Grace (a half Korean, half American girl) are not married shocks Jagan. Such a relationship is unacceptable in a society like Malgudi. The ways and manners of the Hindu society, as Jagan adopts it are pitted against Mali's westernism. Mali has only contempt for the Indian ways and ignores the customs and traditions which are a part of it. The absence of ceremonies in the Mali-Grace relationship, which does not succeed, is significant and in sharp contrast to Jagan's recollection of his own 'bride-seeing' ceremony and marriage which is performed according to the traditional practices. The western admiration for Indian ways is conveyed through Grace who prefers to marry according to the Indian customs. The East-West dichotomy is suggested through their relationship. It is ironic that while Mali (an Indian) is averse to Indian practices and prefers the occident, Grace (representing the West) does not show a similar attitude. Mali brushes aside Grace's idea of getting married as "funny notions" (146), revealing a total break with his orthodox upbringing. Moulded by an orthodox set-up, their relationship appears to Jagan as "living in sin" (135). He even performs actions of a purificatory nature to cleanse the house of the pollution he believes it has acquired due to Mali and Grace's tainted relationship. Jagan's recollections of the ceremonies associated with his own marriage highlight the absurdity and meaninglessness of Mali's relationship with Grace which lacks togetherness. Jagan's own marriage had been carried out according to the customs which accompany a traditional

Hindu marriage. As with most characters in R.K. Narayan's orthodox milieu, Jagan too does not have a say in the choice of his bride. He has to marry the girl of his parents' choice. The preliminary formalities as well as the marriage are in contrast to the absence of customs and rituals in the Mali-Grace relationship. The description of the ceremony is noteworthy as it takes place at a stage when Jagan decides to leave his home and enter the next phase of his life (*vanaprastha*). Jagan seeks shelter in the past and relives the days of his youth. It presents a picture of marriage and domestic felicity under the traditional set-up. The situation is infused with humour and serves to expose the absurdity of the practices. The bridegroom's party is fussed over by the bride's people (as in *The Painter of Signs*). It shows the honour with which the bridegroom and his family are treated at any traditional Indian marriage—"...they [the bridegroom's party] were honoured visitors, on whose verdict would depend the future of the girl; it was a highly serious and important role, and they were expected to carry themselves with dignity..." (150). It becomes an occasion for the display of ceremonial behaviour. While the bride's people try to "judge his intelligence and outlook" (149), Jagan is warned by his elder brother "not to be too communicative, as a certain mysteriousness was invaluable in a son-in-law" (149). In a humorous way the novelist points out the meaninglessness of the customs followed by the orthodox:

> ...the code demanded that their [the bridegroom's] hosts should press the delicacies upon them. Then one would have to break off the jilebi minutely with the tip of one's finger and transfer it to one's mouth, and generally display reluctance or even aversion until pressed again, and then just to please others eat two or three bits in succession and then take an elegant sip of coffee. The essence of behaviour in these circumstances consisted in seeming to do things for the sake of one's hosts. (151)

Jagan's delicate mission is described. Pretensions are kept up, for "although everyone was fully aware of the purpose of the young man's visit, one had to view the main purpose casually, neither side displaying too much interest or anxiety"

(152). The bride appears only after much persuasion. In a traditional society like Malgudi Jagan's plight is similar to that of Chandran and Viswa (*Grandmother's Tale*), for he too cannot voice his opinion regarding his future wife. With a contrary behaviour one would only "cheapen oneself" (155). A similar situation is depicted in Mulk Raj Anand's *Gauri*. The bridegroom, Panchi, is not allowed to have a glance of the bride, nor the bride of the groom, before marriage. Each of them has to depend on rumours regarding the other's appearance. This explains Panchi's impatience at the 'showing' ceremony. Daisy in *The Painter of Signs* is entirely different from the orthodox characters portrayed in R.K. Narayan. She is at odds with the mythological image of the Indian woman. The spirit of change and urbanization which blows over Malgudi is embodied here. It deals with Raman's love and disenchantment with Daisy, an ardent worker at the family planning centre in Malgudi. Daisy effects a readjustment of traditional values, and dominates over her male counterpart, thus manifesting the spirit of liberation. Set against traditional characters, like Savitri (*The Dark Room*) or Bala (*Grandmother's Tale*), her disposition is strikingly modern. She topples the subservience to male authority. The emergence of the active female here is accompanied by the reduction of the male who is a passive character. She rebels against the orthodoxies and approves of a relationship between a man and a woman on equal footing. That Daisy does not believe in marriage rituals or customs indicates a deviance from her brahminic upbringing. Daisy reminds one of Mali in *The Vendor of Sweets*. She has no taboos of any kind. Streaks of feminism have been woven into her character. This is evident when she describes her 'bride-seeing' ceremony:

> My mother called me one day into a side room and told me to be prepared to be inspected by a prospective bridegroom. They had a shock at home when I told my people that I'd not allow anyone to inspect me as a bride and that I'd rather do the inspection of the groom! They felt outraged...and said 'Don't be mad! Don't you know

> that it's not done?' I replied, 'If it is not done, it's better that someone starts doing it now'. (130)

The language is charged with irony and humour when Daisy describes the arrival of the "eminent personage" (131). She says, "What a fuss they made when they arrived. It's hard to get a bridegroom, and when one is available parents treat him as a hard-won prize" (131). For her tradition is a shackle decelerating progress. She goes through the ceremony feeling suffocated. As in any orthodox set-up she is hushed back into the room when she questions the bridegroom. Her overriding nature is similar to that of Bharati in *Waiting for the Mahatma*.

Dowry too is often a deciding factor in the selection of a bride. The gift of the bride (*kanyadanam*) is accompanied by other small gifts. This is associated with the concept of marriage as *dana* (meaning "gift"). It was once a voluntary offering and had its origins in the Vedic times. Though earlier considered as a meritorious act, gradually the custom of *kanyadanam* itself reduced the status of a daughter. She became one of the things possessed by her father—a possession which he could donate at free will, without taking into consideration her choice or opinion. The father or her guardian became solely responsible for the choice of the bridegroom. This "gift of a maiden" slowly gave rise to the notion that it should be accompanied by some *dakshina*, some gift of gold or wealth for the bridegroom. This led to the practice of the payment of dowry in modern times. The dowry system marks the economic dimension of marriage. In *The Bachelor of Arts* Chandran's mother refers to this when she says, "'It is the duty of every father to set some money apart for securing a son-in-law. We can't disregard custom" (85). At the *vagdanam* in *The Vendor of Sweets* the dowry is given by the bride's party with a gentle suggestion to count the cash. The novelist points out the importance which economic transactions are given when a marriage takes place. Apart from this a demand is also made to furnish the nuptial suite. R.K. Narayan's comic irony is at work when Jagan's father passes the cash on to be counted saying, "It was not necessary to count...but since you insisted on it..." (158). The goods gifted are later "examined" and their value assessed by Jagan's relatives. The degradation of a custom (of giving gifts to the daughter by her father on her marriage) is noticed here. Marriage is often reduced to a business transaction. The novelist himself says, "Marriages are, of course, made in heaven, but they are a business in our part of the universe..." (*A Writer's Nightmare* 46). Anita Desai too points out (in *Fasting, Feasting*) how in modern society rituals and ceremonies have become secondary to the economic transaction related to a marriage alliance. Uma's husband (Harish) leaves her because he is already married and had married her for the dowry to save an "ailing pharmaceutical factory" (93) he runs. Harish, an old travelling salesman, accepts the dowry given with "alacrity" (87). The novel humorously adds that the dowry "must have seemed like a bonus to a man who may not have expected more than one dowry in a lifetime" (87). One of the attempts of the family at getting Uma married ends in disgrace as the engagement is broken, and they lose the dowry given to the boy's family. The family loses two dowries for Uma. To avoid further embarrassments there is no 'bride-seeing' ceremony, and the family is portrayed as being frantic to get rid of its unmarried daughter. *Nectar in a Sieve* refers to the wedding ceremonies in a south Indian village. Rukmani's father's declining status is indicated through her recollection of the different marriages which take place in her family. At the opening of the novel Rukmani refers to her elder sisters who are "married fittingly" (1) because her father was the respected headman of the village. They are given plenty of gifts, jewels, and a dowry. As Rukmani recollects, her words draw a picture of the diminishing prestige and fortunes of the family:

> My [Rukmani's] three sisters were married long before I was. Shanta first, a big wedding which lasted for many days, plenty of gifts and feasts, diamond earrings, a gold necklace, as befitted the daughter of the village headman. Padmini next, and she too made a good match and was married fittingly taking jewels and dowry with her; but when it came to Thangam, only relations from

> our own village came to the wedding and not from the surrounding districts as they had done before, and the only jewel she had was a diamond nose-screw. (1-2)

Rukmani's dreams of a "grand wedding" (2) are shattered due to her father's diminished prestige, and she is married off to a poor tenant farmer, Nathan, without even a dowry. Hence she makes preparations for her daughter's marriage from the time of her birth, and brings them out on the occasion. Ira, Rukmani's daughter, too is married off with a dowry they could afford. *The Scent of Pepper* as well as *The Princes* refers to the economic transaction which has become a part of the marriages. Nanji's father agrees to give a dowry to save her from the hands of her stepmother indicating the custom amongst the Kodavas. Besides mentioning the amount set apart for Nanji (at the very beginning of the work), the economic aspect of marriage is referred to later when Subbu expresses his desire to marry Mallige. Nanji then points out that the girl "will be married off with next to nothing" (188). Nanji resents Mallige's modest background:

> Families with prestige gave gold and silver to their daughters, to be displayed on the night of the wedding. Mallige had come with two tin boxes—one filled with clothes and the other with an assortment of vessels not worth more than fifty rupees. Her bridal finery, which had astounded everyone, had been borrowed. Her jewels amounted to no more than a gold chain, pathak and silver toe-rings. Nanji had seen the contempt in the eyes of the guests who went away saying, "The grandson of the Rao Bahadur could have done better". (198)

Like the dowry, the bride price too is a custom associated with marriage. *The Princes* refers to the huge amount given to Abhay's mother's family as dowry. The bride price, a custom prevalent among some of the social groups, gives the bridegroom the right to marry the girl. Mulk Raj Anand's novel *Gauri* alludes to this custom. The novel deals with the story of the eponymous heroine, Gauri, who is beaten, mistrusted and exploited by her husband, Panchi. She finally abandons her home and husband, and chooses to live on her own and to depend on herself. At her wedding, in addition to the bride price given by Panchi's uncle, Panchi gives a pair of gold earrings. The gyrations around the fire are even stopped because of the cheap bride price Panchi gives. The bride price is considered recompense to the bride's kin as well as a means of securing rights over her and her offspring later on. In *Gauri*, Gauri's mother (Laxmi) mentions her intention of using the bride price to start a dairy business. Bride price, resembling the dowry, is a custom which degrades the position of women to the level of an 'object'/'commodity'.

Like the invitation cards, the marriage procession, and the music, the betrothal ceremony also makes the marriage known among the people. Since the marriage agreement is based on word of honour, it is essential that it should be made known to as many as possible to minimize the possibility of one of the contracting parties repudiating the marriage *in toto*. A short description of the Wedding Notice ceremony held at Chandran's house is found towards the end of *The Bachelor of Arts*:

> It was a day of feast and reception in Chandran's house. A large number of guests were invited, and at the auspicious moment Jayarama Iyer [Susila's father] stood up and read the saffron-touched paper which announced that, by the blessing of God, Chandran, son of So-and-so, was to marry Susila, daughter of So-and-so, on a particular auspicious date, ten days hence. (163)

Chandran's failure in marrying Malathi plays an important role in his struggle towards maturity and marks the end of a phase in his life. This forces him to move out of Malgudi to attain a wider experience. The ripples created in his life subside with his marriage and he ultimately accepts life as it is. The ceremony of *vagdanam* (the mutual agreement) is also described in *The Vendor of Sweets*. Priests, a few neighbours and relatives are invited to Jagan's betrothal. The bride's party arrives with fruits, betel leaves, new clothes, saffron, silver plates, lamps, etc. The dowry is given, and the din created by the music party makes it known to the whole town that a marriage is being settled. A feast is held after the ceremonies.

It is only after the approval of the elders, and the preliminary formalities, that the marriage takes place. Invitation cards are then sent, announcing and inviting for the marriage. This traditional atmosphere is woven in a number of R.K. Narayan novels. Many of his works refer to the principal marriage rites. Though the experience in his life makes Chandran lose belief in the sanctity of the institution of marriage, he opts for a traditional Hindu marriage. The preparations for the marriage involve days of intense activity. The novelist avoids a lengthy account of the marriage ceremonies and merely refers to its effect on Chandran, who is once again lost in a romantic world. The failure in love, besides playing an important role in moulding his career and bringing about the transformation in his character, also shows the importance of family relationships in a traditional set-up like Malgudi. The impatience Chandran shows to marry Malathi is later shown in Susila's case too. Regardless of the experience he has gained in life, Chandran's behaviour remains more or less unchanged. Despite making different attempts, R.K. Narayan's characters are unable to escape the grip of outmoded customs, or go against the prevailing practices in their orthodox society. In the caste ridden Hindu society of Malgudi, arranged marriages appear to be the only possibility. Even Chandran's father, though comparatively modern in outlook, is unable to shake off the time-honoured customs and traditions. Brought up in an orthodox brahmin household, the novelist himself seems to uphold tradition. His characters are tradition-bound, superstitious and rooted in the age old practices of their religion. But this is not a deliberate attempt to be traditional:

> Narayan never deliberately attempts to be Indian, but because he deals with convincing human beings in authentic situations, and records their responses honestly, and because these human beings happen to be Indians, he succeeds in achieving that difficult task: writing in a genuinely Indian way without being self-conscious about it. (Mukherjee, *The Twice Born Fiction* 199)

The traditional atmosphere of Malgudi is evoked in *The Vendor of Sweets* with a description of Jagan's marriage ceremony:

> Jagan's whole time was spent in greeting the guests or prostrating himself at their feet if they were older relatives. The priests compelled him to sit before the holy fire performing complicated rites and reciting sacred mantras; his consolation was that during most of these he had to be clasping his wife's hand; he felt enormously responsible as he glanced at the sacred thali he had knotted around her neck at the most auspicious moment of the ceremonies. (160)

The sanctity attributed to Jagan's marriage is lacking in Mali's relationship with Grace. Theirs is a marriage of convenience where each of them can leave when the relationship becomes a burden:

> Mali had proved that there was no need for ceremonials, not even the business of knotting the *thali* around the bride's neck. Nothing, no bonds or links or responsibility. Come together, live together, and kick each other away when it suited them. (175)

Through Jagan the novel asserts the hold of tradition. Apart from the reference to the noise, visitors, and the feasting which go on for three days, R.K. Narayan also risibly refers to the bitterness over the quality of the coffee and the missing gold waist belt included in the list of jewellery. His works give a clear picture of the socio-cultural milieu of Malgudi. The simple characters in his works are conservative, and they closely adhere to the traditional values of their orthodox community. In his works there is "an unadulterated expression of an Indian consciousness" (Dass 212). Malgudi is deeply caste ridden and traditional, and R.K. Narayan asserts the "validity of traditional Indian values" (Ramteke 110).

The practice of child marriage (of Balambal) is described in *Grandmother's Tale*. Balambal (Bala) is married at an early age to Viswa (Viswanath). The novel traces her progress from a school girl to a determined woman and finally to a docile orthodox wife. As in his other works, here too R.K. Narayan has created typical Indian characters who cling on to their traditions and customs. They have the notions and feelings, taboos and morals of India with them. It depicts an orthodox grandmother's tale. Being an orthodox woman it is natural and apt that she describes the marriage ceremonies of her mother as described to her. The child bride, in spite of her reluctance, is forced to go through the ceremonies. The action is taken forward with the marriage between Bala and Viswa. The ignorance and childish nature of Bala and Viswa are conveyed through the ceremony. For a child like Bala the marriage is just "an occasion when she would be showered with gifts and new clothes and gold ornaments" (10). The auspicious date is fixed and she is forced to be indoors, which makes her sulk and weep. In a social set-up where both the bride and the groom are not allowed to express their views with regard to the marriage, Chandran's love affair (*The Bachelor of Arts*) strikes one as modern. The lengthy description of the ceremony hints at the childish nature of the bride and the groom. A picture of child marriage is given here:

> On an auspicious day she was clad in a saree, decked in jewellery and taken to the pillared hall of the temple where had gathered guests and relatives and priests, a piper and drummer creating enough noise to drown the uproar of the priests chanting mantras and the babble of the guests. She was garlanded and made to sit beside a boy whom she had often noticed tossing a rubber ball in an adjoining street whenever she went out to buy a pencil, ribbon or sweets in a little shop. (10)

Viswa ties the *tali* as she sits on her father's lap. There are week long celebrations, feasting and the exchange of ceremonial visits between the bride and the groom's parties. The rigidity of customs does not allow them to meet alone. While the bridegroom returns to his school life, the bride's life changes after her marriage, for she cannot go out freely or play with her friends. According to custom "they could not meet normally as husband and wife. Bala, being only ten years old, must attain puberty and then go through an elaborate nuptial ceremony before she could join her husband" (21). Viswa does succeed in establishing a line of communication with Bala in spite of all the difficulties he has to face. In *Malgudi* Bala is considered a widow when Viswa disappears soon after his marriage to her. She is branded as a widow "pretending to be a sumangali" (29), and prohibited from entering the temple lest she follows the rules of a widow to preserve the sanctity of the temple. Hence Bala leaves her house determined to find her husband. It is difficult to accept this daring act keeping in mind her submissiveness and passivity before and after retrieving her husband. Her marriage to Viswa is in contrast to the "quiet and private" (49) marriage of Surma and Bhatji (Viswa) and the "quiet, and simple ceremony" (90) in which Viswa is married to the maid's daughter. Both these marriages end abruptly, one with Viswa returning to Bala leaving Surma, and the other with his death. It is the tali around Bala's neck which makes her describe herself as the "real wife" (57) and hers the "legitimate home" (57). Her actions are justified by introducing the Savitri legend. Bala is compared to Savitri who brings back her husband from Yama. Savitri in mythology is known for her austerity and purity of mind. Bala too proves to be devoted to her husband. The novel traces the change Bala undergoes. Her marriage plays a major role in this conversion.

The marriage becomes an occasion for enjoyment and revelry in the rural atmosphere. It forms a part of the portrayal of village life in *Nectar in a Sieve*. A large part of the novel concentrates on marriages and the marital life of its characters. The marriage between Nathan and Rukmani is based on love and understanding. It is an ideal one in contrast to the other marriages depicted in the novel. The garland of dry mango leaves which Rukmani sees on arriving at Nathan's house assumes symbolic significance as it prefigures their life and labour growing to bits of withered leaves, and the blows by the calamities of life. When Ira's marriage comes up a matchmaker is appointed to find a suitable groom. The financial position of the bridegroom is ensured. The preliminaries are completed and a day is fixed for the wedding. Ira accepts her parents' choice with docility and after marriage leaves with her husband to begin a "new life" (36). Chapter six of the novel gives a description of the marriage ceremonies which take place in the propitious season. The preparations start weeks ahead. The marriage turns out to be an occasion for the whole village to celebrate. Marriages and similar festivities become rare moments of joy in their lives which are otherwise filled with poverty and the vagaries of nature. It is a symbol of joy, hope (for a new and better future), and happiness. The people come to help the family and celebrate with them. Music and feast accompany the celebrations. The picture of feasting and plenty ends with the marriage. The rains destroy their work and there is little to eat as most of the provisions had gone to make the wedding feast. The bride and the groom sit "uneasily" (37) side by side. The white (a symbol of purity) flowers Ira wears on her hair assume significance in the novel. The picture she presents in the first part is in contrast to the role of a prostitute she is forced to take up later in her life. There is no lengthy description of the wedding ceremonies as the narrator concludes it abruptly with the words, "So they were married" (38). Like most expatriate writers Kamala Markandaya has set her early novels in the land of her origin. The novel beautifully conveys the din and bustle accompanying Ira's marriage and the emptiness thereafter:

> Then the palanquin [into which Ira is lifted] was lifted up, the torchbearers closed in, the musicians took their places. We [Rukmani and Nathan] followed on foot behind, relatives, friends, well-wishers and hangers-on. Several children had added themselves to the company; they came after, jigging about in high glee, noisy and excited: a long, ragged tail-end to the procession. (38)

The noise and bustle end with Ira being taken to her husband's house. But her ceremonial marriage turns out to be a failure. This seems to be indicated at the beginning itself—"The walls showed cracks" (38) soon after the marriage indicating the "crack" in Ira's life with her husband due to childlessness. Her husband deserts her and marries again. In contrast to Rukmani and Ira's marriages is Murugan's (Rukmani's son). While Rukmani and Ira's marriages are arranged by their parents, Murugan marries without the presence of his parents. His marriage too fails. The novelist seems to uphold a traditional marriage based on love and understanding. In the novel, only the Nathan-Rukmani relationship succeeds. M.K. Naik refers to the different relationships in the novel:

> Rukmani's marriage was a sacred covenant which bound the two [Nathan and Rukmani] together in sun and in rain, but not in the case of Murugan [and Ira] who had arranged his own marriage and who, being in the city and without the sanction of elderly people of the village, deserts his wife and takes another woman without any compunction. (Dhawan 215)

Ira's marriage which is arranged by her parents, and is conducted with "the sanctity of elderly people of the village" (Dhawan 213) fails and her husband takes another woman as his wife. Kamala Markandaya's works are more or less free from literal translations of Indian words. Apart from the glossary are the superfluous explanatory descriptions like "across the doorway a garland of mango leaves, a symbol of happiness and good fortune, dry now and rattling in the breeze" (4), and "Ira had been given in marriage in the month of June, which is the propitious season for weddings..." (39) which are familiar to an Indian reader. These may be a nostalgic recollection of the homeland by an expatriate writer. The elaborate descriptions of marriages, festivals, and other customs along with a glossary at the end of the novel makes one feel that the novelist has a western audience in mind—that she is presenting India to the West.

A conventional Hindu marriage is found in Manohar Malgonkar's *The Princes* (the alliance between Abhay and Kamala). It is a traditional marriage brought about after consulting the horoscope, like that of his father and mother, but a happy one. The lavish marriage festivities with brass band, fireworks and dancing girls indicate it to be a royal marriage. As a member of the princely tradition Abhay too has to marry, and make provision for the succession:

> For people in our [the princely class] position...a marriage is a sacred thing. It is not a private, purely

> personal matter at all, but an affair of state, as it were. Even the Political Department has an interest. There is a duty, an obligation to marry someone suitable. Someone whom the people will one day have to accept as their Maharani. (166)

As in any orthodox society, he has to marry after seeing the bride's photograph while the girl is not allowed this and has to observe strictest *purdah*. Abhay mentions how his mother first saw his father during their wedding ceremony when the curtain between them was removed. The women observe *sati* and sacrifice themselves. They thus became goddesses whose names were added to the family shrine. The marriage shatters his plans to marry Minnie Bradley whom his family does not accept. It to them is an "unsanctified marriage" (188). Abhay is married to Kamala in "a purely conventional Hindu marriage" (218). Abhay's emotional detachment at the ceremony is mentioned. He goes through it as "a sort of penance" (219). The marriage emphasizes his return to the princely fold:

> It merely emphasized that I [Abhay] was now within the fold, aware of my obligations to my inheritance. I was taking a wife because a future Maharaja must have a Maharani, but I knew that no other obligations, such as love or marital fidelity, were imposed. (219)

The festivities described here are a display of wealth and extravagance. The marriage plays an important role in the slow but sure transformation which Abhay undergoes. Like his father, Abhay accepts the forces of tradition in his life:

> When I [Abhay] reflect on this [his marriage], I wonder whether there might not, after all, be something to be said for our deeply rooted customs, evolved after generations of trial and error; mine is certainly not an unusual example of how love can flow as a consequence of marriage, living together and the begetting of children. (218)

Actions which do not have the sanction of society are vehemently opposed by its members. In a conservative and traditional society, rituals and ceremonies continue to have their hold, however liberated the people are. Anita Desai's *Fasting, Feasting* hints at how religious ceremonies have lost their significance in the modern world. As against the few references to ceremonies and customs in her other works, *Fasting, Feasting* describes Uma's wedding preparations in a language charged with humour. The novelist seems to convey her dislike for the traditional practices which accompany a marriage ceremony. The action in the first part of the novel centres on Uma, the plain spinster daughter of a close-knit Indian family, smothered by her overbearing parents and their traditions. The first part, set in India, presents a conventional society in which unmarried daughters (like Uma) are a burden to the family. This part is in sharp contrast to the second which is set in America. The novelist concentrates on some of the aspects of a tradition-bound society in the initial section of the work. Unlike her other novels, in *Cry, the Peacock* and *Fasting, Feasting* Anita Desai dwells on characters who are more or less tradition oriented. While Maya is obsessed with a prophecy, Mira-masi is obsessed with the rituals which rule her life from dawn to dusk. The influence of social customs on women is found in some of the works of fiction. While Uma is a mere puppet, Maya's upbringing (marred by superstition) does not give her any choice. The first part of *Fasting, Feasting* provides a description of Uma's marriage. Her marriage is a foil to Aruna's (Uma's sister), for Aruna makes "the wisest, most expedient choice" (100). The description of the ceremonies also contributes towards the Indian atmosphere created in the opening section of the work. Uma's story conveys a sense of Indianness (full of visiting aunts, inquisitive neighbours, ceremonies, etc.) while the second part has an American texture. The language is infused with humour. The account given in the novel implies the significance of marriage in a girl's life:

> There was a time, a season, when every girl in the big, far flung family seemed suddenly ready for marriage. It was as if their mothers had been tending them, in their flower pots, for just this moment when their cheeks would fill out and their lips take on a glisten and all the

> giggles and whispers would arrive at that one decision—marriage. (66)

The novel refers to the various marriages (of Anamika, Uma, and Aruna) which take place in the family. Anita Desai seems to reconstruct an India around her. The absence of bridegroom jokes and gifts from the bridegroom to the children prefigures Anamika's relationship with her husband. The situation is described humorously. Anamika is referred to as "someone brought in because it was the custom and because she would, by marrying him, enhance his superiority to other men" (70). The relationship ends with her death. The bridegroom's conduct at the ceremony indicates his later behaviour towards Anamika. Marriages often mean nothing more than a show of wealth to families. The bride is unimportant and her happiness a minor issue. The traditional upbringing accorded to girls in Indian society is faithfully portrayed in most of the creative works. Through Uma, the novel depicts how in a traditional set-up a girl's unmarried state becomes an "embarrassment" (85) for her parents, and "an obstruction" (85) in conducting other marriages in the family. Uma's mother tries to dispose of her daughter and sends her photographs (even has them touched up) to everyone who advertised in the matrimonial column. The novel describes the wedding preparations and shows how it does not make any difference to Uma whose views are not taken into consideration by the family:

> Mama frantically supervised the cooking of meals and making of sweets for three days in a row. Papa was seeing to the marquee being set up on the lawn, the priest and all his requirements in the way of ceremony and ritual, and the musicians to play during the reception. Uma found herself richer by a dozen saris, a set of gold jewellery and another of pearls, then was handed a garland and posted at the entrance to the marquee to wait for the bridegroom. (87)

The bridegroom arrives with his relatives. The description of the ceremony itself hints that the marriage between Uma and Harish will be a short lived one. Uma herself seems to realize this. Harish asks the priest to cut short the long ceremony and appears reluctant to accept the garland. Uma does not have a choice but to accept her parents' overbearing presence. She is "made to" wait for the groom, "made to drape hers [garland] over his head" (88), and throw rice into the fire at the ceremony. The novel indicates a world where ceremonies and rituals have lost their sanctity. The ceremonies are performed, "not that anyone was listening, apart from Uma and her husband who had no choice" (89). The Sanskrit verses recited by the priest are comprehensible to him alone. After the ceremonies Uma leaves for her husband's house. The relationship ends with Uma's return to her house after a few days. The marriage is cancelled, as arranged, by her parents, while Uma continues to be non-existent to them:

> The marriage was somehow cancelled, annulled. Uma was never told of the legal proceedings involved. It was assumed she would not understand, and was never quite certain if she had never actually married or if she was now divorced. (95)

Another glimpse of the traditional society is presented when, being a divorcee and having "cost her parents two dowries, without a marriage to show in return" (96), Uma is considered ill-fated by all and no more attempts are made to marry her off. Her position thus becomes "that of an outcast from the world of marriage" (96). Aruna's wedding is a "splendid" (101) occasion unlike Uma's which had been "drab" (101). Aruna is more assertive than her sister. She takes time to make a choice, at her insistence a reception is held, and the family even throws a cocktail party to welcome Arvind (the bridegroom) and his family before the wedding. The marriage as well as the preliminary preparations are "chic" (101) and "untraditional" (101):

> ...the wedding was as chic as Aruna had planned it; the ceremony itself brief, its chief features being Aruna's elaborate sari and jewellery and the groom's maharaja-style turban. (102)
>
> The Carlton Hotel provided the dinner, and even if some relatives refused to touch food cooked by who knew

> what
> low-caste cooks in what polluted kitchens, most of the guests were profoundly impressed and grateful and said so in heartfelt tones as they left, compensating Papa somewhat for the shocking expense (102-03).

While Anamika and Uma submit to their parents' wishes, Aruna has her way. Her marriage survives. Aruna's preference for city life is seen throughout the novel and her "untraditional" (101) marriage highlights this trait in her character.

The different aspects of the institution of marriage can also be traced in Kamala Markandaya's *A Handful of Rice*. It presents the life of Ravishankar (Ravi) who flees the countryside and plunges into the turmoil of urban life. The chance meeting of Nalini, and his marriage to her proves a turning point in his life. Ravi becomes a part of the Apu (Nalini's father) household, first as an apprentice and later as a son-in-law. With Ravi's marriage to Nalini the two lives—the rural and the urban—merge. While Ravi does not have a job or an identity of his own in the city his father's presence gives him the "identity and status" (57), and a background and roots that are solid and stable, and reassuring in his in-laws' eyes. There is no dowry, and the day and hour of the marriage is fixed. At the wedding Nalini's bridal finery exposes the poverty of the family. The novelist does not describe the rituals in detail but provides a vivid account of Ravi's wandering thoughts:

> He obeyed, in a trance, with an awkward clumsiness which they indulgently excused as marriage nerves. He got up, he sat down, walked around the sacred flame, and fell at the feet of his father for his blessing. Somewhere beside him in all this was Nalini, but he was not now clearly conscious of her. The fire filled his vision, that and the flowers, flowers everywhere.... From somewhere came the smell of burning camphor...and there was the smell of incense too, wafting up in their blue trails of smoke from incense-sticks.... (59)

The smell of flowers, camphor, incense, and the sound of music fill the atmosphere. Ravi finds it difficult to bear the weight of the garlands he wears. The reference to his "shoulders aching from the weight of the flower garlands heaped upon them" (58) symbolizes the future responsibilities Ravi has to shoulder in the house before and after Apu's death. With Apu's paralytic attack and death afterwards Ravi takes on as his successor. Ravi's psychological condition as he is taken on a nuptial drive after his marriage is skilfully etched. He dreams of a better life, but is jerked out of his reverie. After a brief spell of happiness Ravi has to face poverty and hardship. The drooping plantain stems and the wilting mango leaves and marigolds, which hung on the doorway, too hint at their later life which is full of difficulties. The marriage procession (announcing the marriage) completes a circular movement:

> [They were] back where they had been, nothing changed except perhaps for the worse, nothing to do but put as good a face as possible upon the anti-climax. Enveloped in a sense of incongruity, feeling awkward and slightly foolish, Ravi stepped over the threshold he had done hundreds of times before [but now as a son-in-law]. (62)

With his marriage Ravi attains a new status in the family as Nalini's husband. A feast is held and with his father's return to the village, routine life continues. Unlike the usual marital residence (virilocal, "place of the male") is the one (uxorilocal, "place of the wife") depicted in the novel. Here the couple (Ravi and Nalini) attaches their new household to that of the wife's natal domestic group. For Apu he becomes a son and heir to carry on his work when he dies. Though the marriage brings more problems for Ravi, it also effects a drastic change in his status from a bootlegger, vagabond, and street loafer to a respectable household man. Marriage marks a shift for Ravi from the world of Damodar, into which he had entered after leaving his village, to the human world of Apu and his family. He assumes a new identity and becomes ready to repudiate all that is unworthy. Despite his transition from the rustic to the urban landscape, Ravi is unable to shake off his rustic background. He turns nostalgic for the old ways of life, at the same time projecting a fascination for the new. Ravi loses his freedom after marriage and labours under the burden of Nalini's family. As a member of Apu's family he gains respectability. Ravi's changed status and his awareness of it is conveyed thus:

> He had no friends left. His former associates were nomads, flitting from quarter to quarter as official surveillance tensed or relaxed, and unless one belonged to that band there was no way of locating them. Not, Ravi told himself piously, that he would want to. He would never condemn them of course: never would such heresy fall from his lips: but the fact remained that they were vagrants, seedy failures whom the city had defeated. (111)

As against his earlier existence as a part of Damodar's group is his austere living at Nalini's house. In works like *Nectar in a Sieve* and *A Handful of Rice* the customs and ceremonies add on to the suffering and misery of the peasants described in them. In Indian society, a marriage is celebrated with pomp and splendour even in the midst of hunger and poverty (as in *Nectar in a Sieve*, *A Handful of Rice*, or *Gauri*). Despite their dreadful financial position, Rukmani's father, Rukmani, Nathan, and Apu have to spend a lot on the marriage and the feast which accompanies it. For them the marriage celebrations are occasions of plenty. Though these ceremonies fill their otherwise dull life with happiness, the lavish spending on food, music and the like is wasted as Ira is returned home by her husband in *Nectar in a Sieve*. The happiness is momentary, for both Ravi and Ira have to face the harsh realities of life soon after these festivities.

Novelists (like Mulk Raj Anand and R.K. Narayan) while referring to the customs and ceremonies of the orthodox often apply ancient values to a modern context. While Mulk Raj Anand applies the Sita myth in *Gauri*, R.K. Narayan applies an ancient marriage system to a modern context. *Gauri* opens with a description of the heroine's marriage to Panchi. The relationship later leads to her emergence as a self-reliant woman. With the marriage begins her sufferings. Gauri is restored to Panchi only to be rejected because of the rumours of her life in Hoshiarpur, and she leaves. The novel is an indictment on the society which reduces women to an inferior position. Gauri is presented as a docile cow at the beginning. At the marriage negotiations, her parents repeatedly refer to this quality of hers and say, "'Gauri is like a cow, very gentle and very good'" (11). Panchi himself feels like a "holy bull" (13) going to marry the "little cow Gauri" (13). The story opens with a reference to the marriage procession and the ceremonies associated with it. The marriage brings together two villages—that of Chota Piplan and Piplan Kalan. Suggesting the difference between the two villages the novel points out how the negotiations for the marriage had taken months. One of the difficulties is that the bride is from an ancient village and the groom from a small hamlet. The music played at the ceremony also shows the difference between the two villages. Describing this the novel points out how "the gay band of Piplan Kalan...struck up 'Tipperary' by the gateway of the big village, drowning the 'peenpeen' of the Shehnai flutes of the little band that had come with the bridal party" (9). The groom's party is looked down upon and insulted. The parties quarrel over the bride price as well as the large numbers who accompany the bridegroom. Both the villages try to outshine each other in their rivalry. Some of the ceremonies which accompany an Indian marriage are mentioned here. The quarrels over dowry, jewellery etc. have all become a part of the marriage ceremonies. The groom's party is abused and given food with hemp. Panchi becomes the butt of Gauri's friends' pranks at the 'showing' ceremony. Throughout the ceremony the bridegroom's inferior social status is hinted at. From the very beginning the marriage is doomed to end in disaster. Panchi is considered an inauspicious orphan, and there are hostilities between the two parties. The relationship is broken off and renewed three times before the marriage actually takes place. Bad omens recur—the horse on which Panchi rides tries to throw him off, Panchi steps over the threshold before oil is poured on the corners of the doorway. Life in the village is filled with superstitions and sufferings. The superstitious nature of the villagers is clearly portrayed here. Though oil is poured on the corners of the door way, "just in time to save the marriage from disaster" (18) the villagers feel that the marriage between Panchi and Gauri is doomed right from the beginning. Their superstitious beliefs come true at the end as Gauri leaves her house. As they foresee, bad luck falls into the couple's life with the marriage. Her arrival coincides with the fall in the family fortunes. The joint family breaks up as Panchi fights with his uncle, and a drought strikes the village. Each disaster is seen as the unfortunate result of the ill-starred marriage with the unlucky and inauspicious Gauri. Gauri comes to be identified with goddess Kali (the destroyer). In spite of his disbelief in superstitions, the idea of Gauri's bad stars continue to possess Panchi. In a village filled with superstitions, it is natural for Panchi to believe Kesaro's words that Gauri is the cause of their bad luck. There is a reference to the ceremonial fire and the priests reciting the holy verses at the marriage ceremony. Panchi and Gauri go around the sacred fire and Gauri is "tied" to Panchi from behind with her apron. Mulk Raj Anand seems to mock at and condemn a marriage which lacks the full approval and sufficient knowledge of the concerned partners. The novel also depicts Panchi's comic plight at the 'showing' ceremony. One finds here what Radcliffe-Brown refers to as "joking relationship" (Brown 106). They are the teasing reminder of the social disjunction caused by the marriage, while the social conjunction is maintained by friendliness that takes no offence at the insult. The show of hostility is considered a continued expression of the social disjunction. Joking relationship is thus a way in which persons standing in certain relationships, resulting either from kinship or more usually from marriage, are permitted or required to behave towards one another in a disrespectful or insulting way at which no offence might be taken. In this relationship between two persons one is by custom permitted and in some instances required to take no offence. Panchi himself refers to the custom:

> ...he vaguely knew that such jokes were part of the time-honoured ritual of initiation into marriage, and his

> aspirations to chivalry prevented him from exhibiting bad temper, though great sparks of violence glowed inside him. (24)

Panchi's behaviour at the 'showing' ceremony brings out his naivety and temper which is later the cause for much of the misunderstanding between him and Gauri:

> But [the] first joke at his expense was so crude and violent, and the demolition of his headgear so complete, that he was pale with hurt pride and unnerved, in spite of himself, and could not work up any of the bluff of enthusiasm expected from him. (23-24)

Elements of folk culture are seen in the marriage ceremonies with which the novel opens. As a part of the 'showing' ceremony Panchi is asked a number of riddles. The language used is a mixture of English and vernacular. The custom of partaking of food (signifying oneness) is found here when the bridegroom is given a betel leaf which he puts into the bride's mouth and then has a piece of it himself. Panchi allows himself to be fooled and led by others at the ceremony, as he does later in his life. Much of his later behaviour is prefigured at the marriage ceremony. From the beginning he brooks anger against Gauri and holds her responsible for all his humiliations, indicating his tendency to blame his wife for every mishap. Panchi's curiosity at not being allowed to lift Gauri's *dupatta*, and his wild impulse to satisfy it by pulling aside her *dupatta* show his impulsive nature (later he even beats Gauri at his will and throws her out). Critics like M.K. Naik revealed in similar ceremonies a particular aspect of the peasant character:

> The convention according to which the women folk of the bride's side welcome the groom's party with satirical verses and lampoons; the practical joke of putting hemp in the food served at the marriage feast; and the girlish pranks which the friends of Gauri play on Panchi at the time of the ceremony of "the showing"—all these reveal a robust (if somewhat rough) sense of humour in peasant character. (Mulk Raj Anand 90)

At the very onset the novel indicates the framework of *Gauri* from the Ramayana. The Sita myth is used as a structural parallel like the Bhasmasura myth in R.K. Narayan's *Man-Eater of Malgudi*. Mulk Raj Anand transmutes the myth of Sita who is exiled by her husband Rama on the taunting remark of a washerman that she is impure because she had to live in Ravana's Lanka for some time. But the parallelism between the two stories ends where Panchi challenges Gauri to give proof of her purity:

> It is part of Anand's technique that in his novel a myth should be pursued upto a certain point and then suddenly reversed. This contains an implicit comment on the values of the past, and reveals Anand's rejection of the ideal represented in the particular myth. ...this novel is unique among Indian novels in rejecting rather than extolling the time honoured womanly virtues of patience and submission. (Mukherjee, *The Twice Born Fiction* 164)

The legend is transmuted to suit the modern times as the heroine instead of suffering silently leaves her house to carve out a life for herself. She adopts a path different from the one adopted by her mythic counterpart. The parallel between the two stories, and the past and the present, is hinted at throughout the novel:

> 'Be like Sita...'. (28)

> They [the people] are telling him [Panchi] that Ram turned out Sita because everyone doubted her chastity during her stay with Ravana!... I [Gauri] am not Sita that the earth will open up and swallow me. I shall just go out and be forgotten of him.... (244)

The Sita myth is introduced at the beginning only to be shattered at the end. As in the case of Ira or Uma, Gauri's ceremonial marriage too is not a success. In *Gauri* the "woman who is banished [Gauri] becomes the woman who herself rejects the narrow world of subjections and fears that enslave Panchi despite his better self" (Sinha 69). The heroine becomes a symbol of new womanhood. Mulk Raj Anand does not approve or justify the myth but presents a modern version.

Gauri's plight is similar to that of Girija in Rajam Krishnan's *Lamps in the Whirlpool.* Both the novels trace the transformation which the female protagonists undergo. Girija a middle class girl, and a Hindu wife in a brahmin community has to maintain ritual purity which her mother-in-law insists. Unable to stand the restrictions of a tradition-bound, orthodox set-up she leaves her house only to return to be charged with infidelity. Girija is forced to choose between a crushing orthodoxy at home and the freedom of self-expression outside it. In *Gauri*, the novelist appears a champion of the amelioration of women:

> ...all the old antiquated ideas of India don't apply. The Sita myth doesn't apply. Rama is a coward, not a hero.... (Rajan, *Studies in Mulk Raj Anand* 114)
>
> I [Anand] think it is not the lot of woman to become Sita any more. (Rajan 114)

Unlike Savitri (R.K. Narayan's *Dark Room*) who returns to her house, Gauri shares the qualities of Nora in Ibsen's *Doll's House.* Though Mulk Raj Anand advocates the liberation of women, he seems to stress the need for retaining the traditional aspect of life as well. In the novel he "juxtapose[s] what is decayed and unhealthy and what is still vital and precious in the Indian tradition" (Naik, *Mulk Raj Anand* 87). The transformation Gauri undergoes through the impact of modernity is firmly rooted in tradition. During all her trials "two traditional props sustain her—her faith in the goddess, and her certitude of her own role as a Hindu wife" (Naik 91). Despite the brief spell of modernity Gauri remains firmly rooted in tradition. Through the novel Mulk Raj Anand depicts the unsuitability of an old myth to the modern world:

> My [Mulk Raj Anand] characters were not meant to be revised versions of old mythical symbols of the epics. I think that human beings do change in a changing universe, even if ever so little. So old mythical characters like Sita, or Savitri or Rama, are not eternal types who must be repeated in new incarnations. We cannot live by the good and bad examples of gods and kings of 5000 years ago. (Reddy 26)

According to Mulk Raj Anand there is no return to old myths and contemporary man has to forge new myths for himself which do not approximate to the old ones, but draw their power from India's ancient culture and heritage. The novel which opens with a description of the marriage ceremonies ends with its total break up. But it ends with "the hope of a better order through the successful union of what is imperishable in tradition and what is life-giving in modernity" (Naik 95).

Unlike the other tradition oriented characters in R.K. Narayan is Daisy (*The Painter of Signs*). She does not attach any sentiment to married life, and carves her own separate identity in life. In her is a sort of unmitigated antagonism to the concept of marriage. She discards the institution with its rites and ceremonies. Her short period of courtship with Raman makes it clear that she is not interested in housekeeping, and that her work will always have precedence over her wifely duties. Since Daisy prefers a "very simple ceremony" (158), the Gandharva marriage is chosen to do away with any formality:

> He [Raman] had explained to Daisy the five kinds of marriage he had read about and they had come to the conclusion that the system called Gandharva was the most suitable one for them; that was the type of marriage one read about in classical literature. When two souls met in harmony the marriage was consummated perfectly, and no further rite or ceremony was called for. Daisy said that although she had no faith in any ancient customs, she would accept it, since it seemed to her a sensible thing. (158)

The transition of the image of the Indian woman from the archetypal Sita-Savitri image to that of a modern one is indicated here. The system of marriage they opt for is quite contrary to the traditional one in which the father of the maiden invites the young man to accept the hand of his daughter. A properly bedecked daughter is given away by her father in this brahma form of marriage prevalent among most social groups. The situation exposes Raman's servile nature towards Daisy, and her upper hand in the relationship. Though they decide to live together, the two conditions Daisy lays down—that they will have no children, and that she will be allowed to pursue her social work—reminds one of a similar situation in the *Mahabharata*. There is in R.K. Narayan an extensive use of myths and legends. Through Daisy the Hindu legend of king Santhanu, who marries a beautiful woman on the condition that he is not to question any of her actions, is introduced into the novel. She says, "If you want to marry me [Daisy], you must leave me to my own plans even when I am a wife. On any day you question why or how, I will leave you. It will be an unhappy thing for me, but I will leave you...." (159). Raman himself refers to the legend when he says, "Whatever you say, I will never interfere. I won't question you. I will be like the ancient king Santhanu..." (159). The novelist does not take the point of comparison beyond this and even before Raman questions her, Daisy leaves him. A classical legend is applied to a modern context in the relationship between Raman and Daisy. The juxtaposition of Raman's fate with that of the mythical Santhanu generates an irony of contrast without any attempt to shatter the myth. His characters like Raman and Nataraj find the myth as a spring of consolation. An infatuated Raman agrees to Daisy's conditions. There is no discussion on horoscope, dowry, caste, or status. In Gandharva marriages the parties themselves form the union without the knowledge or consent of their parents or relations. It is settled through mutual understanding as in the novel. There is mutual love and consent between the bride and the groom, and it is usually a voluntary union of a maiden with her lover. Parents and kinsmen have nothing to do in such marriages. But the relationship between Raman and Daisy lacks understanding, and one doubts Daisy's love for Raman. The feeling of oneness is lacking in the relationship described here. It lacks togetherness, and as Raman makes out "the path of peace lay in not contradicting her" (168). Each leads a separate life and the relationship ends even before it begins, as Daisy leaves saying "Married life is not for me" (178). The incident reveals their character. R.K. Narayan seems to point out that such marriages, which do not have the sanction of society, do not flourish. A non-conformist like Daisy, who does not care for traditional customs and practices, does not find a place in R.K. Narayan's milieu. The victory of tradition is ensured in most of his novels. The order which is temporarily disrupted with her arrival is restored once again as Daisy leaves and Raman returns to his own world. In spite of rigid unconventionalism and streaks of feminism shown by Daisy, in the social context of Malgudi she appears an absurd representation of womanhood. While tradition and custom win in Malgudi, the progress of the unorthodox and the unconservative is mostly thwarted. Marriages without their accompanying ceremonies do not thrive here.

The description of the Kodava marriage in *The Scent of Pepper* provides a glimpse of their culture. At the very opening it refers to the marriage between Nanji and Baliyanna. The marriage marks Nanji's entry into the Kaleyanda household. She is received into the house after sprinkling a pinch of saffron rice into a copper pitcher with water. Music, feast, and dancing form a part of their marriage ceremonies. The marriage with a member of the Kaleyanda clan brings with it a new prestige. A short description of Boju's (Nanji's brother-in-law) marriage is also given. It temporarily relieves Baliyanna from his depression, and marks Chambavva's last visit home from the Crystal Palace. Baliyanna refuses to have Appachu (his brother) at the wedding. Appachu's marriage is in contrast to the traditional marriages described here. He marries a Christian and is baptized Appachu Basil Pinto. He defies the Kodava customs only to be deserted by his wife and children, and to return to his roots towards the end of his life. The use of words like *shamiana*, *mantap*, *pujari*, and *muhurtam* serve to enhance the traditional atmosphere created. Boju's marriage plays a significant part in Subbu's transformation into manhood. It also marks a new phase in Nanji's life. As a part of the ceremony Boju touches the feet of his elders and seeks their blessings. Through Clara's presence the East-West dichotomy is hinted at. As at the funeral ceremony, here too she stands apart:

> She wore a blue suit with hat and gloves but in the midst of all the colour and gold [the Kodava girls appear in silks wearing brooches, pendants, chains and diamonds which suggested the solidity of the girl's background, her dress looked too plain and the hat, ludicrous. (114)

The marriage is solemnized at the bride's place and the party returns with the bride to Athur. It suggests the usual post-marital residence which is virilocal. Where a similar custom is followed, the bride generally joins her husband in or near his natal residence, and is received by the women there. Among the Kodavas, as a part of the ceremony, the dancing young men block the path of the bride as she enters the house. The Kodava culture undergoes gradual changes with the passage of time and the old customs are replaced by new ones. The Kodava custom in which a bride is won by a man only after fighting and vanquishing nine suitors is replaced by the custom in which the Kodava groom cuts nine banana trees at his wedding. This is similar to the form of marriage in which the bridegroom is obliged to perform an act of prowess. It is reduced to a mock fight as referred to in this novel. At Subbu's marriage nine banana trees are planted in a row outside the bride's house. Subbu cuts them and dances as if he has really annihilated nine suitors to win Mallige. Ironically he is attacked by one "suitor" who is in love with Mallige, thus reminding one of the actual custom in which a suitor has to defeat his rival. Though injured, Subbu goes through the marriage ceremony. It is significant that the novel provides an elaborate description of Subbu's marriage as most of the later action in it revolves around him. Being late, a furious Kalappa (Mallige's father) keeps the groom's party waiting outside his gate. The incident provides an inkling of the Mallige-Subbu relationship described later. Kalappa's fury "about the indignity of having had to wait for the boy's party" (189) strikes as modern in the traditional Kodava atmosphere. The marriages bring together two families, villages, as well as people. This is seen in the marriages of Nanji, Chinni, Mallige, and Appachu (two different cultures too in his case). The impact of Gandhian ideals and the influence of the Indian political scene on the life of the people of Coorg are found in the second part of the novel. The ongoing transformation which takes place in Coorg is noticeable. A Gandhian, Subbu (in spite of his diminishing faith in congress ideals) refuses to have alcohol served during the two day ceremony. The "dry wedding" (194) creates communal resentment. The ceremonies described throw light on the Kodava culture:

> The barber shaved Subbu using milk to soothe the skin, and was gifted money, rice and the mat on which Subbu sat. Subbu bathed and dressed...and seconds before the muhurtam, [was] led...from the Kaliyanda house to the wedding mantap.... (193)

At Mallige's house the bangle-seller receives his gift of money, rice, and the mat on which the bride sits as he slid the bangles into her wrists. The bride is dressed and adorned with jewels. Mallige enters the house, thus changing Nanji's status in the household. A number of ceremonies are performed as the bride enters the groom's house after the marriage:

> The bride broke a coconut near the well and carried a pitcher of water to the house and, like all Kodava brides before her, stood the trial of patience [prefiguring her patience in dealing with Nanji] and stamina while young Kaliyanda men danced and blocked her path.... Mallige entered the house, sought the blessings of the elders and became a part of the Kaliyanda family. (196)

Unlike Chambavva (Nanji's mother-in-law), Nanji is unable to get along with her daughter-in-law. Nanji gives in to Mallige as Chambavva had done earlier. Though Mallige has none of her mother-in-law's capabilities, she brings about changes in the Kaleyanda household as Nanji had soon after her arrival as Baliyanna's wife. Besides focusing on the customs and ceremonies of the people of Coorg, the novelist also shows its significance in their culture. These practices undergo change with the passage of time.

The social stigma, and seclusion imposed on a widow is portrayed in works like *Kanthapura*, *Fasting, Feasting*, and *The Scent of Pepper*. Through Mira-masi (*Fasting, Feasting*) the novel portrays an orthodox widow obsessed with rituals and ceremonies. An obsession for purificatory rites is seen in her. Her days are filled with rituals like salutation to the sun, ritual baths, prayers, preparation of her vegetarian meal on her own for fear of being polluted, evening ceremonies in the temple, etc. She recites ancient myths and is horrified by pollution or an 'unclean' existence. Apart from the private rituals she performs, she goes to the temple and sits through the rituals there. Mira-masi is one of the few elaborately described orthodox characters in Anita Desai's fictive world. Anita Desai condemns such an orthodox social set-up. In a conservative society widows are believed to bring ill luck and hence looked down upon. They have to shave their head, are not allowed to wear jewels, chew betel, wear coloured clothes, and are forbidden to take part in auspicious occasions. Their very presence is considered an evil omen. The novel provides a detailed account of the rituals and ceremonies Mira-masi seems obsessed with. Like most Indian widows she too resigns to her fate. The description of her activities is humorous. Mira-masi went through these rituals "as casually as if she were dusting her house..." (41). But her obsession with religion (after becoming a widow she had taken up religion as a "vocation" (39)) and purification appears "old-fashioned" (38) to Uma's family. Religion for her is a means to escape reality. She travels all over the country feeling "safe in her widows white garments" (38). Mira-masi even goes to the verge of making a human goddess of Uma, considering her to be "possessed" when she actually has a hysterical fit. Like a widow she spends her life going on pilgrimages. An entirely different picture is found in works like *Kanthapura*, and *The Scent of Pepper*. In the orthodox social set-up of Kanthapura is cast a character like Ratna, who is portrayed as a progressive widow. She is an educated young woman with progressive views. Though a widow, she does not dress and live in the conventional style of a widow. Ratna wears bangles, coloured saris, has *kumkum* mark on her forehead and parts her hair. Though much criticized in the novel for her unconventional ways, she does not care for such criticism and chooses her own path, and sticks to it with determination. Ratna also actively participates in the Gandhian movement, and conducts harikathas, reads out the newspaper, and carries on Moorthy's work when he is arrested and put in jail. In *The Scent of Pepper* the Kodavas allow their young widows to remarry as is evident from Nanji's marriage to Baliyanna. In spite of being a widow Nanji is married according to the customs of the region. The Kodava widows are allowed to live their life, and are treated properly. Thus in a more or less traditional social set-up Nanji is married though she is a widow. Widows for them are a symbol of grief. They (like Chambavva) spend the rest of their lives in the Crystal Palace:

> The inmates of the house knew what it was like to be shackled to a husband, home and society, and that ast experience made them extremely sympathetic to each other's minor vices and addictions. (116)

Like any Hindu widow, the Rao Bahadur's wife, Chambavva, is dressed in white, denuded of her ornaments. The change in Chambavva's status (from a married woman to a widow) creates much discomfort for her. In a humorous way the novel points out that though Chambavva, who had led a life of sloth, sat on a reed mat by the body of her husband "her grief overshadowed physical discomfort. Her status had slipped from that of wife to widow. Even a decaying husband was better than no husband" (14). The mourners offer her flowers and sympathy. In contrast to the usual treatment meted out to widows, the novel shows how the Kodavas treat their widows better than most of the other social groups. They retire from the day-to-day life and live in the Crystal Palace engaging themselves in simple pleasures like singing, games, and drinking, things which the widows in any orthodox society would be denied. Though these Kodava widows lead a mirthful life it was "an expression of rebellion that no one had time or compassion to understand" (20). The treatment meted out to widows varies from society to society. Creative writers often raise their voice against the inhuman treatment meted out to them by society.

Marriage is an auspicious occasion, a sacrament as well as a social institution for the Hindus. There are various social signals (like the procession, feast, and music) which indicate that a marriage is taking place. The actual ceremony is also publicly ratified. An orthodox Hindu marriage is often described as a tiresome affair—very noisy, tediously minute in ceremonies, liable to interruptions from disputes, and often an arena for rival factions to fight out all the ill-feeling, discontent, and jealousy which have accumulated for years. It is not only an occasion for enjoyment but also to show one's prosperity and status in life. The orthodox cling to the ceremonies which accompany a marriage. The marriage becomes a means of bringing relatives as well as friends together. It is a social occasion of happiness and rejoicing, but often becomes a show of wealth and splendour and an instance for establishing one's position and influence. Though the sanctity of the institution of marriage is maintained by the older generation, with modernization much of its significance seems to be lost. More than the ritualistic practices associated the financial and economic significance of the institution gets emphasized in the modern world. These ceremonies are depicted in different ways in a number of Indian English novels. It is a part of the life of the characters depicted in them. Novelists have also brought forth the plight of widows in their works. The Indian woman is often presented as being bound by superstitions and conservative traditions. The hypocrisy of the priests, who are willing to match the horoscopes if money is paid, is exposed in a number of creative works. Creative writers denounce customs like dowry and bride price which have become attached to the institution of marriage. These are dealt with in an ironic and humorous manner (in *The Vendor of Sweets* and *Fasting, Feasting*). While Anita Desai concentrates on the psychological impact of religious beliefs on the human mind, Kavery Nambisan, besides giving one a picture of the Kodava culture, highlights the East-West dichotomy (like Kamala Markandaya). The characters representing the West find themselves out of place in the traditional Indian atmosphere. These ceremonies are central to a traditional set-up like Malgudi in which rebellion is almost impossible. Besides promoting social solidarity and happiness, these rites and rituals play a significant role in Indian life as well as Indian English fiction.

4

The Samskara

There is a remarkable variation in customs with regard to death. While some dispose of the corpse in a very unceremonious manner, others follow elaborate rites. Costly catafalques and cars may be used for the bearing of the body and elaborately wrought and ornamented coffin for its covering. The general objective behind these funeral rites is the disposal of the corpse and the dismissal of the dead spirit. Taboos and limitations of various kinds are usually enforced on the mourners. Like the marriage festivities, the funeral ceremonies often continue through a number of days. As feasting and rejoicing are the main features of the marriage celebration, so feasting and wailing are the prominent characteristics of the funeral week. If the death occurs early in the day the burial usually takes place before sunset, but, if it occurs in the latter part of the day, the burial takes place the next morning. The various funeral ceremonies show the loving reverence for the dead, with a recognition of the continued relation of the dead with the living. Often sorrow is expressed by wailing, mutilation of the mourner or a mourning costume worn for a prescribed period. People go to the graves of their dear ones to weep there, or to adorn them with tokens of their loving remembrance.

Many societies have strange mourning customs. Among some at the very moment of death the nearest relative of the dead gives out a wild shriek, announcing the death to all who are within hearing. This is similar to the function of the church bells which announce the death of a person. In several parts of

India professional mourners are hired. Collecting in a group around the deceased, they commence by setting up in unison the most doleful cries, at the same time, beating their breasts in measured time. They weep, sob, shriek and eulogize the deceased person's virtues and good qualities till the corpse is removed. As soon as the obsequies are over they receive their wages. Beyond the funeral week the period of special mourning for the dead differs among the various social groups. It may even extend from a month to a year or two. A Hindu mourning lasts one year, during which a number of ceremonies are observed. The period of mourning sometimes varies according to how the person has died. In the case of an ordinary death the family may mourn for about a week. During this period they are considered to be in a state of pollution. Work is discontinued during this period of mourning. Apart from the distinctively religious services at the burial, many primitive customs in connection with funerals and burials have been retained among certain groups of people.

The body may be disposed of in various ways. This differs from society to society:

> The body may be eaten with more or less ceremony by relatives or enemies, or flung to the beasts of the field, the birds of the air, or fishes of the sea; it may be buried in the ground full length, or in a contracted position, lying down or sitting up; it may be deposited in a cave, on a platform, or in the fork of a tree, enclosed in a stone cist or wooden coffin, rammed into an earthenware jar, sent adrift in a canoe, or burnt by quicklime or fire. (Hutchinson XX)

The moment a Hindu has breathed his last, the necessary preparations for his funeral begins. As long as the body remains in the house, the inmates cannot eat or drink. U.R. Ananthamurthy's *Samskara* presents a similar situation which the brahmins in an *agrahara* face on the death of an anti-brahminical brahmin, Naranappa, who broke every known taboo. Thus for them, "Alive, Naranappa was an enemy; dead, a preventer of meals; as a corpse, a problem, a nuisance" (3). The last moment of a brahmin's life is associated with a number of ceremonies. They observe very many formalities when their near relatives die. These make one wonder whether they are trying to preserve after their death, that superiority over their fellows which they boast about so much during their life time. The dying man is laid on the ground, for a brahmin must not be allowed to die on bed. Various rites are performed by the chief mourner—the person who is most nearly related to the deceased, or the one who has the right to perform this function. Before his death the dying person has to be expitiated from his sins and has to undergo purificatory ceremonies. Often expensive ceremonies are performed and alms are distributed among the brahmins, apart from a grand feast. All these are done in order to secure the brahmin a place in heaven. The corpse is washed and is often anointed before being conveyed to the funeral ground. The toes as well as the two thumbs are bound together with a small piece of cloth. The body is wrapped in a cloth. Flowers and garlands are sometimes placed on it. After the initial ceremonies, the body is placed on a bier which is borne on the shoulders of four people. The funeral procession sets out with the chief mourner at the head, followed by the bier. The mourning friends and relatives of the deceased also accompany the bier to the funeral ground. They often chant religious sentences in a monotonous and gloomy strain. Hindu women, like the Muslim women do not attend the funeral ceremonies at the funeral ground. The funeral pyre is erected and the corpse covered with a cloth, is laid on the pyre which is ignited with the sacred fire, previously prepared with religious rites. Before lighting it the chief mourner walks around the fire three times carrying an earthen vessel from which water trickles. It is broken afterwards. A lighted torch is then brought to him and he sets fire to the four corners of the pile. The mourners later proceed to perform their ablutions in order to purify themselves of the pollution of having carried a corpse. When the funeral rites are over they have to purify themselves with a bath. But the ceremonies do not end with this. On the following day the chief mourner returns to the funeral ground to collect the ashes which are later immersed in water. Many elaborate rites are sometimes performed in some societies in connection with the disposal of the ashes after cremation. Sometimes it is buried or else it is thrown into the holy Ganges.

The funeral rites for women are nearly the same as that for men. Thus the dead are cremated by the higher castes, and buried or cremated by the lower classes according to the worldly circumstances of the family of the deceased, burial being less expensive than cremation which necessitates the purchase of wood for the pyre. Among some social groups these rites do vary according to the sex of the deceased and also on the basis of other conditions. Amongst certain groups copper coins are thrown into the grave. This is done to propitiate the earth goddess for the disturbance of the soil, and also to help the spirit in its way to the land of death. Sometimes weapons and other articles are placed in the graves. These help to show that the people believed in a life after death.

Burial in a sitting posture is resorted to by many. Robert Towers in his *Necklace of Kali* refers to this practice in Benares. A holy man is lifted into a small boat accompanied by drumbeats:

> The fat old man maintained an awkward and rigid sitting position; the hands were folded in his lap and his bald, shining head was thrust forward at a curious angle, as though he had fixed himself in some kind of cataleptic trance. Very gently and cautiously the young men descended the stairs [of the river] until they were nearly waist-deep in the...water, and then they gently lowered the sadhu into the front of the skiff, maintaining him always in his inconvenient sitting posture. One of them placed a loose garland of white and scarlet blossoms around the sadhu's bare...shoulders. (36)

The corpse was then consigned to the sacred waters. Kavery Nambisan in her *Scent of Pepper* refers to the funeral of Rao Bahadur at the beginning of the novel. Christian funeral rites have also been referred to in Indian English fiction. In *The God of Small Things* Arundhati Roy describes Sophie Mol's funeral.

In certain societies the right of burial was granted only to those who were acquitted of evil doing by a tribunal of their survivors. Lack of burial was often the consequence of a life of sin and crime, as is the case with Naranappa in *Samskara*.

The death of his father and mother must be celebrated by a Hindu all his life without fail. At each new moon it is his indispensable duty to offer libation to his deceased parents as well as his ancestors. These offerings are made at a ceremony called the *sradh*. In the performance of this rite, a ball of rice is offered to the ancestors and then thrown to the crows. It is regarded as a favourable omen if they partake thereof. Among some castes, the clapping of the hands announces to the birds that the rice is being thrown for them to eat. Large numbers of people are sometimes invited to the *sradh* feast. Thus during the funeral ceremonies, which involve not only the family members but also the close relatives and friends, prayers are offered and feasts held for the dear departed ones.

The beliefs and ideals of a civilization are often more explicitly formulated in its rituals than in any other cultural trait. There are rituals to mark the different phases of human life in almost every community. To the living, the dead too belong to their group and a proper disposal of the body has to be carried out. Hence various funeral obsequies (samskara), which mark the final phase of human life, are performed by the living for the dead. These ensure a good afterlife for the deceased. The dead spirits, it is believed, punish the living for their violation of taboos and ritual procedures. Since they play an important role in the affairs of the living, these rites serve to make sure that the dead do not interfere as evil spirits in the day-to-day life on earth. The belief that the dead aid and punish men forces them to pay homage. Along with the proper disposal of the body, these rites confer a new status on the dead. They are reincorporated into the society as dead spirits by virtue of the status they occupied before death. The Indian masses conduct elaborate funeral rites when a death occurs. Drawing on this aspect of Indian life, some of the Indian English novels contain lengthy descriptions of mourning ceremonies and funeral rites. Novelists like Mulk Raj Anand

(*Lament on the Death of a Master of Arts*), R.K. Narayan (*The English Teacher*, *Waiting for the Mahatma*), Kamala Markandaya (*The Coffer Dams, The Nowhere Man*), U.R. Anantha Murthy (*Samskara*), Kavery Nambisan (*The Scent of Pepper*), Rohinton Mistry (*Such a Long Journey*), and Arundhati Roy (*The God of Small Things*) have used these elaborate rituals to attain different effects. The above mentioned works highlight the functional significance of the funeral rites delineated in them.

When death occurs, a great parade of all the external signs of sorrow usually takes place. In several parts of India professional mourners are hired as a part of the mourning ceremony. When called in to attend the obsequies they arrive with dishevelled hair, wearing clothes in a disorderly manner. They collect in a group around the deceased and set up in unison the most doleful cries, at the same time beating their breasts in measured time. The professional mourners weep, sob, shriek, and eulogize the deceased's virtues. This demonstration of affected sorrow lasts until the corpse is removed. As soon as the obsequies are over, they receive their wages and leave. Mulk Raj Anand and Rohinton Mistry have drawn on this custom in *Lament on the Death of a Master of Arts* and *Such a Long Journey* to create a humorous effect. Mulk Raj Anand's *Lament* is an exploration into human suffering and its philosophical implications which preoccupy the mind of the hero (Nur). The existential note is broken by the women who rush in "like fluttering, frightened hens towards a corner of the room" (*Lament* 46). They, like the professional mourners, make a loud demonstration of their grief. The bird imagery used to describe these hysterical women is apt—"frightened hens" (46), they rush towards Nur like "vultures to their prey" (47). In an otherwise serious atmosphere, the wailing and hysterical behaviour of these mourners border on the ridiculous and create a comic effect. The novelist exposes the religious hypocrisy and formalism, and satirizes the human adherence to meaningless customs in most of his works. Like most Anand's heroes, Nur is a severe critic of a religion which is reduced to mere rituals and practices. Nur points out that the Muslim priest is more concerned about the rich food and gifts he gets than the spiritual needs of his community, the *maulavi* shouts at him in a language that does not befit a religious priest, and the hypocrites combine holiness with business. Through Nur the author expresses his own hatred for such hypocrisy. Born into an orthodox Hindu family, he himself rebelled against the practices which prevailed in society. Various manifestations of religious hypocrisy and exploitation are brought out through his characters like Pandit Kali Nath in *Untouchable*, Pandit Bhola Nath in *Gauri*, and the fat yogi of Bhagat Har Das Shrine in *Coolie*. His denunciation is not peculiar to Hindu religion and its practices. Like his brahmin priests, the Muslim priests are greedy, sensual, crafty and gluttonous. Rituals become a means to keep the people in submission, to assert their superior status and to earn money by conducting ceremonies. Anand's novels convey the idea that all the religions are in a similar state. In *Lament* he criticizes Islam. Though Nur's orthodox mind asserts itself in moments of weakness, he considers traditional religion as nonsensical. Faith in God which is deeply embedded in the Indian psyche often reveals itself in times of stress and strain. The novelist satirizes the mourning customs prevalent in India. Nur's neighbours and relatives chant a dirge of lament, similar to those of the traditional mourners at a funeral ceremony. It is ironic that the wailing starts even before the death of the hero, reminding him of his impending death. A realistic and humorous picture of the women, who gather around Nur wailing and shrieking, is presented here. The whole situation borders on the ridiculous. It is like a death rehearsal for Nur. Their cries, "Hai, hai!", and the physical demonstration of grief increase in intensity creating a gruesome picture at the end. An atmosphere full of pathos and philosophical speculation is made humorous with the arrival of these mourning women. They moan, cry loudly and beat their heads. As wailing announces death, the neighbours enquire "Is he dead? Is he dead?" (47), thus heightening the comic effect. Nur, still alive, is embarrassed by these hysterical women:

> [Their wails] grew louder and shriller as his grandmother, his stepmother and the other women of the lane joined the chorus, the loudest of them adding to their shrieks a violent show of beating their breasts, and smiting their foreheads in a rhythmic sequence attuned to the dirge of 'Hai hai! Hai hai!'. (47-48)

Nur realizes the futility of his rage against them. As he says, "...they were only practising a stupid convention that ordained the invocation of cries and shrieks and howls at the barest sign of death" (48). Ironically Nur opens his eyes and merely says, "'I am not dead, I am not dead'" (48). This passivity is something Nur shares with Bakha, the hero in Anand's *Untouchable*. In keeping with the mourning custom the mourners cry out, "'What will happen to us, what will happen to our Iqbal [Nur's wife]?'" (47). Nur is forced to submit unquestioningly to the customs and blind faith in a society where the custodians of religious values have themselves degenerated into hypocrites and shameless epicures. As M.K. Naik points out, "In novel after novel religion is depicted [by Anand] as an affair of hypocrisy and outmoded taboos of avaricious and gluttonous priests..." (Naik, *Mulk Raj Anand* 70). With Nur's death the weeping and moaning reach their climax:

> 'Hai hai!' she [Nur's grandmother] lifted her voice and cried. 'Hai hai! Hai hai!' And she struck the palms of her hands on her breasts, on her forehead, on her face, and moaned and howled and tore her hair as she fell across his [Nur's] neck.
>
> The women...came screaming down, beating their breasts, their thighs, their foreheads, their cheeks and their breasts again and again and cried, 'Hai hai! Hai hai! Hai hai!'
>
> The women of the neighbourhood rushed and, entering the room, began to beat their heads deliberately, crying and wailing, 'Hai hai!'. (64-65)

The image of the dead body, "wrapped in a white shroud..." (8) like a corpse, at the beginning of the story is completed with the wailing and shrieking at Nur's death. The latter part of the novel, full of screaming and crying, presents a sharp contrast to the earlier one filled with Nur's philosophic ruminations. The feeling of grief is lost among the "deliberate" cries of the unconcerned women who gather around Nur. The hysterical scenes serve to heighten the tragic effect of the work, making Nur's plight more poignant. It also serves as a comic relief by illustrating the abstract nature of death itself. The whole episode makes grief more of an absurd convention than an externalization of genuine concern. Mulk Raj Anand's comic sense takes the form of satire and is directed against religious pretence, and meaningless customs and manners in society. The use of an Indian expletive, "Hai! Hai!", serves to heighten the tension in an already gloomy atmosphere. Anand himself revolted against the "claptrap of ritual" (Rajan, *Studies in Mulk Raj Anand* 107) and preferred the "rejection of the barbarous elements" (Rajan 115) that dominate human lives. Adherence to rigid rituals is condemned by him, for religion is not to be equated with ceremonial piety or doctrinal conformity. It is difficult to agree that "[Mulk Raj Anand's] humanistic creed has no place for religion in it" (Naik, Mulk Raj Anand 184). Anand's preference is for a religion that does not create either passivity of narrow orthodoxy or fanaticism in man. Like his other works, *Lament* too depicts Anand's "disgust for" (Naik 14) religious deception. They expose his contempt for the "dead habits and customs and...restrictive religious rites and practices" (Naik 14). A similar humorous situation is also found in Rohinton Mistry's *Such a Long Journey*. The novel, set in Bombay, deals with the lives of Gustad Noble and his family. Here Mistry draws upon the custom of traditional mourners (among the Parsis) in depicting the widow Alamai. Ironically the woman who is never seen beside her husband during his sickness, and whom he refers to as a "domestic vulture" (239), wails and shouts hysterically at his funeral ceremony. This introduces humour into an otherwise sombre atmosphere. In a humorous way he describes the "pathetic exhibition" (251) of grief by Alamai on her husband's death. Her initial composure and silent weeping make Gustad feel the need to hire mourners. Mistry humorously exclaims, "Thank God the quality of afterlife does not depend on the quantity of tears" (245). Gustad ironically refers to Alamai's "histrionic capabilities" (245), which he had underestimated, when she is convulsed by a great sob. She behaves like the professional mourners—"[s]he rocked back and forth, her tall, thin trunk swaying alarmingly in the narrow space, as she clutched her head in her hands and wailed" (245). In India it is the general custom among widows to act in this manner as the signs of deepest grief. The descriptions here are charged with humour and irony, and serve to expose the absurdity and hypocrisy of its practitioners. In one continuous strain, Alamai apostrophizes her husband in a series of questions and addresses the gods, accusing them openly of injustice in depriving her of him. In the manner of a traditional mourner she laments, "'You have left me? Gone away? But why?'.... 'O Parvar Daegar! What have You done! You took him away? Why? Now what will I do? Take me also! Now! Now and now only!' and she smote her chest twice" (245). Like Mulk Raj Anand, Rohinton Mistry too emphasizes the deliberateness of these acts. Alamai's demonstrations expose her hypocrisy and ignorance. The appearance she now projects is quite contrary to the termagnent she had been in her life with Dinshawji. Along with this exhibition of grief she argues with the men who come to perform Dinshawji's ablutions. The women around her, in keeping with the mourning practices, try to pacify her. They "hang...on to her arms" (251), try to "wrestle her down into a chair" (251) and prevent her from rushing to the bier, thus presenting a humorous picture. Exposing the meaninglessness of the whole act Gustad says, "Of course, if tall, lean Alamai had really wanted to, she could have easily tossed aside the four or five gasping women" (251). But she yields to their efforts and suddenly flops back with no more show of escaping out of their hands or rushing to the lifeless remains of her husband. The wailing and moaning makes it known to the people around that a death has taken place. A similar function is played by the gunshot soon after the death of a Kaleyanda in *The Scent of Pepper*. The death of the Rao Bahadur is announced by his son Boju by firing two shots with his father's favourite gun, as Subbu does later for his father, Baliyanna. It announces, like wailing amongst some social groups, the death to the people around. Mulk Raj Anand and Rohinton Mistry use the mourning custom to expose the meaninglessness of these practices and also to point out how religion becomes an affair of hypocrisy and outmoded beliefs and customs. These age old practices which the people do not understand make a mockery of faith.

Owing to their belief in the immortality of the soul, the Hindus perform elaborate ceremonies to ease the problems for the soul's journey to the world of the dead. The dying man is laid on the ground, expiated of his sins (*sarvaprayaschitta*) and a purificatory ceremony is held to free him from all earthly taints. The person who is most nearly related to the deceased has the right to perform the last rites. This is found in *Waiting for the Mahatma*, *The English Teacher*, *The Scent of Pepper*, and *The Nowhere Man*. The chief mourner performs the *samkalpa* ceremony and offers *homam* so that the dead may obtain a place in heaven. After the initial rites, the body is laid on a bier and carried to the cremation ground in a procession, where it is placed on the funeral pyre. The custom is described in *Samskara*, *The Scent of Pepper*, *The English Teacher*, and *Waiting for the Mahatma*. The chief mourner walks around the funeral pyre and finally sets fire to the four corners of the pyre. The pyre is usually lit by the eldest son (the chief mourner) of the deceased, for according to the Hindu religious texts, a son delivers his father from the hell called *pum*. He is called *putra* (son) meaning the deliverer from hell. This belief is expressed in *The Scent of Pepper* and *Samskara*. The son frees his father from whatever wrong he has committed. A number of ceremonies are carried out before and after the death of a Hindu to ensure him a place in heaven. The son also performs the *sradh*, a ritual in annual remembrance of his deceased parents.

Orthodox religion is often ossified through years into empty rituals, and social life is saturated with superstitious practices. Novelists disapprove of the way religion is reduced to mere rituals and dead customs. They critically portray the society where superstitious practices and beliefs reign. Novels by U.R. Anantha Murthy and R.K. Narayan contain references to funeral rites among the Hindus. Though both expose the pretensions of the brahmin community, the funeral rites have been dealt with differently and used for different purposes.

Samskara and *Waiting for the Mahatma* expose the hollowness of the orthodox beliefs and rituals prevalent in the south Indian brahmin community. Samskara provides one with a kaleidoscopic vision of the tradition-bound society with its evils, vices, and ignorant ways. A number of rituals are performed after the death of a person. The novelist shows how the neglect of a dead body over a dilemma of religious laws plays havoc with human life, and plague makes its toll in the village. This exposes the dull and outdated modes of life of the brahmins in the agrahara. The orthodox community clings desperately to its past. The brahmins living in Durvasapura are unable to find a suitable answer to the problem of the last rites of an ostracized brahmin (Naranappa). The novel presents a world in which an act of rebellion brings others with it and quickly adds up to a rejection of piety and reverences that held the society together. There is a delay in cremating the body as well as a controversy about who should perform the last rites. It is significant that Naranappa does not have any children to "save" him from hell. Anantha Murthy's orthodox upbringing seems to be asserting the idea that there is no escape for an unorthodox brahmin (like Naranappa) who flouts all the religious practices. According to their Texts any relative can conduct the last rites failing which any brahmin can offer to carry them out. This only raises the question of Naranappa's brahminhood. A picture of decadent brahminism is presented here. Through Naranappa, the novelist makes way for the disintegration of an agrahara. Though the various meanings of the word samskara are interwoven into the novel, the subtitle, "A Rite for a Dead Man", provides the most concrete of these many meanings. The novel does not provide a detailed description of the funeral rites but dwells on the problems that the need to conduct them creates in a decaying brahmin colony. Ironically the denial of funeral rites for Naranappa necessitates these rites for many more who die due to plague.

The novelist probes into the inner psychological world of his characters to expose the warring impulses and tendencies inside their mind. Unable to change or excommunicate the unorthodox Naranappa, they find in his death a means to punish by disowning him. Here Anantha Murthy creates a world familiar to him—one which he came to hate and rebel against. Born into an orthodox brahmin family he "grew up in an agrahara somewhat similar to what [he] describe[s] in [his] novel *Samskara...*" (Murthy, *Literary Criterion* 58). The picture of the *agrahara* in the first part of the novel brings to light the ritualistic life of the Brahmins. It serves to highlight the decay that has set in. Carrying out the death rites is important to the orthodox brahmins living in Durvasapura. This is implied in their strict adherence to the rituals and practices. The brahmins' lives are ordered by the rituals and festivals they follow. The age old routine is questioned by Naranappa, and hindered by his death. The confusion it creates is thus only natural. The death creates ripples in a seemingly calm *agrahara* and sets their familiar world in confusion. This central event (death) and the rituals it necessitates are used to unveil the ignorance and deception of the supposedly learned brahmins. Hindus observe many formalities when a death occurs. The brahmins in Anantha Murthy's novel refuse to conduct the rites because Naranappa had gone against the ways of brahminism. The various customs and taboos associated with death hinder the disposal of a rotting dead body in the *agrahara*. The ritual bound life of the *agrahara* is turned upside down with the news of Naranappa's death. Being in a state of pollution (because of Naranappa's death) food is taboo till the funeral rites are conducted and the brahmins have their purificatory ceremony. James Frazer refers to this custom in his *Golden Bough*:

> ...both things and words may, like persons, be charged or electrified, either temporarily or permanently, with the mysterious virtue of taboo, and may therefore require to be banished for a longer or shorter time from the familiar usage of common life. (295)

Anantha Murthy uses this taboo to expose the hypocrisy and gluttony of the brahmins in the *agrahara*. As soon as the news of Naranappa's death spreads the brahmins run about preventing others from having food. Children are exempted from this. With a tinge of irony the narrator points out, "[b]y god's grace, no brahmin had yet eaten" (3). The "learned" brahmins are filled with fear and anxiety, for according to ancient custom there can be no worship, food, bathing, or prayers until the body is properly removed. The routine life of the brahmins is set astir, and one by one they break the taboos, still raking up the dead man's faults. What earlier would have been a questionable unorthodox act is now left unquestioned. They even have food with the brahmins of Parijatapura whom they consider inferior. The brahmins had denounced Naranappa's friendship with them. The delay in conducting the last rites means a whole day without food to them. The self-centred Dasacharya, who lives entirely on the meals that the brahmins get at death rites, and anniversaries, finds himself in a paradoxical situation—while the presence of Naranappa's dead body denies him food, carrying out his last rites would ostracize his community from the brahmins around the agrahara. In sharp contrast to these hypocrites, the novelist presents Chandri (an outcaste) who is not tied down by rules or philosophic discussions like the brahmins of the *agrahara*. The food taboo does not restrict her. Chandri has her food when she feels hungry and does not behave like the brahmins in the *agrahara* who are supposed to be fasting. She knows that no rules apply to her:

> She hadn't slept, she was hungry. She wasn't the fasting kind, not in any of her births.... Now she couldn't stand her hunger any more, so she got up and walked through the backyard to the plantain grove. She plucked a bunch of bananas left on the tree for ripening, ate them till she was full, went to the stream and drank a lot of water. (44)

Through Chandri's spontaneous actions Anantha Murthy seems to repudiate the brahmins' decadent value system. Unlike the brahmins who are more concerned with the rules, in

Chandri only one thought surfaces—"It's [Naranappa's dead body] rotting there, that thing, it's stinking there, its belly swollen. That's not her lover, Naranappa. It's neither brahmin nor shudra. A carcass. A stinking rotting carcass" (70). This is something which the brahmins fail to realize till the end. By the "end" of the novel even Praneshacharya, the spiritual leader, breaks the taboo in spite of being in a mourning period. He enters the temple where food is distributed and "pollutes" it. But the breaking of the food taboo which appears as an expression of hypocrisy in the other brahmins is an important phase in Praneshacharya's movement towards spiritual transformation. As James Frazer notes, the various taboos help to "seclude these persons [who are considered polluted] from the rest of the world so that the dreaded spiritual danger shall neither reach them nor spread from them..." (295). Gradually Praneshacharya experiences within himself the condition of Naranappa who was once his opposite. He (like Naranappa) is not able to shed the shackles of his ritual bound existence and remains tethered to it. The brahminism and the fear of defying the rules which have become a part of him prevent him from retaliating against the orthodox practices openly. To an orthodox brahmin community, his taking food in the temple during the period of mourning would be as heinous as Naranappa's unorthodox acts. Praneshacharya breaks the taboo only after drifting out of his accustomed space (the *agrahara*) into the outer world. There is a reversal of roles with his flouting the rules of brahminism. The death of Naranappa and the brahmins' reluctance to conduct the last rites result in the 'rebirth' of the Acharya, and his final decision to conduct the funeral rites himself. His experiences make him ready "to shed the dwarfish Vamana natures of the *agrahara*" (72), and help him in his spiritual upliftment.

The novel is a pungent satire on the hollowness of the contemporary brahmin society. Their familiar world filled with customs and practices is threatened by Naranappa's death. The death betrays a world of complex rituals and taboos which do not spare even the dead. Each brahmin tries to turn the situation to his own advantage and harbours his own reason to hate the dead Naranappa. While a brahmin corpse lies untouched in the agrahara without proper funeral, thwarting every daily duty, the brahmins vie with each other. Like Naranappa, Anantha Murthy also disliked the hypocritical aspects of society and struggled to come out of it. He lashes out against the greedy brahmins who stand revealed when their routinized life is in chaos:

> ...they were afraid, fearful that the lust for gold might destroy brahmin purity. But in the heart of every one of them flashed the question: if some other brahmin should perform the funeral rite for Naranappa, he might keep his brahminhood and yet put all that gold [which Chandri had put forward to meet Naranappa's funeral expense] on his wife's neck. (10)

Anantha Murthy through the death and its repercussions exposes the materialistic brahmins and hints at the deterioration that has enveloped the *agrahara*. The corruption that has engulfed it is highlighted throughout the novel. The novel derides the brahmins with their hypocrisy, and seems to champion the cause of the lowcaste. Though the work does not provide a detailed description of the funeral rites, it exposes the hollow beliefs of a community of brahmins who strictly adhere to complex rituals and taboos without realizing their meaning or significance. It also speeds up the transformation of Praneshacharya, and the downfall of an extremely orthodox agrahara. The brahmins of Parijatapura and the guru at the monastery are all presented in the same light suggesting a similar condition everywhere. As the guru at the monastery clearly suggests, certain simple offerings to remove the impurity would have solved the problem, making one wonder how a spiritual leader like Praneshacharya would fail to note this. Samskara presents "a decadent structure which, once jolted out of its groove, cannot be reintegrated again" (Mukherjee, *Realism and Reality* 168). To the brahmins of Durvasapura the funeral rites serve not only to dispose of the decomposing body but also to get rid of a self they see objectified in him. Naranappa serves the function of a scapegoat to these brahmins. The inner longings of the brahmins are transferred on to Naranappa by them. In this transference and removal is an attempt to expel the accumulated ills of the whole community through a scapegoat on whom the sins of the people are laid. In *The Golden Bough*, James Frazer refers to the expulsion of embodied evils. A man is singled out (here Naranappa) as a scapegoat for the sins of the rest of the village (here the agrahara). It is based on the custom of publicly expelling the accumulated evils of a village, town, or country. This transference of evil is carried out to effect a total clearance of all the ills that have been infesting the social group. Though the evils are "invisible and intangible" (Frazer 753) there is "a visible and tangible vehicle to convey them away" (Frazer 753). A scapegoat acts as such a vehicle and plays a similar role. In *Samskara* the brahmins' attempts are not to obtain a total clearance of the ills that infest their brahmin community, but to get rid of the scapegoat who for them represents all their secret longings. This is in vain, for even in his death Naranappa exposes the brahmins and their weaknesses. The expulsion of a scapegoat "is commonly preceded or followed by a period of general license, during which the ordinary restraints of society are thrown aside, and all offences, short of the gravest, are allowed to pass unpunished" (Frazer 754). The death here (and thus the expulsion of the scapegoat) is followed by the brahmins' breaking the taboos. The "ordinary restraints" (Frazer 754) are violated, but one is not sure whether they will be allowed to pass unpunished. It is paradoxical that along with conveying his contempt for the brahmins' excessive adherence to rituals and ceremonies, Anantha Murthy also suggests that it is impossible to escape the hold of religion. As Chandri recollects, even Naranappa had been unable to shed his brahminism completely. On his death bed Naranappa shows the tenacious hold the orthodox beliefs of brahminism have on him. This only dampens a lifetime of deliberately postured defiance. The vehemence of his repudiation of brahminism suggests an unconscious attachment to it, as well as a sense of guilt at abjuring it. A conflict must have always been in his mind between the orthodox ways of brahminism and the unorthodox life he led. Brought up in the rituals and beliefs of brahminism, Naranappa (as well as the Acharya), like Moorthy in Raja Rao's *Kanthapura*, is unable to rid himself of the brahminic creed. What Meenakshi Mukherjee says of Moorthy can be applied to Naranappa as well:

> Brahmanism in India, and especially in the south, is perhaps more than a caste distinction: It is a special mode of apprehending reality, an experience that pervades all aspects of man's life, growing beyond his conscious mind. The episode in Raja Rao's *Kanthapura* where the Gandhian protagonist Moorthy, who has repudiated caste, still trembles as he enters a pariah house and cannot drink water there, points to the unconscious and instinctive conditioning of a brahman which makes his caste indistinguishable from his self. (Mukherjee, *Realism and Reality* 179)

This conflict between the orthodox beliefs and the desire to break away from them was felt by Anantha Murthy himself:

> The most intense experiences of my boyhood, which later became a preoccupation of my writing, were my attempts at demythifying reality.... I had to prove to myself that the sacred shrines under the trees, idols of Gods in the temples, the all powerful saffron clad Swamis and such other sacramental object of worship that surrounded me were not really potent. (Murthy, *Literary Criterion* 59)

Apart from the conflict between the brahminic and the unorthodox ways of life, the superstitious fear regarding a dead body remaining unattended, without proper funeral rites, turning into an evil spirit is also found in the novel. A contrast to the brahmins' concern for rituals is offered by the outcast hutments where the people are not obsessed with ritualistic practices. As the low castes die due to plague, they set fire to the huts with the bodies inside them. To them what matters is the immediate disposal of the body. These outcastes do not indulge in long philosophical debates like the brahmins. Questions which rock a whole *agrahara* do not bother them. The brahmins as well as the lowcaste people fear Naranappa's ghost roaming about demanding a proper burial. The widespread belief that a body left uncremated without proper funeral rites turns into an evil tormenting spirit is deeply ingrained in their psyche. The presence of vultures, plague, and every disaster is considered a result of Naranappa's untimely death and the brahmins' dereliction of duty in not performing his final rites. Through Manjayya of Parijatapura Anantha Murthy discloses the foolishness of the orthodox brahmins who, obsessed with the rites and customs, bring about their own doom by not properly disposing of a body infected with plague—"Being inert all this while, bound to some blind belief and not doing the dead man's last rites—was like drawing a slab of stone over one's own head" (104). The apprehension, that Naranappa would become a brahmin demon, is repeatedly expressed by Chandri too. While the brahmins fear the disrepute if a low caste conducts the last rites, the body is unceremoniously carried in a cart and burned in a field by Chandri and Naranappa's Muslim friend. This is in contrast to the funeral rites given to the other brahmins in the novel who, unlike Naranappa, have been "insiders". With a deft handling of words, Anantha Murthy conveys that the last rites of the dead brahmins have been conducted in a brahminic way. Various instances like "[Naranappa] didn't even come to the funeral rites" (7) on his wife's death, Praneshacharya's wife is "ritually cremated" (85), and the "wet dhotis [referring to the bath subsequent to the funeral rites]" (85) after Dasacharya is cremated, indicate this. It is only towards the end that the actual preparations for the funeral rites take place. Still quarrelling, the brahmins decide to conduct the dead man's last rites unaware that the body has already been disposed of. Firewood is brought to the cremation ground, a fire is kindled in a clay pitcher outside Naranappa's house. The pitcher is carried by the chief mourner who leads the funeral procession. A stretcher made of bamboo is prepared for the dead body. Ironically the physical problem of the body's disposal ceases to be relevant. The brahmins, engrossed in their philosophic discussions do not enquire about it, thus exposing the meaninglessness of their acts. The concern with rituals and ceremonies highlights their ignorance. As in life, in death too Naranappa upholds the unorthodox ways to which he clung in his life. Being a rebel, cast out by his own community, he is neither expiated of his sins nor are the final purificatory ceremonies performed. Appachu in *The Scent of Pepper* too has to face a similar predicament on his death. Through his death, Naranappa exposes the brahmins whose heads are filled with chants they do not understand, and their desire to maintain Brahmin supremacy. The situation makes Praneshacharya realize the disintegration that has set into the agrahara. He is filled with disgust for the brahmins who are not interested in the rites or the Books, but mechanically perform the rituals and recite the verses. The novel is an attack on the excessive adherence to meaningless rules and rituals. Fire symbolism recurs in the second part of the novel. In Indian thought fire has been given the attributes of both life and death. In *Samskara*, fire signifies death, destruction, and through it, the purification and regeneration of an *agrahara*. Fire represents the intense sexual desire in Praneshacharya and also keeps reminding him of Naranappa's body awaiting disposal. To the brahmins, consigning the libertine's body to the flames is not only a means of disposing of a decomposed body, but also the removal of the selves they hate to see revealed through Naranappa's actions. The "flapping flaming fire" (70) to which Naranappa's body is consigned represents his rebellious life. To expose the brahmins of Durvasapura, the novelist also employs Hindu mythological allusions. Along with references to classical myths and characters like Trishanku, Vamana, and Menaka, the metaphysical thoughts and philosophical speculations here also serve to heighten the hypocritic and outmoded life of the brahmins living in the *agrahara*.

Like Anantha Murthy, R.K. Narayan too exposes the hypocrisy of the brahmin community to which he belongs. He portrays in his works a world regulated by rituals where much of the behaviour is ceremonial. A microcosmic India, caught in conventions, traditions and social changes is found in his works. A realistic picture of Indian life is charged with gentle irony and light humour in them. Like all R.K. Narayan's novels, *Waiting for the Mahatma* depicts an orthodox society with its taboos and restrictions. The orthodoxy here is represented by Sriram's Granny. A product of the Hindu high caste family, R.K. Narayan and his characters share the beliefs and practices of his society. In his Malgudi, even a child like Swaminathan (*Swami and Friends*) imitates the perverted ways and manners of the adults. The sense of sacredness which runs through the Indian mind is revealed through this orthodox school boy's act of throwing a little mud on the ant which is drowned—"He [Swaminathan] took a pinch of earth, uttered a prayer for the soul of the ant, and dropped it into the gutter" (*Swami and Friends* 33). R.K. Narayan's novels present a world which is deeply traditional and caste ridden. It is inevitable that in such a society, death is accompanied by a number of rituals. In *Waiting for the Mahatma* Sriram's grandmother's "death" is followed by a number of rituals. The episode marks the end of his political life as a Gandhian and a revolutionary. Through the description of the rituals, the comic element is introduced into an otherwise drab political novel. The news of his grandmother's death brings Sriram back to his familiar household. Besides expressing Sriram's love for his grandmother the words, "I can't believe she is dead" (173) appear ironic as Granny returns to life later in the novel. As against the wailing and shrieking, one finds in *Lament on the Death of a Master of Arts*, and *Such a Long Journey*, is the "mournful silence" (173) in *Waiting for the Mahatma*. The absence of relatives does not deter Sriram. He feels only hatred towards his money minded kin who did not have any genuine grief. Kanni, his friend, and the other neighbours come to Sriram's help and make all the necessary preparations for the funeral rites. According to custom, her body is wrapped in white. In the absence of her relatives, women from the neighbouring houses keep vigil. The body is laid on a bier made of bamboo. It is carried by four professional carriers, and is accompanied by a few other mourners. The chief mourner (Sriram) is asked to bathe in the river and come back with wet clothes on. R.K. Narayan, through his description of Sriram's grandmother's funeral rites, gives one a glimpse of the materialistic society where men haggle even at the funeral ground. Money minded people like Kanni try to make the most of the situation. When Sriram asks Kanni to meet the expenses of his grandmother's funeral, Kanni's reply reveals this—"Yes, I know. I can always get my debts. I have kept your account in full detail. You should have no misgiving even about an anna, I have even put into the account what I have been paying the doctor from time to time" (177). The haggling which goes on with the fuel supplier reminds one of the ironic words of the firewood supplier in Raja Rao's *On the Ganga Ghat*:

> "The less it [firewood] burns," says he, "the more they'll buy." But the brahmins are keen masters in this choice of good firewood. Their tasks have to be finished quicker. Otherwise they would lose their next client. So between the firewood sellers there was, as it were, an ancient pact.... That made firewood costlier for the dead. But then who will not pay dearer prices for the dead? (27-28)

The situation reveals the hypocrisy of the priest who conducts the last rites. He tries to extract more silver coins apart from the agreement on a lumpsum for performing the rites. The priest even explains the significance of the rituals. He says, "It is said to smooth out the passage of the soul into further regions. I am only repeating what the shastras say.... I am merely a mouthpiece" (179). Through the dialogue between the priest and the mourners, R.K. Narayan gives the situation a comic turn. The conversation is charged with irony. Realistic questions, like "what happens to the coins [the two extra silver coins which the priest demands]?" (179), are avoided by the priest. Kanni's humorous reply that it goes the way of other coins, "that is into a priest's money-box" (179), further exposes the priest, who becomes angry and gives the situation a philosophical twist. He retorts, "Do you expect the soul to carry the silver with it?" (179). These hypocrites exploit the ignorant and superstitious masses. They thus assert their authority and maintain supremacy in society. Rational explanations are shunned by the priest, for they expose his greed. Here the novelist shows how none contradict such a priest even when aware of his deception and greed. He portrays a group of people who, steeped in superstitions, lack the courage to question. This is but natural in an orthodox set-up like Malgudi. Reared by religious rituals and beliefs of an age old tradition R.K. Narayan describes similar situations with ease. His comic vision is ironical. But his irony is free from the satiric spirit of condemnation and censure. The vehement opposition to injustice and hypocrisy found in Mulk Raj Anand is absent here. R.K. Narayan conveys his hatred for the meaningless beliefs and rituals in society through his works in his own detached manner. His works show "an intricate alliance of the serious and the comic" (Kantak 180). As a social realist, the novelist has a keen eye for the various customs and traditions which shape the life of man in society. R.K. Narayan's humour can be comic even at moments of high tragedy, as seen in *Waiting for the Mahatma*. Being a wanted revolutionary, Sriram attends the funeral in disguise. The initial preparations for the funeral rites are carried out by his neighbours, while Sriram (who is unable to take part in it) waits for the funeral procession at the cremation ground. The hero is indifferent to the customs and rituals he has to carry out. There are a number of instances in which the rituals have not been properly carried out—Sriram is unperturbed about the food taboo usually imposed on a Hindu mourner (the novel does not mention such a taboo), neither Sriram nor his relatives take part in the funeral procession, it is Kanni who carries the pot of fire which the chief mourner has to carry, and Sriram refuses to shave his moustache and the top of his head. It is only at the cremation ground that Sriram takes on as the chief mourner (Kanni hands over the pot of fire to Sriram). These violations lose their seriousness in the light of his grandmother's return to life. They seem to prefigure the later action in the novel. As Granny returns to life, the absence of Sriram and her relatives to mourn and carry her body relegate to the background. Sriram refuses to go to the barber because of his fear of being caught by the police than from imbibing modern trends. Through the priest the novelist portrays a Malgudi in the throes of change. The priest, due to his greed and fear of losing a customer, exempts Sriram from the ritual. He quotes the shastras to establish that it depends on the person to follow or modify a ritual. Modern life "makes it difficult to follow all the rules, and people have to adjust themselves" (180). The priest acts as a foil to Sriram's Granny who is presented as a woman bound to tradition. She accepts the dictates of the tradition-bound society in which she lives. The last rites for her are performed. But, confusion fills the place as Granny shows signs of life. The situation reveals Sriram's love for his grandmother, for without heeding anyone he pours water over the pyre and takes her out. Sriram's actions throw light on his character and show him as a person not obsessed with rituals and ceremonies. His passivity at certain moments—first becomes a follower of Gandhi under the influence of Bharati, then a revolutionary because of Jagadish, and finally, though he prevents his Granny from being burned alive, he does not react to the decision of her not being allowed into the village—makes one realize that he too, like the other inhabitants of Malgudi, is not free from the clutches of tradition and customary practices. His refusal to shave his moustache and to let his Granny burn to death are two of the rare moments in his life when he asserts himself. He even defies the priest and saves his grandmother. A realistic, but humorously ironic portrayal of the Indian reality is found here. The orthodox social set-up of Malgudi refuses to take Granny back into its fold, for if by any chance the supposed corpse should revive after reaching the pyre, dire consequence would result to the village. Hence the person is not allowed to enter the village and is expelled altogether. In a humorous way the novel denies the possibility of Granny being a dead spirit—"Her personality seemed to have returned from the other world unscathed by the contacts there" (186). As feared by Sriram, the whole commotion leads to his being caught by the police. The phase of his life as a revolutionary too comes to an end. The novelist points out how conventional society forces its beliefs on the orthodox people who comprise it and meekly submit to its dictates. Sriram's grandmother being an orthodox woman comprehends the situation, and respecting the views of the people around her decides to spend her last days in Benares. As in any orthodox society, the people of Malgudi including Sriram passively accept the priest's decision to keep Granny out of town. This submissive attitude is an outcome of the traditional atmosphere in which they are brought up. Apart from a few attempts at rebellion, and being modernized, R.K. Narayan's society is by and large orthodox. His novels are "intensely Hindu" (Naipaul, *The Wounded Civilization* 22), and his humour and irony are "part of a Hindu response to the world" (Naipaul 21). He concentrates on the transformation of his central character be it Raju, Krishna, or Sriram. *The English Teacher* depicts the life of Krishna, an English teacher whose life changes with the death of his orthodox wife Susila due to typhoid, and his loneliness thereafter. The novelist takes him farther from the western intellectual frame of mind in which he is embedded at the opening of the novel, and further towards native Indian spiritual practices (after his wife's death). The autobiographical element in the novel cannot be missed. The atmosphere of happiness at the beginning is broken by her death and its accompanying rituals. Various customs associated with death, like the Hindu practice of laying the dead on the floor, and making of the bier fill the gloomy atmosphere of death created here. Priests, bearers, and wailing relatives and friends fill the scene:

> Neighbours, relations and friends arrive, tears and lamentations, more tears and lamentations, and more and more of it [suggesting monotony and weariness]. The priest roams over the house, asking for one thing or other for performing the rites.... The corpse-bearers, grim and sub-human, have arrived with their equipment —bamboo and coir ropes. Near the front step they raise a small fire with cinders and faggots—this is the fire which is to follow us [the mourners] to the cremation ground. (95)

An elaborate picture (unlike in *Waiting for the Mahatma*) of the funeral rites is provided. In both these novels, the body in spite of being disposed of with proper funeral rites returns to the living world, one alive (Sriram's Granny in *Waiting for the Mahatma*) and the other as a dead spirit (Susila in *The English Teacher*). A vivid account of the rites is found in *The English Teacher*—the body is laid on the bamboo stretcher to be borne upon men's shoulders, saffron is touched on her face, vermilion on the forehead, and a string of jasmine on her head (all indicating her married state, but Granny being a widow is denied all this in *Waiting for the Mahatma*), rice is placed on her lips and Krishna her husband is given a pot containing the fire to cremate her. The jasmine (a symbol of purity) symbolism runs throughout the novel. The imagery subtly woven into the lives of Krishna and Susila is important in their relationship which progresses from the romantic to the "spiritual". It symbolizes the purity of their love which continues even after Susila's death. While describing Susila's last rites R.K. Narayan also refers to the commercialization which has crept into the life in Malgudi. Here too people haggle over the price and quality of fuel. As a routine, a man comes and writes down the name, age, and disease on a notebook, "collects a fee, issues a receipt, and goes away" (96). The novelist points out how one finds it difficult to evade the "trappings of trade" (96) even in death. He lays bare the routine, unsentimental life in modern society. It is only after purifying himself (by taking a plunge in the river) that Krishna performs the rites. He also "mutter[s] a lot of things" (96) the priest asks him to repeat revealing his ignorance of their meaning, and his disturbed state of mind. The body is laid on the pyre and lit. The fire in the funeral ground fills in him the desire to die, thus expressing his lovelorn state and pain. Susila who enters the house with various ceremonies leaves it with her death rites. Rituals mark every aspect of human life in a tradition-bound society like Malgudi. The death rites also serve as initiation rites for Susila into the world of the dead. The idyllic, paradisical relationship between Krishna and Susila ends with the funeral rites carried out for her. Susila takes on the role of a dead spirit, giving the last part of the novel a mystical turn. For Krishna, the death brings in a new role to play. He is forced to take on the role of a mother to his daughter. He gradually dons his wife's role. This reversal of roles is described:

> In three or four months [he] could give her a bath with expert hands, braid her hair passably, and wash and

> look after her clothes, and keep correct count of her jackets and skirts. [He] slipped into [his] double role with great expertness. It kept [him] very much alive to play both father and mother to her at the same time. [His] one aim in life now was to see that she did not feel the absence of her mother. To this end [he] concentrated his whole being. (97)

Even after the cremation, Susila's dead spirit continues to exist. Though her body is consigned to the flames with proper funeral rites, Krishna starts "receiving messages" from her through a medium. This is ironic for the rites are believed to ensure the smooth passage of the dead spirit from the world of the living to that of the dead. Krishna gradually reconciles himself to the idea of her bodyless presence around him. The *deus ex machina* saves him from feeling the absence of his wife too intensely. The grim and comprehensive account of the funeral rites marks the transformation in the Krishna-Susila relationship. There is a clear break between the domestic life, where their love deepens and intensifies in the midst of household chores, and the final "spiritual" section where he directly communicates with her spirit. With the funeral rites the novel takes on an 'other' worldly nature. The death leaves Krishna shattered. With the disposal of her dead body there is a change in the husband-wife relationship, for they meet again on a mystical plane. Krishna's mind keeps buzzing with her thoughts and memories. As Freud states, "[t]he loss of a love-object is an excellent opportunity for the ambivalence in love relationships to make itself effective and come into open" (Gay 587). One wonders about the veracity of Krishna's mystical communions with his wife. The descriptions of his state—"blind, dumb, and dazed" (95), he feels like "an imbecile, incapable of doing anything or answering any questions" (96)—raises the question whether these "psychic" portions are hallucinations of a troubled mind. Krishna himself wonders whether his attempts at communicating with his wife were all "self deceptions" (164). The latter half of the novel tries to bridge the gulf between life and afterlife. The Hindu belief in a life after death is conveyed. It is difficult to label the latter half of the novel as "spiritual". Krishna's mind, filled with Susila's thoughts and memories, feels an echo of her voice or speech, or sometimes her moaning and delirious talk in the sick-bed. Psychologists have pointed out that delusions and neurosis often pass for religious feelings without one's knowing it. They hold that utterances of persons in deep meditation cannot be regarded as divine revelations or occult messages. The communication of Krishna with the soul of Susila though hard to believe, is based on R.K. Narayan's own experiences after his wife's death:

> The 'English teacher' of the novel, Krishna, is a fictional character in the fictional city of Malgudi; but he goes through the same experience I [R.K. Narayan] had gone through, and he calls his wife Susila, and the child is Leela instead of Hema. The toll that typhoid took and all the desolation that followed, with a child to look after, and psychic adjustments, are based on my own [R.K. Narayan's] experience. (*My Days* 135)

Critics have pointed out that Krishna "turns to occult" (Narasimhaiah, *The Swan and the Eagle* 146) and that R.K. Narayan uses it as a substitute for the profoundly spiritual. Krishna behaves like one obsessed with the phantasy of his dead wife. It is difficult to agree that the first and the second halves blend naturally (though there are connecting links like the jasmine imagery). The novel clearly depicts the transformation Krishna undergoes as a result of these experiences in life. The pattern of order, dislocation of order, and reintegration is traceable—the domestic harmony in the first part of the novel, its dislocation with Susila's death, and the final reconciliation which is achieved with Krishna and Susila meeting on a "spiritual" plane. R.K. Narayan is at his best when he deals with the superstitions in Indian society. Susila's mother's belief in the "Evil Eye" (83), and the "malignant spirit" (83), the headmaster's belief in the astrologer's "month-to-month report" (162) giving him the exact date of his death, or Krishna's belief in the "ghost" (165) and in other worldly affairs show that the novelist is closely acquainted with the manners of the south Indian community.

His characters are rooted in their orthodox set-up, and the old and the new are interwoven into the life of Malgudi. A minute observer of the traditional society, R.K. Narayan neither condemns nor reacts violently against the superstitions, and prejudices found in society. While depicting the Hindu rites and rituals, he mixes satire with his gentle humour to present the ridiculous foibles and eccentricities of human nature. In an alien language R.K. Narayan communicates with complete ease an Indian sensibility.

The life of the inhabitants of Kodagu (Coorg, who assimilated a form of the Hindu religion) portrayed in Kavery Nambisan's *The Scent of Pepper* is loaded with religious observances and superstitions. They form an integral part of Kodava life and their description in the novel is apt and significant. The second chapter provides a detailed account of the death rites of the Rao Bahadur who falls prey to acute mental depression, a disease endemic to the area. The Rao Bahadur is given a funeral befitting his status in life and the financial position of his family:

> The dead man wasn't just anyone, he had married a diwan's daughter and he had received the title of Rao Bahadur from the British for his loyalty. Such solidity of background. He deserved a splendid funeral, and the family could afford to give him one. (13)

Kavery Nambisan provides a lengthy description of the last rites given to him. Besides familiarizing the reader with the rituals and practices of the Kaleyandas, the novel also makes one realize how these rituals are inherent to the life of Kodagu. As in Hindu funeral rites, the sons take the lead in the last rites of the Rao Bahadur. His body is laid on a stone slab near the well and purified with water. Neighbours, relatives and others join to offer help to the family. The purificatory rites prepare the dead man for the after life. In the Rao Bahadur's case it also removed the "dirt-encrusted clothes and washed away the slime and accretions of eleven years of decay [which had set in due to his illness]" (13). The novelist gives a clear picture of the initial preparations for the last rites:

> They dressed him like a bridegroom in kupya-chale, with the peeche-kathi at his waist, covered his wispy hair with the gold-lined turban and put a mirror in his hand. They stuck a gold sovereign on his forehead and sat him up on a divan in the centre of the front room because the Kaleyanda men never take anything lying down. (13)

In spite of having committed suicide (swallowing his diamond ring) the Rao Bahadur is given a proper funeral rite. This is but natural as many Kodavas became victims of "the contagion of mental depression" (10) and the Rao Bahadur had ended his life in a way fit for nobility. An entirely different practice is found among the African Igbo tribe rendered in Chinua Achebe's work. They detest suicide. The last rites are not carried out for such a clansman as his body is considered evil. Only strangers touch it. Unlike the Igbo tribe in Achebe's *Things Fall Apart*, the Kodavas give the Rao Bahadur's body a proper funeral rite. Suicide to the Kodavas is just the termination of a life which has succumbed to a contagion prevalent among them. Mourners arrive in large numbers. White is their colour of mourning. The mourning attire is a disguise, being generally the reverse of the ordinary wear. The Kodavas refrain from work during mourning. As a part of the last rites the mourners touch the dead man's feet and drop a rupee coin in the brass plate at the foot of the divan. The atmosphere is filled with incense sticks and garlands. Food is served (indicating that there is no food taboo, except on items like milk, meat, and spices which Chambavva, like any other Kodava widow, refrains from) to the mourners by Nanji, the Rao Bahadur's daughter-in-law whose "tears were for the splendid diamond ring that the Rao Bahadur had used as his instrument of suicide" (14). It meant the loss of a family heirloom which her husband would have inherited. The mourners fill every inch of space in the house and bear the discomfort, expressing their love and respect for the dead man. The Rao Bahadur's death creates confusion among the Kodavas who are now deprived of a leader. There is no one to direct the course of the rituals. Young men dressed in black appear with their guns ready for the funeral honours. The Rao

Bahadur's body is carried on a bamboo chair, to the area reserved for the family funerals, by his sons and cousins. As the Kodavas cremate their dead, firewood is kept ready for the funeral. There is no haggling over the prices as in Raja Rao or R.K. Narayan's works. The Kodava women too attend the funeral rites. The body is carried three times around the pyre. Chambavva follows it with a cracked mud pot on her head, water trickling from it. The ritual of the cracked pot symbolizes the termination of her married life. A description of the Kodava life will be incomplete without a reference to their customs and practices. It is the son who lights the pyre among the Kodavas. Baliyanna, the eldest son, lights the Rao Bahadur's pyre. Baliyanna accepts his brother, Appachu (who had converted to Christianity and accepted English ways) because his mother denies him the right to conduct her funeral rites otherwise. It is significant that Baliyanna, who succumbs to depression, commits suicide only after giving his mother's body the last rites. The taboos are followed until the 'eleventh-day' ceremony. According to custom, Chambavva could not comb her hair or sleep on her bed. She also abstains from milk, meat, and spices, and eats only once a day after offering food first to the spirit of her dead husband and then to the crows. The crows are considered the souls of the departed, by the Hindus, and are summoned while offering the *sradh*. Similar to this is the custom performed by Chambavva in the novel:

> With Nanji, she walked to the backyard with the food wrapped in banana leaves, laid it near the well and clapping her hand, called: 'Ka! Ka! Ka!' The crows were only too happy to feast on the food; death meant little to these realists who believed only in survival. But to the grieving family, the fact that the crows enjoyed the food meant that the dead person too was satisfied. Chambavva did it for eleven days until the soul of her husband joined his ancestors and had no further need for worldly victuals. (16)

The situation is described in a humorous manner. Among most social groups the funeral feast is obligatory. It must be observed even if it consumes every item of property the man possessed, and leaves the wife and children to starve. Besides the workers, Yeravas, and multitude of wanderers, beggars, and derelicts, the Rao Bahadur's family feed a hundred guests at the 'eleventh-day' ceremony. Marking the end of the period of mourning, the family also follows the Kodava custom of a pilgrimage to scatter the Rao Bahadur's ashes in the river. With their return from this pilgrimage the family puts an end to the personal period of abstinence by eating breakfast. They then break the various taboos imposed on them and return to their normal life. A number of changes occur in the Kaleyanda household after the Rao Bahadur's death. Nanji's new role (the one Chambavva had occupied earlier) is indicated by the name Baliyakka she assumes. Descriptions of death rites recur in the novel though not with the elaborateness as at the beginning. This avoids repetition and boredom. Terse references are made to these rites when deaths occur later on. When Nanji's sons die, Kavery Nambisan refers only to the "never-ending rituals of mourning" (135) which leave her no time to brood. A short account of Baliyanna's last rite is also provided. Nanji wipes off her *kumkum* and announces the death of her husband. Mourners dressed in white fill the place. The descriptions throw light on Nanji's character. She is portrayed as a woman of strength tiding over the grief and hardships in her life. The picture she presents is in sharp contrast to that offered by Chambavva. The various rites described also indicate the passing of time, the old generation making way for the new one. While Baliyanna conducts the Rao Bahadur's last rites, it is Subbu who accepts words of sympathy from the mourners and carries out Baliyanna's funeral rites. As a part of the funeral rites Subbu shaves his head, bathes and prays for his father's soul after scattering the ashes. For Clara, Baliyanna's English friend, the death marks the end of a phase in her life—the end of a relationship she had cherished amidst loneliness and antagonism from her own people in an alien land. She returns to England, her homeland, soon after it. Entirely different is the funeral rite given to the Rao Bahadur's brother Appachu, for he (like Naranappa in *Samskara*) is an "outsider". He marries Marjorie, a Christian, and converts to his wife's religion. His funeral is in contrast to the ones described in the novel. There are no mourners and descriptions like "doves of peace" (14), "stacked white linen" (15), and "the sea of white" (184) to describe them are avoided to indicate this:

> It [Appachu's funeral] was a mourning to mourn about. Never in the history of the Kodavas had a death not been grieved for by neighbours. Mourners always came to stay with the family until cremation. Till the eleventh-day ceremony, there was never any need to cook, because the neighbours brought food. Relatives...would come to share the burden of grief. (244)

The villagers avoid the family as an expression of faith in a tradition which Appachu had once left behind. Appachu presents the picture of a man who gets uprooted from his native cultural traditions and values. His position as an outcast and an unaccommodated alien is clearly portrayed. The villagers feel it unwise to burn the body of an outcast in the family funeral ground and prefer it to be given a Christian burial. Nanji decides to carry out the rites indicating her divergent views. For her the funeral is neither a social occasion nor a ritual but the "culmination, the final full stop to a life" (244). A few villagers give a rupee coin from the gate for the funeral expenses but do not enter the house or take part in the rites, thus expressing their protest. Instead of flowers and garlands are the fumes of putrefaction which begin to permeate the sandalwood and incense aroma. The body is carried in a bamboo chair, to be cremated before sunset. Patrick (Appachu's son) lights the pyre and Appachu is cremated like his other family members in the family cremation ground. The ashes are gathered and scattered according to the Kodava custom. With his cremation in the family *smashana* Appachu is taken back into the family's fold despite protests from the people around. Appachu, in spite of his brief departure from the Kodava culture, is unable to separate himself from his native culture.

The Kodavas worship their ancestors, who they believe hover over Kodagu, and guard them, is evident in the novel. Elaborate funeral rites are conducted to enable a good afterlife.

Baliyanna conveys this belief while planning his own death—"He wrote his will, shared the property between his sons and wife, [and] cleared away any obstacle that might harass them after his death..." (179). The various instances convey the Kodava faith in a life after death. They have complete faith in the ancestors, and pray for the goodwill of these dead spirits who according to them reside in the clouds and bless their land with plentiful rains:

> When the ancestors were happy with their progeny, the rain fell vertically and nourished the land; if the spirits were displeased, the rain slanted at an angle when it fell and a lot of water was wasted; if the ancestors were truly incensed—as when a Kodava married an outsider—the rain fell transverse, beating horizontal tracks of such fury that it cut through persons who dared go out, it slashed its way past fields, it broke doors and windowpanes, lifted entire roof tops and fell in shuddering waterfalls from the slopes of the hills. (177)

The absence of rain after Appachu's funeral hence makes the villagers consider it a curse of the ancestors due to the disregard of a custom by the Kaleyanda family. The coming of rains is taken as a sign that the ancestors had forgiven the Barrister and his people. As the community accepts new found ways rains fail, implying that the "ancestors had given up on the super-mart, English-speaking, sophisticated" (252) Kodava race. Like *Things Fall Apart*, Kavery Nambisan's *The Scent of Pepper* presents the picture of a society in the throes of change; changes which wipe out much of their culture. Her characters consist of those who accept change as well as those who prefer to cling on to the old. A third type returns after wandering in a world outside their own. Through Appachu and Subbu the possibility of the errant Kodavas returning to their culture is conveyed. The novel familiarizes one with the Kodava life which is filled with rituals, beliefs, and practices. A number of Indian words like *payasam*, *smashana*, *tulsi*, *thirtha*, and *agarbathis* and those associated with the Coorg life help to create the local colour.

Like in Chinua Achebe, Kavery Nambisan refers to the changes which the British advent in Kodagu brings with it. One of the important results of this inwave in Kodagu is the building of a local cemetery (for their convenience) to bury their dead. The local cemetery marks the establishment of the British rule (and of Christianity) in Kodagu. Hinting at the East-West dichotomy, the novelist makes the cemetery an important part of the world the Britishers create for themselves in an alien land. This difference between the two cultures is hinted at throughout. The making of a cemetery is an expression of the different values cherished by the two groups. Subbu's actions reveal the meaninglessness of the British practices for the Kodavas. This is also brought out in Kamala Markandaya's *Nowhere Man* and *Coffer Dams* through a reference to the funeral rites. In *The Nowhere Man* the British characters are unable to comprehend the Indian custom of cremating the dead. For the British (with their love for the finer aspects of life) who are unaccustomed to such sentiments, Srinivas' act of scattering his wife's ashes in the Thames is just "household rubbish" (41) which will pollute the river. For Srinivas "the fine array of floating debris" (41) is his wife. The sauntering policeman (a Britisher) feels awkward at Srinivas' display of emotions and walks off. Through the incident Kamala Markandaya hints at the disparity between the oriental and occidental attitudes, values, and customs. *The Coffer Dams* also presents the clear rift between the Indian and the British values of life. Just as the Kodavas join to conduct the funeral rites of their dead, the British families in Coorg are represented at the funeral of Rupert Fox who looks after the coffee estate in the area. He is buried in the cemetery. The rites bring the Britishers together in an alien land. In contrast to the Kodava mourners, the Britishers are dressed in black to mourn the dead. The mourning attire too indicates the difference between the two cultures. The colour symbolism employed highlights the difference between the natives and the 'aliens'. Clara's (Rupert's wife) mind is filled with the ridiculousness of the symbol—she is dressed in black, mourning the death of a husband she had never loved. The funeral indicates her estrangement from her fellow countrymen because of her intimacy with the natives (reminding one of Clinton's wife, Helen, in *The Coffer Dams*), especially Baliyanna, whom the Britishers consider inferior. The descriptions reveal Clara's utter unconcern for it. To her the wooden crosses appear "the sad testimony of her people" (92) and the inevitability of the influence of religion even at death. These "faked symbolisms" (92) become a means by which the Britishers assert their unity in an alien land. The "collective sympathy" (184) and "the strength of communal grief" (184) among the Kodavas marvel Clara who goes to attend Baliyanna's funeral. Clara dressed in black (representing the western culture) looks incongruous like "a gawky crow" (184) among the Kodava mourners. The wide gulf between the two cultures is repeatedly hinted at. Like the other British characters portrayed (except Clara) Patrick, Appachu's son, too has only contempt for the natives. He and his sister Emerald are unable to understand the Kodava customs and prefer a Christian burial for his father. They reveal a total alienation from their father's culture. As a son he gives his father *thirtha* to absolve him of his sins. He finds the Kodava rituals irritating and feels only hostility towards his father. Patrick reveals a disregard for the sentiments of the dead and hates to have to be around for his father's funeral. The contempt of the British for the native beliefs and customs is vividly presented in *The Coffer Dams*. The story revolves around a dam under construction over a turbulent hilly river. The superstitious natives of the area propitiate it with ceremonies and sacrifices. They do not blame God in times of drought or floods, and accept it as their fate. Like the Britishers in *The Scent of Pepper*, here too they build a cemetery, "which they had faithfully copied from the home model so that the dead could lie easily...if the dead were British of course" (107). The reference to Indian customs by the Britishers reveals their attitude towards it. The Indians, according to them, prefer "not to lie and moulder" (107), and carry out their last rites punctiliously. The ashes are sent "bowling merrily along on the river" (108). While the British give proper burials to their dead, they show utter unconcern for the dead Indians. They do not even send letters of condolences for them. This attitude is revealed through the accidental deaths which occur at the work site. Burial services for the two dead Britishers, Bailey and Wilkins, (who die during the first accident) are conducted by their fellowmen, revealing the British preference for their countrymen. The bodies are retrieved and brought in coffins by the pallbearers. The corpses are washed and laid. The Bible is read and the coffins are lowered. Clods of earth are put on the coffins and the British make for their two countrymen simple graves to rest in. They are given proper last rites. The Union Jacks stencilled on the coffin lids reveal the English sentimentality about dying in a foreign land. Like Vasantha (*The Nowhere Man*) the British too hate dying in an alien land. The second accident in which a few Indian workers are killed creates an entirely different situation. The situation exposes the social tensions prevalent. The novelist highlights one of her favourite themes through its portrayal. The natives, like the Britishers, need the bodies of their dead men to perform the rites for their souls to depart in peace. The workers, led by Krishnan, demand the retrieval of the bodies defying Clinton (their superior) who had decided to carry on the work without retrieving the bodies. They are adamant (having a precedent when the fatalities had been British and the bodies had been retrieved) and demand equal treatment for the dead Indians. While for Clinton the delay means an inability to complete the dam, for Krishnan it becomes a struggle between the 'oppressor' (Britishers) and the 'oppressed' (natives), and a chance to assert his power. It becomes a struggle between "them" and "us". For the workers it is a "matter of equality" (179), "the same done to us as to you. Whether in life or death" (179). The Britishers consider this merely as a question of the disposal of a few dead bodies. The incident brings the natives together for they have a "common aim" (180), and Krishnan emphasizing the need to be unified says, "[i]t is our turn to be strong. Power can shift. They must learn that it has, it is for us to teach them" (180). The dead bodies and the last rites become secondary and the focus shifts on to the power struggle between the Britishers and the natives. The difference between the two cultures is further emphasized by the sound of drums (similar to the tolling of church bells in the West) which indicate the native's ceremony of death, of mourning the loss.

This appears "uncivilised" (174) to the Englishmen. Indicating the difference in practices Mackendrick says, "It is a matter of country. Bells, cymbals, or drums,...one takes one's choice" (174). Like the "tom tom" in Eugene O'Neill's *Emperor Jones* the sound of the drums signify the impending trouble. Unlike the other British characters is Helen, who understands the Indians' belief. More than the death it is the desire to be treated equally which makes the natives insist on recovering the bodies. The incident reveals Clinton's different temperament not only from the natives but also from his wife. Though Clinton decides to incorporate the bodies into the structure he is finally forced to give in to the natives' demand. The bodies are recovered with Bashiam's (a native) help, and given the last rites. The incident is significant as it brings Bashiam, who had renounced his roots, back to his society and makes him help them in regaining their dead. He comes forward to help his men not only because he is one of them—"I must do it, since they are my people, whom I cannot shed, although I have tried" (182)—but also because of Helen, and Clinton "whose wife he had taken, to whom a debt was owed" (183). The Bashiam event furthers the plot towards a crucial phase in the narrative. It has two consequences, "(1) The crippling of Bashiam; and (2) the realisation on both sides that human values lend meaning to progress, regardless of differing cultural matrices" (Prasad, *Perspectives on Kamala Markandaya* 166). The situation highlights the conflict between the eastern sensibility and the western indifference. It exposes Clinton's jealousy, disregard for the natives, his inhuman nature as well as the tussle in him between the jealous husband and the builder who wants to save the dam. The East-West confrontation figures prominently in Kamala Markandaya's works. *The Coffer Dams* depicts the British officers who fail to respect the natives' sentiments regarding their dead but are particular about giving a decent Christian burial when their own men succumb to accidents. Though Kamala Markandaya denies considering herself as an expatriate writer, one finds in her works an understanding of both the oriental and occidental values of life. It signifies the presence of the two cultures, the dual experience, in the novelist's own mind. They reveal an awareness of the native culture, its rituals and practices which are often coloured by her status as an expatriate writer.

The Nowhere Man too refers to the funeral rites. Though the descriptions lack the elaborateness in works like *The Scent of Pepper*, it highlights one of her favourite themes—the East-West confrontation. It serves to expose an expatriate's predicament. The rites have been dealt with differently in *The Coffer Dams* and *The Nowhere Man*, but both bring home the point that the two cultures (the East and the West) have their own values, customs, and practices which are ingrained in its people. An expatriate even after facing an alien culture prefers to establish a coherent link with his own roots. Through Vasantha in *The Nowhere Man*, Kamala Markandaya presents the emigrant dangling between the memory of his homeland and the exigencies of his secondary, preferred country. Like her creator, Vasantha is an outsider in an "alien" land (London), and away from her native place. The novel presents the story of Srinivas and his family who have emigrated to London. Srinivas and Vasantha are depicted as Indian emigrants following Indian habits, dress, beliefs, and rituals in a foreign land. While Srinivas feels alienated from India, Vasantha, in spite of being uprooted from her country, lives rooted in Indian values and ways of life. Acquisition of a new culture is frequently associated with frustration and tension to come to terms with a foreign culture and the desire to retain the essential native heritage in the adopted environment. Vasantha is an Indian to the core and refuses to adopt the alien customs and practices. Clinging to her Indian identity and refusing to be anglicized she had brought with her the festivals and practices to an unfamiliar land and observed them. But Srinivas is unable to adjust like his wife. Unlike Vasantha he finds himself "[a]n alien, whose manners, accents, voice, syntax, bones, build, way of life—all of him—shrieked alien!" (241). Even in an alien land when death occurs (as when Srinivas' son dies) people gather, their faces pale with the strain and misery of fellow-feeling. The novelist deals with Vasantha's death (due to consumption) at the very beginning of the novel. Her desire to return to her homeland culminates with the death in London.

Outside the crematorium Srinivas is handed a casket with her ashes. The attendant asks him to scatter the ashes, for it would not "do any good brooding over them..." (40), expressing his stance. Srinivas carries out her last rites. Along with the ashes, he carries her sandalwood box containing the earth from India, and her hair oil bottle half full of Ganges water. Srinivas tips her ashes into the river Thames. He sprinkles the earth and the Ganges water on to the ashes which were being borne away on the Thames. The merging of the ashes in the Thames functions as an attempt at merging the East and the West. The act prefigures the relationship between the Indian Srinivas and the English Mrs. Pickering which develops later in the novel. He tips the ashes "leaning out as far as he could so that they should not be washed back" (40). This also indicates his later connections with the Englishmen. The racial prejudices he puts up with only lead to his death—hinting at the impossibility of merging the East and the West. Like Vasantha, Srinivas longs for his homeland. The rite makes him feel one with his wife. The earth and the Ganges water which Vasantha carries with her to England show her deep-seated attachment to India. The act not only suggests the transformation of the Thames into the holy Ganges but also Vasantha's indomitable will to zealously preserve her cultural moorings. The Ganges water is usually kept in small sealed copper pots. Vasantha stores it in a hair oil bottle exposing a hollow attempt to cling on to something which one has lost. Vasantha's life is entrenched in the Indian values and practices. The drops of Ganges water sprinkled on her ashes is an attempt to make a Ganges of the Thames. By adhering to the Indian way of life she had made a little India around her. The indigenous customs and values are so integral to Srinivas' psyche that he cremates even a dead rat placed at his door. He prepares a bier and a pyre of crumpled paper and twigs for it. The feelings of intolerance and racial prejudices lead to disharmony and destruction thus causing the death of the victim (Srinivas) and the victimizer (Fred). A repeated reference is made to the fire which becomes a literal fact at the end. Words from religious terminology, like consecrate, vestment, psalm, dirge, incantation, too abound in the novel. Through Vasantha, Kamala Markandaya conveys her own displaced predicament. For an expatriate Hindu writer, as for Vasantha, the native country's epics, deities, and rituals represent the ethos and the culture one has left far behind.

A similar status (that of an expatriate Indian writer) is held by Rohinton Mistry. An insider's account of the tradition-bound Parsi community is provided by Rohinton Mistry's *Such a Long Journey.* As Salman Rushdie points out in his *Imaginary Homelands*, exiles, emigrants, and expatriates "are haunted by some sense of loss, some urge to reclaim, to look back..." (10). This is true of writers like Kamala Markandaya and Rohinton Mistry. The nostalgia, the irresistible attempt to write a novel about one's native country reveals the desire for a lost home among emigrant writers who have been cut off from their ethnic roots. The novel deals with an authentic portrayal of the Parsis, and the customs and rituals related to their community. The novelist accustoms one to another way of life, and graphically describes the Parsi religious customs, prayers, and funeral rites. The cultural distinctiveness is asserted through the use of untranslated, specifically Parsi words. He creates a Parsi ambience with the description of Dinshawji's death rites. Ironically Gustad is reminded of Dinshawji's words—"'No need to take me to the Tower of Silence when I die. My domestic vulture [Alamai] will pick my bones clean ahead of time'" (239). Alamai's actions reveal her attitude towards her husband. Her actions, words, and loud demonstrations of grief make one doubt the genuineness of her grief. The situation throws light on Alamai's character. This character is a sharp contrast to Dina Dalal (*Fine Balance*) who behaves in a dignified manner on her husband's death—"No wailing, no beating the chest or tearing the hair like [one] might expect from a widow who had suffered such a shock, such a loss" (*Fine Balance* 46). Alamai, in between her grief, finds time to argue with the men who come to perform Dinshawji's *suchkaar* and ablutions, forbidding them to follow the traditional method of sponging the corpse with gomez. The deceased are usually given a final purificatory bath. This purificatory ceremony with the cow's urine (gomez) reminds one of its similar use (for purification) by the Brahmins. The *panchagavyam* which the brahmins use to remove both external and internal defilements too consists of cow's urine. Those who attend Dinshawji's funeral wash their face and other parts of the body that are exposed with water to purify themselves. Humour is introduced into an otherwise grim atmosphere when Alamai bursts out, "'All this nonsense with bull's urine is not for us.... We are modern people. Use water only, nothing else'" (246). The situation becomes more humorous when she insists that the water used for purification be warmed as Dinshawji (now dead) had a habit of catching chill if he bathed in cold water. Instead of revealing her love and concern for her husband, the actions only present her in a comic light, and expose her ignorance and hypocrisy. She had never shown similar concern when her husband was alive. Alamai appears in the novel only after her husband's death and her behaviour and words prove Dinshawji's description of her as true. The pallbearers appear in white, and place the body clad in white on a platform. At the funeral everything appears to be well organized. Gustad ironically suggests that everything proceeded "efficiently" (247) as though "Dinshawji died every day" (247). The various rites and prayers are carried out methodically by the priest. The dustoorji's prayers are beautifully described. They take Gustad under their spell. The description of the priest at his prayers adds to the atmosphere. Rohinton Mistry uses well chosen words to convey the effect the situation has on Gustad:

> The dustoorji was not praying loudly, yet, little by little, in ever-increasing circles, his voice touched every point of the prayer room. Now and again, he added a stick of sandalwood to the thurible, or sprinkled loban....
>
> The prayers filled the dark room slowly. Slowly, the prayer sound was the dark room. And before he [Gustad] was aware of it, Gustad was under its gentle spell. He forgot the time, forgot Alamai, forgot Nusli. (247)

Through Gustad the novelist conveys the plight of the ordinary man who mutters his prayers and performs the rituals without understanding their meaning. The priest's words make him feel at one with the nature around. Rohinton Mistry evokes a similar atmosphere through his description of the scene with words. Gustad comes under the soothing and gentle sway of the prayers and listens to them reverently, though he is unable to understand them. For him the funeral rites become a kind of cleansing process that pushes him closer to an intense spiritual experience. According to custom, a funeral notice is published, and a good number of people turn up at Doongerwadi. This is in sharp contrast to the funeral given to Jimmy Bilimoria, Gustad's friend. His funeral is shrouded in anonymity. Gustad is the solitary mourner who attends it. A large number of friends, who are shocked and surprised by his death, come for Dinshawji's funeral and through their presence express their love for him. The women draped their saris over the dress and men who forgot their prayer caps borrowed or used handkerchiefs. The situation revealed that though despised by his wife, Dinshawji was a man loved and respected by his friends into whose lives he had brought laughter and happiness. The novelist exposes the frailty of his characters with his gentle humour and eye for the comic in human nature. Alamai's hypocrisy is further highlighted when she tries to implement her plans for Nusli, her sister's son. She tactfully tries to get him a job, thus revealing herself as a practical woman devoid of love for her husband. Here the novel refers to the custom, among childless Parsis of adopting a child as the heir. Apart from this he also mentions the 'ceremony of the dog' in which a dog (the *char-chassam* dog) is led to the bier. It is believed to contain the evil of death (*nassoo*) and to assist the forces of good. The gloomy is punctuated with humour by the novelist. Though a tinge of satire or pathos presents itself felt here and there, mostly humour provides the comic relief. The ceremony discloses Alamai's ignorance and mistaken notions as she expects the dog to make some sound as a sign that Dinshawji's spirit is present. Rohinton Mistry avoids harsh satire and gives the situation a comic turn. He invigorates his work with an uncanny sense of humour in the comic mode. One does not fail to perceive the pervading loneliness and alienation that his characters sense. This in a way is reflective of the psyche and loneliness the author himself undergoes in a foreign land. The novel also contains references to Parsi prayers like Yatha Ahu Varyo, Ashem Vahoo and Ahunavad Gatha. Alamai, the family members, and relatives pay their obeisance to the dead man before the nassasalers, dressed in white, come to carry the bier to the Tower of Silence. The mourners follow the bier holding a *paiwand* (connection) between them in the form of a handkerchief:

> They [the mourners] stepped up in twos or threes, linked by white handkerchiefs, in keeping with the wisdom of the ancients—that there was strength in numbers, strength to repel the nassoo, the evil which hovered around death. (252)

The journey motif echoes in the reference to the mourner's movements—"Crunch, crunch, crunch. Grinding, grating, rasping. The millwheel of death. Grinding down the pieces of a life, to fit death's specifications" (253). The mention of death also fills Gustad's mind with similar memories:

> A sound to stir the past, to stir up sleeping memories, to whisk them all into the flux of the present, all the occasions when I [Gustad] marched thus, up the hill, upon the gravel walk, as though to crunch, to grind, to crush all loss, all sorrow, into dry flakes, pulverize it into nothingness, be rid of it for ever. (253-54)

After these ceremonies Dinshawji's face is covered and his bier is carried to the Well of Vultures. Women are not allowed to accompany the procession. For people like Mr. Madon, the Manager, with a silk handkerchief and expensive perfume, it becomes an occasion to show off their wealth. The body is placed on the platform and the face uncovered for one last time. Finally four pallbearers enter the Tower of Silence with the bier and close it. Though the mourners could see no more, they are well aware that the body would be placed on a *pavi* (the outermost of three concentric stone circles). Using hooked rods they would tear off his clothes and leave him "naked as the day he had entered the world" (254). Along with a detailed and authentic description of the Parsi funeral rites Rohinton Mistry also describes the vultures that descend while the mourners recite prayers for Dinshawji's ascending soul. He refers to the vultures "graceful in flight" (255) their bodies hunched, their "serpent-like necks" (255) and bald heads rising from their plumage. The Parsis revere the sun, moon, fire, water, earth, and all creations of God. In Zorastrian religion fire is considered sacrosanct. Fire is worshipped in all forms from the sun to the household fire, and no Zorastrian worship is complete without it. This is similar to the Hindu practice of worshipping Agni, the central deity in the Vedic sacrificial ritual. The Sanskrit word *agni*, meaning "fire", refers to both the sacrificial fire of the brahmins, and the Hindu God of Fire. Through the meditation of Agni, the gods receive sacrifices and oblations offered into the fire by the officiants. It occupies a very predominant and indispensable position in the Hindu religious tradition since ancient times. As Dinshawji is given the status of a dead spirit, the mourners wash themselves, do their *kustis* and rejoin the world of the living. The materialistic world is humorously referred to through the two women at the funeral place who wanted to shoo off the vultures to get a diamond ring they had forgotten to remove, for its "sentimental value" (316). Being a Parsi himself, Rohinton Mistry is aware of the rites and rituals of his religion. The novel is strewn with words from Parsi life, like *kusti*, *dustoorji*, *loban*, *gomez*, *bungalee*, *nassoo*, *char-chassam*, *sezdoe* etc. which help to create the atmosphere. These words relate to the Parsi life which a non-Parsi may find difficult to comprehend. Along with a description of the funeral rites he also points out the ecological problems created by the Parsi funeral rites. The green acres of Doongerwadi which consist of luxury buildings are made filthy by the vultures. The religious rites lose their significance, as the human flesh scattered by the vultures become "rubbish" (316) to the people around who complain about it. The whole description is charged with humour and irony. As against the flat owners are the relatives of the deceased who protest "that they were not paying funeral fees to have their dear departed ones anatomized and strewn piecemeal on posh balconies" (317). In a humorous way it reveals the modern worldly life in which human sentiments and religious rites have lost their sanctity. Suggestions of either training the vultures, or importing more vultures (so that all the flesh can be consumed) to avoid surplus are introduced. The problem even leads to debates between the orthodox and the reformists. The orthodox defend it as "a pure method, defiling none of God's good creations: earth, water, air, and fire" (317), while the reformists favour cremation and denounce the customs as a "ghoulish system" (317), unsuitable to the twentieth century. According to them it is not in keeping with the community's "progressive reputation and a forward-thinking attitude" (317). Rohinton Mistry here writes against the rituals and practices which create environmental crisis. The Parsi religious rites which sanctify the atmosphere are in contrast to the occult practices described in the sub-plot woven around Gustad's wife and Mrs. Kutpitia. A rich culture along with the customs and traditions of a marginalized community are recreated here. The passages describing the Parsi death rites and other practices associated with the Parsi life give one a glimpse of the Parsi culture and customs. The Parsi words used in the novel convey the sensibility and nuances typical to their life. There is no conscious or unconscious idealization of values the novelist has become alienated from in real life in *Such a Long Journey*. The Parsi religious observances promote social harmony and philanthropy. It projects a magnificent panorama of the cultural and religious richness of the community. The detailed account of Parsi rites and rituals create a world of authentic ethnic revelations. The use of the unique Parsi idiom is notable in Rohinton Mistry's writings. This is nothing unexpected in a novelist who is himself a Parsi.

The Christians have their own rites associated with death. Unlike the Hindus and the Parsis, they bury their dead with the proper funeral rites. Arundhati Roy describes some of the rites she is familiar with in *The God of Small Things*. The opening chapter of the work describes Sophie Mol's funeral. The death foreshadows the gloomy atmosphere created therein. A major portion of the action revolves around the past of the Ayemenem household. The story is intricately woven around the central incident of Sophie Mol's death by drowning. The novelist herself has stated that the opening chapter of the novel is an enigmatic nutshell. A large part of the novel is seen through the consciousness of the children—Rahel and Estha—around whom the story revolves. This is found in expressions like "Satin-lined" (4), "Brass handle shined" (4), and "coffin-cart wheeler" (251). When Sophie Mol dies, she is given a proper Christian burial, which can be used as a yardstick against the funerals given to the other characters here. The congregation gathers around the coffin. While the family stands huddled together at the funeral, the twins—Rahel and Estha—are made to stand apart. Indicating the treatment meted out to them at Ayemenem. Their mixed parentage rules out possibilities of their being either complete Hindus or Christians. The stigma of mixed parentage, disgrace of a divorcee mother, all undermine their position at the Ayemenem house. Sophie is the only character in the novel to be given a proper funeral rite. Though destined to live only for a brief spell of time her presence is felt throughout. The funeral is presented through the children's eyes. A child's way of registering, using, uttering and remembering a word is used here. Sophie Mol is buried in the old church at Ayemenem. In a humorous and childlike manner the children conclude that the government did not pay for the funeral because Sophie Mol did not die on a zebra crossing which to them was a condition for free funerals. The description of Sophie's coffin—"Special child-sized coffin" (4), "Satin-lined" (4), and "Brass handle shined" (4)—indicates the novelist's style and hints at the experiments with language attempted. It also reveals a deft handling of English language with elliptical sentences and new coinages. Comparisons like, "the yellow church swelled like a throat with the sound of singing" (4) and "Her face was pale and as wrinkled as a dhobi's thumb from being in water for too long" (4) are true to a child's mind. A child's view of the adult world is offered. The priest with the frankincense, the candles on the altar, the "funeral junkie" (5) who often surfaced near the body, put cologne on a wad of cotton wool and applied it on Sophie Mol's forehead, the prayer books, Mammachi's dark glasses and off-white sari, the Christian prayer when the body is committed to the ground, all pass their eyes. Though dead, Sophie Mol points out the church dome and the bat to Rahel. The newly painted high dome of the church, which Rahel felt was easy for Sophie Mol to see from her coffin, reminds her of Velutha "[l]ying broken on the hot church floor, dark blood spilling from his skull like a secret" (6). This prefigures the events (which culminate in Sophie Mol's death) that are later told in the novel. An inkling is given of the incidents preceding the funeral and of those later depicted. It is significant that though the coffin is lowered Rahel feels Sophie Mol's presence. At the funeral Rahel feels Sophie Mol scream from inside the earth. In a childlike manner she concludes, "Sophie Mol died because she couldn't breathe. Her funeral killed her" (7). The coffin seemed to carry a secret to Rahel (that she is alive), a secret knowledge which is shared by none. Signifying her short life her tombstone said, "A Sunbeam Lent To Us Too Briefly" (7). The funeral rites mark Estha's growing sense of alienation from his family and society after giving false testimony against his friend Velutha who later dies in police custody. Sophie's death leads to Velutha being falsely implicated in spite of the fact that everyone knew Sophie Mol's was an accidental death. Unlike Sophie, Velutha's body is dumped in the *themmady kuzhy* (the pauper's pit where the police dump their dead) and is not given proper last rites. Like Naranappa (*Samskara*) and Appachu (*The Scent of Pepper*) he is an "outsider" who has gone against the dictates of society. He is cast out and punished. The two children—Rahel and Estha—play games at Sophie Mol's funeral. Frazer points out in *The Golden Bough* that many of the funeral rites arose from games. A cryptic style, as when Rahel feels Sophie Mol's presence throughout even after her body is disposed of with the proper funeral rites, is found in the first chapter. While Estha is returned to his father after Sophie Mol's burial, the death marks Velutha's end too. Shroud-related images recur. The drapes and curtains in the novel symbolize the shroud. Estha plays Caesar with his sheet wrapped around him and falls down playing a dead body. When Ammu dies she is "wrapped in a dirty bedsheet" (162) before her cremation. Sophie Mol's death also puts an end to the possibility of their (the twins) stay at Ayemenem. The reference to the skull in the novel also signifies death. Ammu, another "outsider", too is denied a Christian burial. She is ostracized due to her relationship with a Paravan (Velutha). Ammu dies in a grimy room in a lodge. The church refuses to bury her. So her body is taken to the crematorium by Chacko (her brother), and Rahel (her daughter). The novel humorously describes her as of a "die-able age" (3). Chacko and Rahel are given her ashes—"The grit from her bones. The teeth from her smile. The whole of her crammed into a little clay pot. Receipt No. Q498673" (163). Like Velutha, she is given a last rite similar to those of derelicts. Ammu is thus reduced to a numerical value, on the receipt, shorn of all human dignity and individuality. The description of Sophie Mol's funeral abounds in single word sentences, capitals, and repetitions. Arundhati Roy also brings the English language under the influence of the vernacular. Malayalam words, like *themmadi kuzhy*, are embedded in the novel. The use of the native tongue gives a local colour. The priest's funeral song at the burial and the epitaph on Sophie Mol's tombstone are in italics to make them stand apart from the rest of the narration. Observations like "Her funeral killed her" (7) followed by "Dus to dus to dus to dus to dus" (7) in italics also stand apart. Italicization serves different purposes (like give emphasis, make ironic statements, make comic effects) here. One also notes the use of capitals along with italicization, as in "A Sunbeam Lent To Us Too Briefly" (7) signifying her early death. Through the use of capitals—"She showed Rahel Two Things" (5), "Thing One was the newly painted dome..." (5), and "Thing Two that Sophie Mol showed Rahel was the bat baby" (6)—while describing the events at the funeral service, the novelist seems to be conveying that Sophie Mol being dead would not be able to do what she was doing. The use of brackets in describing the funeral—the reference to an "old lady masquerading as a distant relative (whom nobody recognized), but who often surfaced next to bodies at funerals (a funeral junkie? a latent necrophiliac?)..." (4-5), or "She [Rahel] heard (on Sophie Mol's behalf), the soft sounds..." (7)—seem to be authorial comments used as an effective technique.

Funeral rites have been depicted in Indian English fiction in innumerable ways. Novelists indicate how rituals and prejudices are exploited by man to suit his selfish ends. Death becomes a social occasion for people to come together and share their grief. Every religious group has its own funeral rites. The Muslims and the Christians bury their dead while the Parsis place their dead on the Tower of Silence for the vultures to consume. Despite the differences, these rites and rituals help in bringing the living together, in accepting the loss and carrying life ahead, in the readjustment of social roles and relations, and sometimes even involves a redistribution of property and wealth. Funeral rites consist of elaborate rituals involving many individuals. The dead leave behind not only physical property to be redistributed but also a bundle of roles and statuses which have to be dismantled and reallocated before the breach in the social fabric, caused by the death, is filled in. The position he held is gradually taken up by his successor and he (the dead) is invested with the status of a spirit which helps and guides the living on earth. The creation of the new is always preceded by the destruction of the old. Death is the way in which any transition to a new state is conceived. The death rites enable the proper disposal of the dead body as well as the readjustment of life among the living. These rites mark the end of their life on earth. In a way they serve as initiation rites for the dead who are thus ushered into a new world. Death rites open up a new beginning for the dead as well as the living.

5

The Carnival

The diversity of the Indian population has given us a large number of festivals. The people celebrate many colourful festivals, both religious and social, throughout the year. These festivals reflect the inherent feelings of a nation with a long cherished historical and rich cultural background. Each festival is an occasion for celebration beyond religious barriers. These festivals often assume great social and political importance. They even help to arouse mass appeal. Every religion has its own festivals. The Muslim festival Id is celebrated as a public festival. The streets are decorated and processions are taken out in large numbers. Hindus celebrate colourful festivals throughout the year, during which deities like Vishnu, Shiva, Ganapati, and Durga are worshipped with devotion and joy. Some festivals are celebrated within the family while others tend to be group celebrations or social functions, as is the case with Ganesh Chathurthi. During this festival devotees install the Lord's clay idols in their houses, decorate them and perform puja. After weeklong festivities, the idols are immersed in the sea. Being a nation riven with caste and class differences such processions and social ceremonies become grounds for religious and political strifes. But festivals and the ceremonies associated with them are often "the means by which the society acts upon its individual members and keeps alive in their mind a certain system of sentiments" (Banton 119). These sentiments of attachment in the minds of the people in a group is essential for its solidarity and permanence. One of the means of ensuring solidarity is to give them occasional collective expression. Rituals express this collective expression of social sentiments.

The various rituals and ceremonies are carried out by the priests, who act as intermediaries between man and the supernatural. The priest is a central figure in any Hindu household. He is called in to settle lucky days on which to begin or put off an undertaking or expedition, to avert evil influences, for purificatory ceremonies, to give names to newly born children and to draw their horoscope. The most important of their duties is the celebration of marriages and conducting funerals. They take care to keep themselves clean, to prevent any sort of defilement and to purify themselves from any uncleanness that they may have contracted.

During festivals, prayers are offered and sacrifices made to appease the deity. The concept of sacrifice which was a part of many ancient barbaric rituals have undergone change with the passage of time. Now human beings are substituted with animals during sacrifices. Rituals to placate the planets are carried out not only during marriages and festivals to avoid evil influence, but also by the sick and unfortunate who suppose themselves to be under their baneful influence. The ceremony of walking on fire or a shallow pit filled with glowing embers is performed during festivals like Moharram. Sometimes it is undertaken as a purificatory ceremony or a vow. This practice is seen among the Hindus also. Sometimes the hot embers are substituted with flowers.

The Indian masses being deeply religious, religion was freely exploited by Indian patriots all through the freedom struggle. Political propaganda is often carried out in the guise of religion. Festivals are used as suitable instruments for educating the masses making them politically conscious. In Raja Rao's *Kanthapura* the religious, political, and social life of the people are inextricably woven together. There are recitals of Kathas and Harikathas. It is under the guise of a religious procession that the people of Kanthapura try to escape.

Festivals are held throughout the year in honour of various gods and goddesses, trees, mountains, rivers, and snakes. Gods and goddesses are thus periodically worshipped and propitiated. Annual festivals and sacrifices are carried out to ward off evil spirits. There are many ceremonies and rituals associated with these festivals, some of which are found in creative writing.

The worship of Nature is an integral part of many religions. The people who worship the forces of Nature believe in the power of these forces and their influence on the people. These forces have to be appeased for granting favours, and for protection against their wrath. The people believe these forces to be benevolent as well as malevolent. Festivals at which these gods are worshipped are often held at the commencement of the agricultural year. As a mother, earth is considered stable, fecund and moist, always feeding the millions that live off her. Festivals cover such operations as ploughing, sowing, planting, and harvesting. When the seed is sown at harvest time the farmers seek her blessings. A long description of a similar ceremony is found in Kanthapura. In seasons of drought prayers are offered to the rain god, who is supposed to be angry with the people. Rukmani, the narrator in Kamala Markandaya's *Nectar in a Sieve* says, "That year the rains failed. A week went by, we stared at the cruel sky, calm, blue, indifferent to our need. We threw ourselves on the earth and we prayed. I took a pumpkin and a few grains of rice of my goddess, and I wept at her feet" (72). Thus the people strongly believe in the powers of their gods and goddesses, their efficacy to bring rains to a parched village.

The vegetable world supplies us with the annual cycle of seasons which is often represented by, or identified with a divine figure which dies in autumn, or is killed with the gathering of harvest, disappears in winter, and revives in spring. Death is seen as a necessary preliminary to their revival. Rites are often performed to guard the dangers of winter and to promote spring fertility. Sacrifices and offerings are made to placate the natural forces. In these sacrifices, it is not the taking of life that is important, but the giving of life to promote and preserve life, and to establish union between the individual and the unseen forces that surround him. In Kanthapura the villagers join to celebrate the coming of rains in Vaisakh. The people plough their fields and sow the crops. An auspicious day is chosen, camphor is lit and offerings are made. The people offer the first rice to their goddess Kenchamma. The practice of offering first-fruit is common among most agricultural communities. This is done to protect the crops, by thanking and propitiating the deity. Such customs and practices provide occasions of social festivity. The people of the community join together and celebrate this festive occasion. James Frazer in his *Golden Bough* observes, "In some of the festivals...the sacrament of first-fruits is combined with a sacrifice or presentation of them to gods or spirits, and in course of time the sacrifice of first-fruits tends to throw the sacrament into the shade, if not to supersede it" (640). The corn goddess is said to make the crops grow or to blight the grains of those against whom she has a grudge. The offering of first-fruits to the gods is a "sufficient preparation for eating the new corn; the higher powers having received their share man is free to enjoy the rest" (640). The offering is regarded as a gift bestowed by the gods upon man, who is bound to express his gratitude by returning to them a portion of their bounty.

Chinua Achebe refers to the agricultural festival, Feast of the New Year, among the Ibo tribe in his *Things Fall Apart*. They observe the Week of Peace before planting the crop. The earth goddess, if insulted may refuse to give a rich harvest, and they would perish. Those who break the Peace are punished, as is the case with Okonkwo, "for if the clan did not exact punishment for an offence against the great goddess, her wrath was loosed on all the land and not just on the offender" (106). The Feast for the Ibo people is thus an occasion for thanking their earth goddess. It is also an occasion of joy. The people invite a large number of guests from far and wide.

Among certain agricultural communities, rites connected with warding off drought are carried out. In Bengal this rite is called 'the wedding of the frog'. A man smears clay over his body and along with his companions goes from house to house. The housewife throws bucketsful of water on the clay smeared body. This rite they believe ensures rainfall. Frazer in his *Golden Bough* refers to a custom observed by young girls in the Kanagra district of India, which closely resembles some of the European spring ceremonies. Here, small, painted earthen idols of Shiva and Parvati are worshipped. At the end of the ceremony, the idols are thrown into the river. The deities, Shiva and Parvati, are conceived as spirits of vegetation. Thus the divinities of vegetation are represented in duplicate by plants or by puppets. The immersing of the idols into the water and mourning for them are similar to the European customs of throwing the dead spirit of vegetation into the water and lamenting over it. The spirit of vegetation is believed to have a quickening and fertilizing influence on the life of man as well as plants. Hence these ceremonies, it is believed, help to procure husbands for the girls (421-22). Baisakhi, celebrated especially in Punjab, is a time of great joy. It marks the ripening of the rabi harvest. The people offer prayers and are attired in their best clothes.

In South India Pongal, also known as Maha-Samkranti, is an occasion of great rejoicing. The feast lasts for three days. The first is called Bhoghi-Pongal during which the people visit friends and relatives. During the second day, called Surya-Pongal, the sun is worshipped. Rice is boiled in milk on a fire in the open air. After offering a portion of it to the gods and the cows, the rest is eaten by the people of the house. The third day is the Pongal of the cows, called Mattu-Pongal. The people worship the cows. The horns of the cows are painted in various colours and garlands are hung around their necks. Then they are allowed to graze everywhere.

Festivals like Onam and Vishu are referred to in Sethu's *Pandavapuram* (translation from Malayalam). Vishu is celebrated as the Malayali New Years Day. Gifts are exchanged and various ceremonies associated with the festival are followed by the people. During the festival of Onam, which is celebrated all over the country, people make flower carpets and enjoy themselves in numerous ways.

Shivaratri and Navaratri are celebrated by the Hindus. The month of Ashwin begins with Navaratri festival, celebrated for the first nine nights of this month, followed by the tenth day or the Vijaya Dashmi. In Bengal it is celebrated as the Pooja festival. The goddess of learning, Saraswati is worshipped on the seventh day and the goddess of prosperity, Lakshmi, on the eighth day. On the nineth day goddess Durga is worshipped. In Uttar Pradesh the festival is celebrated as Ramleela. Songs describing the heroic deeds and virtues of Rama are sung and effigies of Ravana are burnt on Dasera. Weapons, books, and tools are worshipped. The farmers, carpenters, blacksmiths, all worship their respective tools. It is a custom to begin new work on this day of Dasera. The festival marks the victory of goddess Durga over Mahishasura, and of Rama over Ravana. The festival thus symbolises the victory of good over evil. People visit temples and arati is performed. The sound of drums, cymbals and bells fill the air. Every home has a display of kolu. A decorated platform is prepared and covered with dolls and clay figurines representing gods and goddesses. Elaborate processions are taken out. At the end of the festival idols of the goddess are taken out in great pomp and immersed in water amidst huge crowds.

Lakshmi, the goddess of wealth, is worshipped during Diwali. She is considered the protector of harvests, and offerings are made during the harvest time. Every Hindu home is cleaned a few days before Diwali. People illuminate their houses, courtyards, gates, roofs and gardens with oil-filled earthen lamps throughout the night to welcome the goddess. Markets, streets and all public places are decked with small glittering lamps. The festival of Diwali is described in *Kanthapura*. The mythopoeic imagination of the narrator Achakka, lets the gods freely jostle with men in her account of the festival. Offerings are made and the people pray for the God's blessings. A colourful description of the Festival of Lights is given in the novel. The narrator speaks about the "white lights from clay-trays and red lights from copper-stands, and diamond lights that glow from the bowers of entrance-leaves; lights that glow from banana-trunks and mango twigs" (87).

Holi, the festival of colours is celebrated by all the people in the country. On the night preceding Holi, people light bonfires, and offerings of coconuts and food are made. The people go around the Holi fire. An effigy of Holika, made of bamboo and straw, is set on fire. This festival is said to mark the end of winter and the beginning of spring. On the next day, the people indulge in merry making and enjoying the festival. They amuse themselves by throwing handfuls of coloured powder on their friends and relatives, or spray coloured water on them.

Certain groups celebrate the Churuk Puja or Hook-Swinging festival. The devotees are swung up in the air by means of hooks, thrust into the flesh below the shoulder blade. It is a painful ceremony and has been prohibited by law.

The Muslims have their deceased saints who have to be propitiated. They celebrate festivals like Id and Ramadan. Id is the festival of sacrifice celebrated to commemorate the incident of Abraham's sacrifice of his son. Ramadan is the holy month of the Muslims during which they fast from dawn to dusk. During this period they abstain from food and drink. It was in this month that the Koran was revealed to Prophet Mohammed by angel Gabriel. At the end of the mourning observed to commemorate the martyrdom of Husain, Muslims immerse a replica of the tomb of their saint which is taken out in processions with pomp and splendour. This is similar to immersing the idols of Hindu gods and goddesses during festivals.

Most of the festivals are celebrated by people all over the country, irrespective of caste and creed. The devotees invoke their gods and goddess with flowers, fruits, sweets and incense. They blow the conch, wave prayer lamps around the idol and ring the bell. Sometimes during these festivals public entertainments are conducted.

The eleventh day of the moon is religiously observed by the Hindu women. This is called *ekadasi*. Many of the Indian writers have referred to this in their works. The women keep a strict fast on this day and abstain entirely from rice. It is the day set apart for the worship of Lord Vishnu. To fast on this holy day and to offer puja to the Lord is to ensure the forgiveness of sins and the gratification of one's wishes. On the tenth day only one meal is eaten. The night of the eleventh day is usually spent in a temple dedicated to Lord Vishnu. Those who faithfully observe the fast of *ekadasi* are sure to achieve salvation.

Many of the Indian English novels include descriptions of festivals, and the ceremonies associated with them. R.K. Narayan's *The Dark Room* has a description of the Navaratri festival, Raja Rao's *Kanthapura* describes the festival of Diwali, while Vani Subramanian's *Reminiscences* describes the festival of Pongal.

Most of the Indian villages have their own deities, and shrines dedicated to them. Lamps are lit and offerings ranging from coconuts to animal sacrifices are made regularly to them as part of a propitiation and appeasement rite. The temples and churches in the country have their own feasts, recurring at intervals during the course of the year. During temple festivals the gods are brought out of the temple with much ceremony. The idols are taken out in decorated chariots. Long ropes are attached to them. Thousands of worshippers struggle for the honour of holding them. The crowd shouts and music fills the air. Colourful processions are taken out during these festivals. These festivals are often coloured by the socio-political situation in the country.

Festival days are devoted to rejoicings. Relatives and friends meet and celebrate the occasion. Houses are decorated and feasts are often held. People appear in their best clothes and spend the time in games and entertainment. The thrust is certainly on enjoyment coupled with cleansing and rejuvenation.

Myriad arbitrary rules and regulations are adhered to even by the most liberated people. These regulations however trivial, help to order the world. They provide a feeling of control. Ambiguity and the unknown increase our anxiety, whereas order reduces it by making our environment more predictable and controllable. Human beings follow certain rites and rituals from cradle to grave. Perhaps it is a reflection of the need to make the world more predictable and therefore more secure. Sometimes religion is reduced to mere repetitive acts. For the

Hindus it may thus come to mean just caste and cow-protection, for the Muslims circumcision, and for the Parsis fire worship and feeding vultures. But rituals and ceremonies have potential social value through influence over group attitudes.

Myths often help when rituals or festivals demand justification. They give meaning to rituals. Many of the myths remain valid if their central interests have been transmuted or presented in continuing celebrations. Each nation has its own myths. Some of the characteristics of the human psyche get revealed through myths. Often new explanations are given to old myths. According to R.K. Narayan, the gods of our mythology should be looked upon "not as some remote concoctions but as types and symbols, possessing psychological validity even when viewed against the contemporary background" (Dass 212). Works like Shashi Tharoor's *The Great Indian Novel* treat old myths against a contemporary background.

There is a close connection between myths and rituals, as myths account for many of the rituals, customs and cycle of seasons. Many of the festivals have myths associated with them. Thus myths provide explanation where reason fails to help us. It is one of the oldest elements of human heritage. Emile Durkheim even points out the social function of myth—that it binds a society together. Myths often help to reveal or bring to focus some exciting feature or aspect that would otherwise be overlooked. It is a means of enlarging and intensifying what would perhaps be put in more matter of fact terms. Some rituals find meaning in myths. But they have been manipulated for power, prestige and political ends. It is sometimes used as an instrument in the political struggle for power. Beliefs are manipulated for political ends, in order to validate his or her group's claim to power and authority.

Northrop Frye in his *Anatomy of Criticism* stresses the fact that myths often give meaning to rituals when he says, "Ritual, by itself, cannot account for itself" (106). According to him the myth "accounts for, and makes communicable, the ritual" (106). The vegetative world also has myths to support its cycle of seasons which follow the birth-death-rebirth pattern. The ancient myths were considered psycho-therapeutic to the people who believed in them. The preoccupation with myths reveals a yearning for order in the midst of disorder. For Jung myths and rituals reveal the "transcendental symbolic forms found universally in the psychic life of man, embodied in a collective unconscious in which the individual psyche unknowingly participates" (Righter 17). These archetypes, as Jung calls them, while finding expression in myths and legends of particular communities also characterize the universal experience.

Ritual is not only a recurrent act, but it also expresses "a dialectic of desire and repugnance: desire for fertility or victory, repugnance to drought or to enemies. We have rituals of expulsion, execution, and punishment" (Frye 106). Frye draws a parallel between rituals and dreams in his work. In dream there is both the wish-fulfilment dream and the anxiety or nightmare dream of repugnance.

Writers enrich their works with mythological allusions. Myths not only describe things but often explain how it came into existence. Some of them find a new explanation in works of creative writing. The mythical technique has been used successfully in *Kanthapura*. The past and the present mingle freely in the novel, and gods and goddesses of epics jostle with contemporary personalities.

Many of the Indian festivals have myths associated with them. The Vijaya Dashmi day is celebrated to commemorate the victory of Lord Rama over Ravana. It was also on this day that Arjuna became a charioteer to drive away the enemies from the kingdom of Virat. The festival of Diwali is celebrated to signify the victory of Lord Krishna. Lord Krishna killed the demon Narakasur on this day and returned home victorious. The ladies of the town greeted him and his warriors with lamps in their hands. The people decorated their houses and lighted up the city with rows of light. *Ekadasi* too has certain myths associated with it. Women worship the banyan tree, observe fast and pray for the long life of their husbands. These rituals are associated with the Savitri-myth. Savitri in the Hindu mythology is known for the devotion towards her husband. On Shivaratri Lord Shiva is devoutly worshipped. People observe fast and keep awake throughout the night, praying to the Lord. Fasts are undertaken and offerings made. According to the myth a hunter, who felt tired after killing his prey, climbed a bilva tree and spent the night there. At the foot of the tree was a lingam, the adored symbol of Lord Shiva. While changing positions frequently the shaking of the branches of the bilva caused some flowers and leaves to fall on the lingam. This fortunate incident helped him to win the Lord's favour. The Lord was much gratified at the offering thus made to his adored symbol and rewarded the hunter. This myth is referred to by Raja Rao in his novel *The Cat and Shakespeare*.

Rituals cluster around the cyclic movements of the moon, the seasons, and human life. Every crucial experience, harvest, seed-time, birth, initiation, marriage, death, have rituals related to them. Men make oblations of blood, chant hymns and prostrate themselves before God intoning his praises, and fill his temples with costly gifts. These offerings, sacrifices and prayers are aimed at pleasing the deity. Myths often help one to have a better understanding of the rituals associated with them.

Rituals related to superstitious beliefs and practices also play an important role in human life. Man will cease work, return from a journey, break an appointment, if anything ominous occurs. They follow various rituals to avoid ill-luck. These concrete acts of religious observance help to reinforce human faith. The desire to avert evil influences has given rise to numerous rituals. As soon as the child is born its eyelids are sometimes smeared with soot to render it unattractive. The ceremony of *arati* is performed on several auspicious occasions. It is usually performed by married women at marriages, victories and other such functions. It consists of incense sticks, a lighted lamp, flowers, vermilion powder, turmeric powder and betel-nuts. The woman holds the plate containing these and raises it to the level of the person's head for whom the ceremony is being performed. She then makes a specified number of circles with it. It is one of the commonest religious practices and is observed in private and in public. The ritual is usually done to avert bad influences. *Arati* is also performed for the idols in homes and in the temples. Another practice to avert evil influences is the rangoli. It is a design drawn using the rangoli powder and is considered very auspicious. These auspicious symbols are usually painted on walls, or doors, or on the floor of temples and houses. Coloured powders are used to make colourful designs. Of all the Hindu rites *puja* is one that occurs most frequently in all their ceremonies. Every brahmin is obliged to offer it at least once a day to his household gods. Offerings are made and the worshippers often prostrate themselves before the deity. These rituals are conducted to avert ill-luck and to achieve the blessings of the deity. To avert evil influences women often crack their knuckles and wave the lamp over the bride and the groom during marriage ceremonies. The belief in evil-eye which raises the jealousy of the spirits and causes it to do mischief to the object admired is thus widely prevalent. Eclipses are supposed to have a bad influence on the expectant woman. Among some groups the woman is kept in a dark room till the eclipse is over. She also has to abstain from food and drink during this time.

The tendency of the people to submit their bodies to severe and often cruel tortures, or to spend their means in costly offerings is manifested whenever they find themselves in critical circumstances. In times of sickness or trouble they make vows to perform some ritual on condition that the person is delivered safe and sound from his unfortunate predicament. The rich even make vows to celebrate solemn festivals at temples. The offerings made vary according to the person's social status. It may be a piece of cloth, gold, a buffalo, or a cow. If the eye, nose, ear or any other organ is afflicted, they offer to the deity an image of it in gold or silver. This superstition mania causes numerous offerings to flow into the temple, in gratitude to the deity for recovery from sickness or other benefits conferred. Representations of the human figure or part of the body which has been affected are often presented as votive offerings. Belief in the efficacy of charms or talisman is widely prevalent among the people. Such rituals related to superstitious beliefs are found in works of fiction. Rohinton Mistry's *Such a Long Journey* contains references to certain Parsi beliefs and practices. Superstitious beliefs are also current with regard to every animal. In spite of developments in the field of science and technology, and increasing rationalisation, people cling to such superstitious beliefs and practices.

Often people have to undergo purificatory ceremonies. There are rituals associated with restoration to caste, after being expelled from it as a punishment for some crime. This varies from society to society. Sometimes the person prostrates himself with signs of repentance, listens without complaint to the rebukes showered on him and pays the fine imposed on him. When the expulsion is the result of some heinous crime the guilty person, to be readmitted into his caste, may have to undergo ordeals like branding with hot iron, burning his tongue and walking bare-footed over red-hot embers. He has to thus purify himself. Women undergoing their periodical uncleanness are isolated and may have no communication with anyone during the days her defilement is supposed to last. After this she purifies herself by ablutions. She puts on a clean dress after purifying herself. She has to immerse herself in water, for till then her very glance would defile any person on whom it fell. Often the priest is called in to complete her purification and she receives the consecrated water from him. The network of rituals and observances like *madi* occupy a central role in Rajam Krishnan's *Lamps in the Whirlpool.* During the purificatory ceremonies the person concerned is thus secluded. The period of seclusion may vary from a few days to a year, depending upon the type of impurity involved. In *Kanthapura*, Moorthy who enters a pariah house has to undergo certain purificatory ceremonies before entering his house again. He has to wash himself with hot water, put on new clothes and change his holy thread. But, since he could not change his holy thread everyday it was decided that on similar occasions he could purify himself with a little Ganges water.

Each group may have its own rites connected with ancestor-worship. Ancestor-worship consists of rites carried out by the members of a lineage for the deceased members of the lineage. Offerings of food and drink are often made. In these rites of commemoration of the ancestors, the participants express their reverential gratitude to those from whom they have received life. These acts of piety towards the deceased are caused by fear, or love, or solicitude for the spirit of the departed. Offerings of food and various other articles are often left in a person's grave. The dead it is believed, needed these in their afterlife. The survivors perform the requisite obsequies, go into mourning and observe the traditional taboos and customs to be quiet of the dead spirits. They resort to various methods to propitiate and keep quiet the spirits of the dead. Animal sacrifices are sometimes made to ward off their baneful effect. Stones representing the deceased members of the tribe are worshipped in the belief that the spirits of the departed will protect and even guide the living. Sometimes these ancestral spirits are propitiated during the marriage rites. Others do this by performing *sradh* or other ceremonies.

The members of a group may join together and make offerings or sacrifices to the spirit of the dead relative. Sometimes feasts are held. It is only after the dishes have been exposed for some time and the spirit has finished with his spiritual share that the food is given to friends and relatives. Thus, maintaining a constant round of ritual supplications became the principle means by which the living sustained obligations to their ancestors and provided for their own comfort in the afterlife. As Carl Becker says, "Each generation must inevitably play on the dead whatever tricks it finds necessary for its own peace of mind" (Muir 1).

The dead are thus chosen as objects of worship. Prayers are held for these ancestral spirits who, it is believed, keep watch over the behaviour of their living kin. They are worshipped during marriages also. It may be due to fear of the dead spirit or the danger of the evil influences which may render the union infertile. The dead are the recipients not only of expiatory offerings but also of acts of thanksgiving and commemoration. These rites are said to ensure the deceased, his rightful position in the world of the dead. They regulate his relationships with the living for whom he has relevance by virtue of the status he occupied at the point of death. Hence sacrifices and offerings are made to appease them and to discourage them from evil.

The solidarity and continuity of the lineage helps in giving stability to the social structure. For the individual his primary duties are those to his lineage. These include duties to the members now living, to those who have died, and also to those who are not yet born. These rites serve a social function, for "by giving solemn and collective expression to them the rites reaffirm, renew and strengthen those sentiments on which the social solidarity depends" (Brown 164).

Among certain groups these rites mark the son's gradual assumption of his father's authoritative role in the domestic domain. Thus the dead person's progress to ancestorhood is paralleled by the son's assumption of the father's role, he has vacated in this world. He replaces his father as an elder of the lineage. Some of the tribes in South Africa feel themselves dependent on their ancestors, for "from them he has received his life and the cattle that are his inheritance. To them he looks to send him children and to multiply his cattle and in other ways to care for his well being" (Brown 175). According to them the ancestors watch over their conduct and, "if he fails in his duties they will not only cease to send him blessings, but will visit him with sickness or some other misfortune" (Brown 175). Thus they cannot stand alone and depend only on their efforts. They depend on their ancestors for everything.

Periodic commemorative rites, expiatory sacrifices and offerings are made to the ancestral spirit to avoid sickness and disaster. Amongst certain societies in South Africa a portion of the cattle received for a girl on her marriage is sometimes taken by her mother's brother. This bride price is held by him on behalf of his sister's children. If one of his sister's sons or daughters falls ill, he is required to offer a sacrifice to his ancestral spirits from this herd held as bride price (Brown 26). In certain groups ancestor-worship is patrilineal. Sometimes each family has two sets of gods, those on the father's side and those on the mother's, both equal in dignity. Ancestor-worship thus consists of the relations of the living persons to their deceased kindred. Works like *The Scent of Pepper* refer to ancestor-worship. The *egwugwu* represents the ancestors of the Ibo tribe in *Things Fall Apart*. The people of this tribe make offerings to appease the ancestor spirits during their ceremonies.

Rituals and ceremonies thus influence almost every aspect of Indian life. They sometimes acquire a socio-religious, or a religio-political configuration. Psychologically, man finds it difficult to evade their hold. An objective study of Indian English fiction will help to throw light on the various rituals and ceremonies prevalent in Indian society from times immemorial.

Social customs and practices are considered an expression of communal will and the crystallization of communal experience. Festivals bring people together and strengthen their bonds of union. Some of these festivals have in course of time become so deeply rooted in the consciousness of the people, that they constitute essential and inseparable elements of culture. Rituals and myths associated with festivals enhance their meaning. Various festivals are celebrated throughout the year in India. Festivals held in honour of various deities play an important role in the life of the Indians. They become occasions for rejoicing and reunion and are celebrated either as private worship at a household shrine or as public festivals. Everyone takes part in these public festivals which serve to strengthen social solidarity. The celebrations at home are usually restricted to family and close friends. Festivals like Deepavali, Navaratri, Dussera, and Holi attract large crowds from all over the country. Some of the festivals are more regional in their popularity. Temples celebrate the annual festival of the deity to which it is dedicated. The various festivals and ceremonies, besides establishing routines and schedules, also mark the passage of seasons. They are occasions of collective observances which help to foster unity and strength.

Festivals are a part of the life of the Bengalis of Tarasankar Banerjee's *Ganadevata* as well as the orthodox Hindus who inhabit R.K. Narayan's Malgudi. They form a part of the life, of both the urban and the rural folk, depicted in creative works (like *Two Virgins*, *Golden Honeycomb*, and *Nowhere Man* by Kamala Markandaya). The religious and agricultural festivals are an inseparable part of Indian English fiction as of Indian life. The descriptions form an integral part of the plot and serve different functions in the works in which they are portrayed. For the Indian emigrant festivals become means of clinging on to the Indian values in an alien land. In some of the works, it becomes a means of highlighting the East-West dichotomy, to show how the Indian festivals mean nothing to the western mind. While some of the novels make only a passing reference to the festivals and ceremonies associated with them, others describe them in detail. R.K. Narayan's *Dark Room*, *Guide,* and *Man-Eater of Malgudi*, Raja Rao's *Kanthapura*, Kamala Markandaya's *A Handful of Rice* and *Nectar in a Sieve*, Kavery Nambisan's *Scent of Pepper*, and U.R. Anantha Murthy's *Samskara* makes it a part of the narrative.

The tradition of celebrating festivals runs almost throughout the year in India. They are occasions for the people to come together. The life of an orthodox Hindu consists of the observance of a large number of fasts and festivals. Deepavali (*deep* meaning "light" and *awali* meaning "row") is celebrated in the country as the Festival of Lights. The women fast, worship the cow with its calf, and pray for the well-being of their children. Lanterns are lit in front of the houses. According to a myth associated with this festival, when the demon Narakasur was killed by Lord Krishna he was greeted with lamps. The houses were decorated to mark his victory. The festival came to be known as Deepavali. It begins with the day commemorating the killing of Narakasur, and ends with the day of the killing of Tripurasur by Lord Shiva (which is another myth associated with the festival). The festival thus marks the victory of good over evil. It also marks the victory of Lord Rama over Ravana, the victory of Truth. Every house is lit with lamps to celebrate the occasion. People clean their houses, wear new clothes and illuminate their houses with colourful lights. The focus on purification and newness are symbolic of the casting off of the old and the hope for a new life. Crackers are lit and celebrations continue late into the night. The fireworks displayed are believed to ward off evil spirits from the area. The lighting of lamps is one of the most beautiful aspects of Deepavali which is celebrated on the darkest night of the year. The lamps signify enlightenment or upliftment of the mind. These lamps usually made of clay or banana leaves, symbolize the removal of darkness/evil from the human mind and enlightening it with knowledge. The festival is mentioned in works like *Nectar in a Sieve*, *Kanthapura*, *Two Virgins*, and *A Handful of Rice*. It is one of the rare moments of happiness in the rural life (of Nathan and Rukmani who have to face poverty, floods, drought, as well as the effects of industrialization in the form of the tannery) in *Nectar in a Sieve*. Through the festival, the novel refers to the better economic position of Nathan's family. They could afford to buy firecrackers which they had been unable to do the previous year. The narrator, Rukmani, describes the festival as she recollects it:

> As it grew dark we lit the tapers and wicks and encircled our dwelling with light. A feathery breeze was stirring, setting the flames leaping and dancing, their reflections in the black glistening oil cavorting too. In the town and in the houses nearby, hundreds of small beacons were beginning to flash, now and then a rocket would tear into the sky, break and pour its riches like precious jewels into the darkness. As the night went on, the crackle and spit of exploding fireworks increased. (54)

The bond between Selvam (Rukmani's son) and Ira is also indicated here. The villagers come together and celebrate the festival. In their otherwise gloomy life, these are rare moments of joy and happiness. Men, women, and children come out dressed according to their economic position. A bonfire lit in the town as a part of this festival is described:

> In the centre of the town the bonfire was beginning to smoulder. For many weeks the children had been collecting firewood, rags, leaves and brushwood, and the result was a huge pile like an enormous ant-hill, into

> which the flames ate fiercely, hissing and crackling and rearing up as they fed on the bits of camphor and oil-soaked rags that people threw in. (55-56)

Deepavali is the Festival of Lights and fireworks. A bonfire is usually lit during the festival of Holi. This is considered a lapse on the part of the narrator who recaptures her past in a reminiscent mood. It has also been attributed to the novelist's (an expatriate Indian, writing about her "home") confusion, though she does refer to a bonfire during the festival of Holi in *The Golden Honeycomb*. Kamala Markandaya presents here a Dionysian atmosphere of excitement, joy, and drunken revelry. The atmosphere is charged with the scent of jasmine flowers mingled with the fumes of camphor, oil, and the smell of toddy. Rukmani loses the company of her husband and children in the throng indicating their later separation. Her husband dies, Arjun and Thambi (her sons) leave for Ceylon, Murugan settles in the city, Raja and Kuti die. The novel highlights, the urban-rural dichotomy. The novelist has been frequently criticized for trying to explicate Indian customs and beliefs. This is found in the reference to the festival of Deepavali—"Deepavali, the Festival of Lights, approached. It is a festival mainly for the children, but of course everyone who can takes part" (54). *A Handful of Rice* too refers to the festival of Deepavali (Apu's family visits the shrine and makes offerings of flowers and coconuts) but focuses on the fire-walkers who arrive soon after it. In *Two Virgins*, the novelist through the description of the festival hints at the East-West dichotomy as well as the urban-rural theme. To Lalitha's teacher, Miss. Mendoza, Deepavali means nothing (as she is a Christian). She plans to take Lalitha to the city during this "Hindu holiday" (119) as she would be away from school as little as possible. For Lalitha's Appa and Amma it means not having their daughter on a special festival occasion. Mud saucers with oil and wicks light up the darkness. The whole village celebrates the festival. Those who cannot afford to have fireworks, like Manikkam's children, are helped by others. The festival brings the villagers together. Various instances in the novel support this—"The children scrounged round, collected what neighbours gave them. As soon as it was dark they trooped off down to the river where families in like straits pooled their resources" (120). The family is able to afford only a few lights and fireworks, due to the expenses on Lalitha's visit to the town. Besides the reference to fireworks, there is also a reference to the bonfire made of rubbish, as "nobody would burn good fuel or firewood" (121). Saroja, her parents, and her aunt celebrate the festival with Anand who comes to share his fireworks with Saroja. In the midst of this joy and happiness everyone tries hard not to be reminded of Lalitha. This prefigures her later separation from the family, though she does return for a brief spell to the village. The difference in temperament between the sisters is hinted at throughout. While Lalitha celebrates the festival in town, Saroja enjoys herself in the village. Lalitha describes her Deepavali as a "grand affair" (124). In the city guests are invited, fireworks set off by the servants, and tableaux depicting scenes from the epics carried out. The urban-rural dichotomy is depicted through Saroja (with her preference for the ways of the village) and Lalitha (with her craze for city life).

A poetic description of the month of Karthik is found in *Kanthapura*. The novel which deals with the impact of the Gandhian freedom struggle in a remote south Indian village (Kanthapura) contains details of the various festivals and ceremonies celebrated by the people, and their ardent faith in goddess Kenchamma (the village deity). Emphasis is laid on the impact of religion on the life of the people. Even politics comes under the influence of religion here, and political activities become elaborately celebrated festivals. At the very outset the novel provides a swift sketching of the locale, its socio-economic divisions, superstitions, caste prejudices, and blind faith in gods and goddesses. The mythical technique is used to juxtapose the past with the present and to make the past heighten and glorify the present. The people being deeply religious, festivals are used as a suitable medium for educating the people and making them politically conscious. Religion is the most potent force in Kanthapura. Making an old woman (Achakka) the narrator enables the novelist to mingle fact and myth in an effective manner. The Indian sensibility is clearly manifest in the installation of the *lingam* (and its consecration which ushers in a more religious life for the people of Kanthapura), the Sankara Vijay, Sankara Jayanthi, the cycle of festivals etc. The action begins with the unearthing of a half-sunken lingam by Moorthy and its consecration which is celebrated with a feast. The poetic imagination of the narrator is visible here. It is natural for a narrator like Achakka to remember the various festivals and ceremonies which form an essential part of the life in Kanthapura. The mythopoeic imagination of the narrator makes the gods freely mix with men in her account of the festival. The evocative and descriptive passage is a "brilliantly sustained piece of rhythmic prose" (Iyengar 395). The social, political, and religious are inextricably woven into the complex story of the regeneration of Kanthapura as a result of the freedom struggle. A beautiful description of the coming of Karthik which is "a month of the gods" and a "month of lights" (87) is provided:

> Kartik has come to Kanthapura, sisters—Kartik has come with the glow of lights and the unpressed footsteps of the wandering gods; white lights from clay-trays and red lights from copper-stands, and diamond lights that glow from the bowers of entrance-leaves; lights that glow from banana-trunks and mango twigs, yellow light behind white leaves, and green light behind yellow leaves, and white light behind white leaves...and gods walk by lighted streets, blue gods and quiet gods and bright-eyed gods, and even as they walk in transparent flesh the dust gently sinks back to the earth, and many a child in Kanthapura sits late into the night to see the crown of this god and that god, and how many a god has chariots with steeds white as foam and queens so bright that the eyes shut themselves in fear lest they be blinded. (87)

There is "a lilt and seductive rhythm, curious incantatory power, in this kind of speech which coils round one more and more, and involves one inextricably in the experience" (Iyengar 395). The children in the village light the clay pots, copper candelabras and glass lamps. A re-enactment of the ancient myth is seen here. The happiness is marred as it is followed by a series of arrests. The life of the entire community revolves around an endless cycle of festivals and ceremonies. These festivals indicate the passage of time. The Gandhian movement itself is absorbed into the ritualistic pattern. The novel juxtaposes the contemporary situation with the attitudes and values of traditional Indian life. Politics is gradually ritualized. The satyagrahis have to fight against the puritanical forces of orthodoxy as well as the tyrannical rule of the alien government. Kanthapura is a festival ridden village in keeping with the tradition of India where social reformers have been profoundly religious men:

> Both the religious bhajans and the national movement have helped the novelist penetrate into the deeper layers of human nature and perceive the pettiness, greed, jealousy and in some cases callousness and inhumanity of the so called spiritually-bent Indian. (Narasimhaiah, Raja Rao 57)

The political and social activities gradually become celebrated festivals. On being arrested the people feel they have "walked the holy fire at the Harvest Festival" (134). They look up to the local deity (goddess Kenchamma) to release Moorthy from jail, and vow to make offerings on his return. The people take a dip in the river and cook payasam and chitranna on the occasion of Mahatma Gandhi's manufacture of salt "as though it were Gauri's Festival" (126). The picketing of toddy booths is celebrated with drums and trumpets in the village. The country's variegated religious and political activities are mirrored. The warmth, nearness, and feeling of well-being for others are manifested among the villagers in their religious functions, festivals, marriage ceremonies, and in difficult situations. The basic faith in God sustains them in hours of adversity. As the revolutionary spirit seizes the people of Kanthapura, the celebration of festivals, the recital of bhajans, kathas, and harikathas become linked with politics. It is through them and the religious functions that Moorthy creates nationalistic feelings in the minds of the uneducated villagers.

It is under the guise of a religious procession that the people of the village finally try to escape. The mythical technique is at its best in the harikathas, where the contemporary events and personalities mingle with puranic gods, and epic heroes and heroines. The reading of the Gita and hand spinning are elevated into a daily ritual like puja. The people of the village relate to the political situation in the country through similar situations in the country's epics:

> He will bring us Swaraj, the Mahatma. And we shall all be happy. And Rama will come back from exile, and Sita will be with him, for Ravana will be slain and Sita freed, and he will come back with Sita on his right in a chariot of the air, and brother Bharatha will go to meet them with the worshipped sandal of the Master on his head. And as they enter Ayodhya there will be a rain of flowers. (183)

Religion becomes politicized in the village—on the eve of the election to the Congress Committee the villagers are busy washing the gods and preparing flowers, wicks, and crowns for the gods, religious prayers and processions are accompanied by political slogans like "Mahatma Gandhi ki jai!" and "Vande Mataram", it is in the temple that the women take refuge during their political activities, and a picture of Gandhi is placed at the feet of Satyanarayan during the Satyanarayan puja. The villagers organize prayers and bhajans, and gather at the temple. They come together to celebrate the Rama Festival, Krishna Festival, Sankara-Jayanthi, and Ganesh-Jayanthi. Flowers and fruits are offered during these occasions, camphor is lit, coconuts are broken, and the conch is blown mingling the religious and the political:

> As a 'Purana' it [the novel] appeals to legendary memory and enshrines archetypal experience. The divine and sacred processes mingle freely with the ineffable socialities on the historical and secular plane at which all mundane human action is projected as a ritual continuum. (Rao, *The Fiction of Raja Rao* 49)

The myths associated with festivals enhance their meaning. As Leslie Fielder has pointed out, each generation will temper the myths of the past to meet its own needs. Psychologists also agree to the "extraordinary sense of release" (49) which one feels when an archetypal situation occurs. At such moments "[we] are no longer individuals, but the race since the voice of all mankind resounds in us" (49). Similar archetypal situations or characters (considered universal) are portrayed in literary works:

> Whoever speaks in primordial images speaks with thousand voices; he enthrals and overpowers, while at the same time he lifts the idea he is seeking to express out of the occasional and the transitory into the realm of the ever-enduring. He transmutes our personal destiny into the destiny of mankind, and evokes in us all those beneficent forces that ever and anon have enabled humanity to find a refuge from every peril and to outlive the longest night. (Marudanayagam 49-50)

The political turmoil is transcended and assimilated into the racial heritage as myth and legend. The various myths prevalent among the people of Kanthapura help to "direct [their] emotions, mobilize [their] will, [and] give purpose to all that [they] are and do and make" (Righter 10). The political battle described is reminiscent of the eternal battle between good and evil which is a part of the Indian thought and continues to live in the collective unconscious of the people as an archetype. The technique of mythicising used is significant:

> The mythicising of facts serves a two-fold purpose in *Kanthapura*. Its narrator is an old illiterate woman, and mingling of myth and fact would be her natural manner of observation and reflection. Thus, it is a device of characterization. Secondly, Raja Rao adheres to the Indian classical tradition by idealising or mythicising the central character.... A myth necessarily deals with an idealised man or a man larger than life and Raja Rao uses the device of mythicising facts in order to give his hero that exalted status. (Mukherjee, *The Twice Born Fiction* 146)

Conventional mythology gets mingled with the contemporary reality in the village. Apart from the religious and agricultural festivals, an air of festivity surrounds much of the political activity described in *Kanthapura*. While the festival of lights ends with the people being arrested, the ceremony of ploughing ends with the news of Moorthy's return from jail. People gather at the temple and make offerings on every occasion, political or religious. The temple becomes the centre of their activities. The action culminates in the Satyanarayan puja and procession described at the end of the novel. Gradually the words "Satyanarayan Maharaj ki jai!" (169) are replaced with "Vande Mataram!" (169). Another instance where politics and religion mingle is the reference to the Gauri's night:

> ...when lights come floating down the Rampur Corner, lights come floating down from Rampur and Maddur and Tippur, lights lit on the betel leaves, and with flowers and kumkum and song we let them go, and they will go down the Ghats to the morning of the sea, the lights on the betel leaves, and the Mahatma will gather it all, he will gather it by the sea, and he will bless us. (182)

Durgapuja or Navaratri (The Festival of Nine Nights) is also a festival celebrated in India. It is held in honour of goddess Durga who is the personification of "Shakti" and goes on for nine days symbolizing the fight against the demon Mahishasur (beginning on the first day until he is defeated on the ninth). The festival is an enactment of the myth of Mahishasur who was given a boon of not being killed by a man. He conquers the world and sets out to conquer the heaven, but is killed by goddess Durga. The tenth day is celebrated as Dussera signifying the victory of Rama over Ravana. The nine days are for the worship of goddess Durga (the goddess of Strength on the ninth day), goddess Lakshmi (the goddess of Prosperity on the eighth day) and goddess Saraswati (the goddess of Learning on the seventh day). goddess Durga is worshipped in the form of Mahishasur Mardini. People visit temples, exchange gifts, and perform arati. The air fills with the sound of drums, cymbals and bells. Houses have a display of *kolu*—a decorated platform covered with dolls and clay figurines representing the gods and goddesses. Mahishasur represents the forces of evil and the fight is the archetypal struggle between good and evil, that of light overcoming darkness. Goddess Durga is the female deity representing power. This festival, which is a part of the Indian culture, is referred to by R.K. Narayan in *The Dark Room*. Malgudi serves as the setting. Chapter four mentions the preparations for the Navaratri festival in the Ramani household. The south Indian kolu which is an important part of the Navaratri ceremonies is described at length. At the opening Savitri (the heroine) is depicted as an orthodox woman. The festival indicates the passage of time to her. The sight of the dolls makes Savitri nostalgic. The streets ring with the cries of hawkers selling dolls. These are the earliest intimations of the coming Navaratri festival. To the children it is a time of excitement and happiness, as they look forward to buying new dolls. The dolls are brought out a day before the festival, arranged, and displayed:

> There they were—dolls, images, and toys of all colours, sizes, and shapes; soldiers, guards, and fat merchants; birds, beasts, and toys; gods and demons; fruits and cooking utensils; everything of clay, metal, wood, and cloth. (33)

The festival becomes "an agreeable change" (32) from the monotony of everyday routine. The atmosphere is filled with fun and playfulness. Savitri is presented here as a Sita figure in contrast to her later rebellious nature. Through the various incidents during this festival the novelist hints at the later happenings in Savitri's life. The broken elephant (one of a pair of the dolls) symbolizes the later separation of Ramani and Savitri (though only for a brief period). The Navaratri celebrations end in a quarrel, with Savitri retreating to her dark room. Significantly at the very beginning of the preparations for the festival she is reminded of "a particular Navaratri which was completely ruined because she and her sister had scratched each other's faces and were not on speaking terms" (34-35). Through the sibling rivalry (between Babu and Kamala) described an implicit reference to the patriarchal set-up is made. This is also seen in Ramani's words, "'Who asked you to go near the dolls' business? Are you a girl? Tell me, are you a girl?'" (47). Babu takes charge during Ramani's absence. He makes the platform for the display of the dolls. Towards the end of the chapter Janamma too points this out when she says, "You should either let your words out or feel that everything your husband does is right.... What he does is right. It is a wife's duty to feel so" (59). Conditioned by a similar society, Janamma's words make Savitri feel foolish at the thought of her own resentment, and she emerges out of the dark room (only to return to it later). The description of the making of the platform and the fixing of bulbs indicate it to be a man's job. The dolls which are kept for nine days create "a fantastic world" (39):

> ...a world inhabited by all God's creations that the human mind had counted; creatures in all gay colours and absurd proportions and grotesque companies.... Here and there out of the company of animals and vegetables and mortals emerged the gods.... Mortals and immortals, animals and vegetables, gods and sly foxes, acrobats and bears, warriors and cooking utensils, were all the same here, in this fantastic universe conjured out of coloured paper, wood, and doll-maker's clay. (39-40)

The serenity of the gods who are unaffected by the company about them is in contrast to the quarrels which rock the Ramani household. There is a repeated reference to "fights" in this part which finally culminates in the Ramani-Savitri encounter. Apart from the decorations and festoons, Babu (with the help of his friend) fixes coloured bulbs (indicating the changes Malgudi has undergone) to make their kolu look unique. Friends and neighbours are invited to celebrate the festival. The atmosphere becomes dim and gloomy as the lights go out, and with the arrival of Ramani it becomes tense. The happenings throw light on the husband-wife relationship around which the novel revolves. A submissive Savitri does not respond to her husband's cynical remarks. She is unable to put up a fight against her husband, though she glares at her husband and feels "faint with anger" (48). She finally bursts out crying. Submissiveness pleases Ramani and restores the situation to normalcy, while Savitri helplessly looks on. Though Savitri makes a feeble attempt to save her son from Ramani's anger, Ramani brushes aside the incident as a "sentimental show" (48) and "stage-show" (48). The dissension of domestic harmony at the time of the festival prefigures the later separation of Ramani and Savitri, when Savitri does not merely sulk in the dark room and refuse to come out, but leaves her house and embarks on her own. Like his father, Babu too is nurtured by the patriarchal society. His words reveal this. Ramani's and Savitri's behaviour at the festival throws light on their character as well as relationship. Prefiguring his later attitude (towards Savitri's leaving the house) Ramani decides to ignore his wife's absence—"He was going to show her that sulking would not pay. He demonstrated his calm indifference by humming a little song, whistling loudly, and by talking to his daughters..." (53). He is bent on making her realize that she is not indispensable. Life continues to be normal for him, while the children suffer in silence. The festival turns out to be an utter fiasco. It prepares the readers for the later break up in the family which also evokes a similar response from Ramani. The chapter ends with Janamma bringing things to normalcy. It is ironic that in spite of all the shouting and sulking Savitri says, "'There is no quarrel. I never uttered a single word'" (59). As at the end of the novel here too it is the thought of spoiling the happiness of her children which makes Savitri return and restore normalcy. This temporary withdrawal from the household chores is repeated in the novel. Ramani himself declares that the final leaving is "a different version of the sulking in the dark room" (142). Navaratri is a festival celebrated to obtain perpetual happiness and prosperity, but the happenings in the novel turn out to be an inauspicious one. Goddess Durga who is worshipped during this festival is a representation of Shakti, a source of life and energy. Those in distress turn towards the goddess to inspire courage for the struggle against the forces of evil. But Savitri is a docile woman and not a representation of Shakti. She does not even put up a real fight but protests silently. This only results in the restoration of routine life. Savitri's return shows R.K. Narayan's "unflinchingly traditional outlook" (Mukherjee, *Considerations* 81). R.K. Narayan here (and at the end when Savitri leaves her family) operates within a framework of traditional Hindu society. Through the episode the plight of the traditional Hindu wife in Indian society is brought out. The description of the festival is not merely informative but serves the purpose of advancing the plot. The novelist's attempt is not to present a Sita image through the heroine but to focus on the tradition-bound society in which any attempt to go against the prevailing social tradition and customs is impossible. His female characters range from the docile, suffering, and helpless Savitri to the dominating ones like Bharati (*Waiting for the Mahatma*) and Daisy (*The Painter of Signs*). It is able to trace the transformation in his portrayal of female characters. While Savitri's silent suffering is broken by a temporary rebellion, Bharati and Daisy have a will of their own thus reducing their counterparts to a passive role. The various religious taboos and practices have a tremendous influence on the orthodox women. In R.K. Narayan's Malgudi, women are steeped in blind beliefs and superstitions. Rituals and ceremonies form a part of their life. They propitiate the gods, observe festivals and holidays while the men join them in their observances (though some male characters like Ramani and Krishna do not show any interest). The women who feel frustrated (either because of marital disharmony or loneliness in life) often indulge in social or religious activities and try to submerge their unhappiness and dissatisfaction in religious activities. It may not be a conscious effort on their part to sublimate their frustration in personal life. In the orthodox set-up Savitri (unable to cut off her links with her family) has no other alternative but to return to her husband and children. A woman with liberated views, who fights against her husband's injustice, cannot carry on her struggle in a society like that of Malgudi. *The Dark Room* makes an attempt to break away from the mythological image of Indian women. The women in some of R.K. Narayan's novels dare to be different in a traditional patriarchal society. Though Savitri's rebellion against the callousness of her husband awakens her from a soporific state, she is not able to put up a real fight. The break from the ordinary domestic world only shows how difficult revolt is for an Indian woman haunted by the Sita image that rules the society as well as her own psyche. As Meenakshi Mukherjee observes, "[n]othing could be more provincial and localized than the life of Malgudi town, yet R.K. Narayan successfully achieves a universal vision through it" (*The Twice Born Fiction* 25). Savitri's return at the end of the novel, like her sulking during the Navaratri festival, does not have any effect. Her name recalls the archetypal constant wife of the Hindu legend. However, Savitri in *The Dark Room* is timid, weak, and vacillating. She is an ironic counterpart to the legendary Savitri and merely gives vent to her feelings by making fiery speeches.

The reason for performing a rite is the desire for a particular fruit or effect. Divine powers are also attributed to Nature. The power of the elemental forces of Nature is considered uncontrollable. Because of the uncertainties and risks involved in the works of agricultural production, the deities of Nature are usually propitiated. Various ceremonies are performed by the agricultural community—like the ceremonial furrowing, ceremonial planting, and invocation of the Rain God—as it is believed to ensure a good harvest. Rain drops are believed to impregnate the earth, as a result of which life comes on it. Worshipping the forces of nature is a part of many religions since ancient times. People believe in the influence of these forces and hence propitiate them to prevent any harm. The divinity is considered an embodiment of the earth or the corn. They see in Nature the manifestation of God and worship those forces of Nature whose favourable disposition is indispensable for their survival. People in agricultural communities worship the Rain God. In *Nectar in a Sieve* the farmers accept the vagaries of Nature as a part of their life. In contrast to the picture of plenty when they have abundant rains, Rukmani recollects a year when the rains had failed and they had made offerings to placate the Rain God:

> That year the rains failed. A week went by, two. We stared at the cruel sky, calm, blue, indifferent to our need. We threw ourselves on the earth and we prayed. I

> took a pumpkin and a few grains of rice of my Goddess, and I wept at her feet. (72)

Their lives being closely linked to Nature the villagers worship its various forces. Their simple faith does not fade even when the gods in whom they repose their faith remain unmoved by their prayers. Reeling under the year's dry spell, the hapless villagers (be it in *Nectar in a Sieve* or *Gauri*) leave no stone unturned to propitiate the Rain God. Offerings and sacrifices are made and the ceremony becomes a social event after which the villagers return home in the belief that rain will soon fall. The agricultural activities are delayed due to the irregular rainfall. In Raja Rao's *Kanthapura* a commonplace yearly event like the coming of rains in Vaisakh is described in highly poetic terms, so that it seems something uncommon and unfamiliar. An evocative description of the first rain is given. The importance of water in the life of the villagers is emphasized at the beginning of *Nectar in a Sieve* when Nathan and Rukmani name their first daughter Irawaddy—"We called our daughter Irawaddy, after one of the great rivers of Asia, for of all things water was most precious to us..." (15). Mulk Raj Anand's *Gauri* too refers to the invoking of the Rain God, Indra, by Panchi and his wife:

> ...he [Panchi] began to perform some rites to invoke the Rain God, Indra, which his mother used to carry out, with Gauri as an assistant, on the riverside, offering coconut and milk to the deity, at the dawn of everyday, which was supposed to be the propitious hour.... (68)

Even when prayers fail to bring the desired result the villagers continue to believe in the powers of the gods and goddesses. These instances bring out the plight of the farmers whose lives are dependent on Nature. The absence of rains aggravates their poverty and makes life miserable. In such moments the villagers (as in *Gauri*) resort to various superstitious beliefs prevalent among them. Panchi even starts blaming Gauri as inauspicious in spite of his disbelief in such superstitions. The drought worsens the situation. The Kodavas in *The Scent of Pepper* too face periods of drought. Due to their superstitious beliefs, the people attribute it to the disregard of custom by the Kaleyanda family (they carry out Appachu's last rites). The drought is regarded as a curse of the ancestors, and when it rains the villagers consider it a proof that the ancestors had forgiven the Barrister and the Kaleyanda family. The novel also refers to their belief that the spirits of the best among the Kodavas reside in the clouds. If happy with their progeny, the spirits bless them with plentiful rain. The gradual change which engulfs the clan is indicated at the end, in their adoption of the artificial irrigation system:

> The ancestors had given up on the super-smart, English-speaking, the sophisticated mediocrity that was now the Kodava race; the clouds could no longer be relied upon to bring rain, so it was practical to supplement rainwater by artificial means. (252)

The various festivals mentioned show the importance of ancestor worship in their life. R.K. Narayan refers to the practice of placating the Rain God in *The Guide*. The ritual fasting which Raju undertakes (because of the drought in the village of Mangala) creates a festival like atmosphere in Malgudi. The novel revolves around Raju who is in turn a vendor, a tourist guide, an adulterer, a manager, a swindler, a jail bird, and an ascetic. It traces the hero's growth from a tourist guide to a spiritual guru (to the ignorant and superstitious villagers of Mangala). Here fasting is undertaken to propitiate the Rain God. Raju, the trickster figure, falls a victim to the personal identification and is "caught in the coils of his own self-deception" (Iyengar 378). The gullible villagers soon crowd around the fake swami. It is ironic that the fasting thrust upon the hero ultimately leads to his spiritual transformation. The forced sainthood ultimately transcends his control and obliterates his former self. When drought strikes the land the villagers turn to their "swami" for help and consider him as their saviour. The life of the villagers who depend on agriculture for their livelihood is affected due to the failure of monsoon. The situation in Mysore offered the novelist a setting to the story:

> A severe drought had dried up all the rivers and tanks; Krishnaraja Sagar, an enormous reservoir feeding

> channels that irrigated thousands of acres, had also become dry.... As a desperate measure, the municipal council organized a prayer for rains. A group of Brahmins stood knee-deep in water (procured at great cost) on the dry bed of Kaveri, fasted, prayed, and chanted certain mantras continuously for eleven days. On the twelfth day it rained, and brought relief to the countryside. (*My Days* 167)

In Mangala, crops are scorched, seedlings destroyed, and the water level in the river falls. The earth becomes dry and cracks appear. Quarrels break out in the village. Raju tries to escape the situation only to be dragged further into it. He undertakes the fast (not due to a genuine concern for the welfare of the villagers) because of the fear that a disturbance might attract public notice to the village. Raju is forced to get involved in the villagers' life and activities. Finding himself cast into the role of an ascetic, "he attempts to perform the act with gusto partly for the sake of self-preservation, and partly because it suits his personality wonderfully" (Mukherjee, *The Twice Born Fiction* 123). Velan gives Raju a clear account of what a saviour was expected to do:

> [He has to] stand in knee-deep water, look to the skies and utter the prayer lines for two weeks, completely fasting during the period—and lo, the rains would come down, provided the man who performed it was a pure soul, was a great soul. (109)

It exposes the ignorance and simplicity of the villagers. Sacrifices are carried out to gain God's favour. This is depicted in a number of literary works:

> An archetypal situation encountered in many novels is a sacrifice done in order to gain divine favour, for example fasting unto death to end a drought as in *The Guide*, or the fasting of Moorthy in *Kanthapura* for the purification of self.... (Mukherjee 137)

The drought affected Mangala is suddenly transformed. People start coming from all directions, and all facilities from tea-stalls to efficient postal system are made available. Film shows, music and gambling booths, pedlars and press reporters appear in the area. Raju's fasting brings the villagers together. It is ironic that Raju undertakes the fourteen day fast reluctantly to avoid publicity. He stands in knee-deep water in the artificial basin made for the purpose. Flowers and festoons are hung and the whole atmosphere is transformed as people light lamps and decorate the floor with patterns in coloured flour. The various festivals like Dussera, Deepavali, harvest or the Tamil New Year help Raju to keep count of time. The "collective faith" (Mukherjee 128) of the villagers compel Raju to be true for once to his public image and he makes an earnest effort at fasting, finally succumbing to the role Velan has destined for him:

> He [Raju] felt moved by the recollection of the big crowd of women and children touching his feet. He felt moved by the thought of their gratitude. (111)
>
> He [Raju] would not like to cheat them altogether about the fast if he could help it. (111)

The collective force of the traditional orthodox society as well as the co-operation of the people in times of crisis is seen in *The Guide*. It gradually transforms Raju:

> [The incident transforms Raju] from what he really is, into a worthy object of...devotion. Towards the end Raju loses the feeling of an actor performing an act; the act becomes the reality, the mask becomes the man, and Raju the guide turns into a guru. (Mukherjee 128)

Though on the last day of fasting he says, "Velan it's raining in the hills" (247), one wonders whether his fasting brings the rain or not. The incident does transform Raju and bring about his redemption. Water is a time-honoured symbol of purification and regeneration in the Indian context. The rain symbolizes his spiritual regeneration. Though Raju does not undertake the fast to purify himself (as Moorthy does in *Kanthapura*), it brings about his inner transformation. The fasting undertaken marks the transformation of the former tourist guide and prisoner. Fasting is a symbol of sacrifice and detachment from worldliness. The concept is inherent to many of the religions in the world. Fasting or abstaining from food is often undertaken for religious purposes. It may be done with the purpose of expressing one's reverence towards God and to seek His blessing. Refraining from eating is also symbolic of controlling one's desires and thereby bringing peace of mind and happiness. R.K. Narayan creates humour by exposing the absurdity of human situations. The way sainthood is forced upon Raju is in itself comic. Raju accepts the role thrust on him as it provides him a supply of food. Ironically, taking him to be on a fast, the villagers stop bringing food and Raju is forced to starve. The narrative shifts between the past and the present, and with his undertaking the fast the action focuses on Raju's transformation.

Various ceremonies are performed before harvesting the crop. When the crops are ready for harvesting, the cultivators offer prayers and the first-fruit to their deity. The deity is thus thanked for ripening the crops and making it fit for the food of man. This is mentioned in *Nectar in a Sieve*, *Gauri*, and *Kanthapura*. Offering of the first-fruit is an important part of agricultural ceremonies. The sacrament of the first-fruit is accompanied by a presentation of them to the gods:

> The mere fact of offering the first-fruits to the gods or spirits comes now to be thought a sufficient preparation for eating the new corn; the higher powers having received their share, man is free to enjoy the rest...they are regarded no longer as themselves instinct with divine life, but merely as a gift bestowed by the gods upon man, who is bound to express his gratitude and homage to his divine benefactors by returning to them a portion of their bounty. (Frazer 640-41)

The people of Kanthapura vow to offer their local deity the first-fruits:

> O Kenchamma! Protect us always like this through famine and disease, death and despair. O most high and bounteous! We shall offer you our...first fruit, and we shall offer you saris and bodice-cloth for every birth and marriage.... (9)

Agricultural rites are based on the primitive conception of the identity of earth and woman. They are usually sexual in character (as fertility rites)—the identification of the sky as the male moistening and fertilizing the female, earth. The idea is based on the primitive notion of the supposed identical relation between the fruit bearing earth and the child bearing woman. Mother Earth is the life giver, supporter, sustainer and source of life. The ceremonial practices referred to in *Kanthapura* are reminiscent of this. The ceremonial sowing of seeds found in *Nectar in a Sieve* and *Kanthapura* contain references to the sexual imagery seen in agricultural practices:

> As soon as the rains were over, and the cracks in the earth had healed, and the land was moist and ready, we took our seed to our goddess and placed it at her feet to receive her blessing, then we bore it away and made our sowing. (Markandaya 79)

After the initial ceremonies are performed at the ploughing ceremony in Kanthapura, "the plough cuts the earth and spatters the clods" (117). In *The Golden Bough* Frazer refers to the sexual union at agricultural rites to secure the fertility of the fields. The woman's child bearing power is believed to have a sympathetic effect on the growth of the plant. This helps the land to yield a good harvest. The association of sexual union with agriculture—that sexual act assists the promotion of abundant harvest—is universal. Frazer cites examples in Java, New Guinea, Central America, Greece etc. to support this. The collective agricultural rituals often become a sign of prosperity or greatness of a single person. The land and its people rejoice in the generosity of Mother Earth. They celebrate the plenitude of the harvest and the gifts of Nature. These rites "program groups through changes in the seasons, intensify their ordinary social relationships, and often allay their anxiety about their relations with the environment..." (Moore 119). Social solidarity may be a recognized function of religious rites but the intention of satisfying this functional requirement may not motivate its performance. Even if the efficacy of the rituals for the attainment of their end is not sure, it serves as a cementing force and allays fear. The rational ordering of time is expressed in the calendrical rites. The cyclical movement of death and birth or disappearance and return is found in the vegetative world. The divine activity is usually identified with one or more of the cyclical processes of Nature. As Frazer points out some of the agricultural communities have a general clearance of demons at harvest:

> But, at whatever season of the year it is held, the general expulsion of devils commonly marks the beginning of the new year. For, before entering on a new year, people are anxious to rid themselves of the troubles that have harassed them in the past; hence...in so many communities the beginning of the new year is inaugurated with a solemn and public banishment of evil spirits. (754)

In the Hindu pantheon animals and plants are considered sacred and placed on a high pedestal. Every custom is infused with the spirit of intense devotion. There exists a close tie between the animal and the vegetable world. The annual death and revival of life in autumn and spring found in the vegetative world finds a parallel in the animal world. This symbolizes the supposed death and resurrection of the deity. In the life of the ignorant and superstitious villagers rituals and ceremonies hold an important place. Most of the novels which portray rural life refer to the undiminishing faith of the villagers which carry them through the trials and tribulations of life. Superstitions and age-old customs sway their minds. Bondage to age-old customs takes the extreme form in the general resentment to Moorthy's free mingling with the Pariahs in Kanthapura. Belief in superstitions is also exemplified in the blind practices of the labourers at the Skeffington Coffee Estate. The ploughing of fields at the first rains is an important event in Kanthapura. The forces of orthodoxy and conservatism are strong in this village. During the month of Vaisakh they plough the fields and sow the crops on an auspicious day and time. The local deity Kenchamma presides over the seasonal ploughing. A brahmin priest conducts the agricultural rite. The ceremonies, which reflect the social structure of Kanthapura, are performed and prayers are offered to goddess Kenchamma. The month of Vaisakh marks the beginning of summer. Life goes on smoothly in the village during the time of the harvest, but when crops fail hunger, poverty, and quarrels spring up. Life becomes relentlessly hard on a land that depends on rains. The benevolence of Nature is stressed here. The river Himavathy is described as a living presence. The perfect empathy between man and Nature is seen when the remains of the saint is burnt on the bank of the river. The river pays homage to him by rising and sweeping the bones and ashes away. On the Rohini star the villagers yoke their bulls to the plough. An auspicious day is chosen to bless the ploughs for a grand harvest. The whole village is stirred to activity and the political activities are suspended. The villagers' bathe, wear new clothes, make offerings to the local deity, and pray to the Sun God for a good harvest. Similar ceremonies form an important part of the life of the agricultural community in the country. Their lives being dependent on the various forces of Nature, the farmers make offerings to placate them and ensure a good harvest. The bulls are washed and flowers are tied to their horns. People gather at the temple courtyard. A caste ridden social set-up in which the brahmin priest (Rangappa) occupies a significant place exists in Kanthapura. The goddess is bathed and adorned with flowers. The horn is blown indicating the beginning of the ceremony. The Pariahs, and even those who do not have either plough or bulls, come to participate in the event. The narrator conveys the excitement that fills the air. The sound of the conch, hymns, and temple bells fill the atmosphere. It is only after worshipping the goddess that the bulls are blessed by splashing holy water on them. The yoke is tied to the youngest bulls of Subbe Gowda. The appearance of the eagle, the vehicle of their tutelary deity, is taken as a sign from the goddess. After breaking a coconut and throwing flowers and coloured rice the ploughing begins. The people give nickel coins to the priest. He scatters the holy water in the eight directions. The sexual imagery in the descriptions here is explicit as agricultural rites are often considered fertility rites. The earth is the receptive female principle and the ploughing correspondingly represents the active male principle. The plough through the breaking of the earth, in preparation for the sowing of the seed, unites the two principles. This symbolizes the union of these two outwardly apparent opposites. It is but natural for the narrator (an old woman) to nostalgically remember the festivals she has celebrated in Kanthapura:

> Thus the reference to the rituals of ploughing, of worship and sacrifice, becomes a means of establishing the atmosphere in which the villagers live, as well as a device for concretizing the 'point of view', i.e. delineation of the character of the unsophisticated narrator who can assimilate all facts into a mythical structure, for whom no fact becomes really significant unless it can be identified as part of a myth. (Mukherjee 146-47)

The ploughing is carried out according to the appropriate ritual. It is considered successful when favourable omens are seen. The prayers for proper rains expose their dependence on the vagaries of Nature, and helplessness in the face of natural calamities. For the old narrator, festivals become a means of realizing the passage of time. The poetic descriptions of festivals do not appear as digressions.

The Kodava festivals, and their observance with gaiety and co-operation, also have a larger intention of promoting, establishing, and sustaining the harmonious relationship in the community. The festivals promote harmony and brotherhood in the village. Highlighting the Kodava culture, *The Scent of Pepper* refers to festivals like Sankramana and Puthari that are a part of the Kodava life. The novelist does not describe the festivals in detail. Baliyanna describes the festival of Sankramana to Clara. It is a festival held in the month of Tula that signals the end of the monsoons. The reference to the festival also highlights the East-West dichotomy. The difference in the eastern and western sensibility gets revealed. Festivals are an occasion to rejoice in different parts of the world. This is true of Coorg too. Preparations for the festival of Puthari begin early among the Kodavas. There is much activity during the period. After the festival, paddy is sold and coffee picking begins. For them it is "the best time of the year" (107). The festivals also indicate the passage of time. It is during a Puthari that Boju tries to win Chinni and later on it is on a night before Puthari that Baliyanna dies—"It was the month after Puthari; the Kaliyanda family did not celebrate the festival that year" (185). Hence that year coffee picking is not preceded by any celebration. For Boju the festival becomes an occasion for showing his valour and impressing Chinni whom he loved. The festival is celebrated with liquor, crackers, dance, feasting, and village sports:

> On Puthari night, the first sheaves of paddy were cut to the cries of 'Poli, Poli Poli Deva...!' ...When the sheaves were tied to doors and bed-posts, food and drink offered to the ancestors [showing their belief in ancestor worship] and crackers burst in the front yard, the men quenched their thirst with toddy. (108)

On the auspicious night of the full moon, when the crop is ripe the Kodavas cut the first ripe sheaves of paddy and tie them to the doors and bedposts. They enjoy themselves during this agricultural festival. Another festival celebrated among the Kodavas is the Kailpodh. Various preparations are made for the festival. A feast is held and the photographs of ancestors and icons of the gods are worshipped. After the guns are worshipped, food is offered to the deities. Various sports like *pariakali* (during Puthari) are held during the Kodava festivals. A gun sport is held, during Kailpodh, in which the young show off their skills while the old look on. The festival marks Subbu's transition into the role of a household elder after his return from the army. Nanji realizes her growing age, as Subbu does during the later years. Without a reference to the festivals of the Kodavas Kavery Nambisan's novel would have been only a partial account of their life. The work is not a mere anthropological study of the race. The novelist has combined her narration of the customs and rituals with the different facets of Kodava life. The description of the Kodavas, the Kaleyanda family, the East-West relationship, the customs etc. familiarize one with the life in Coorg. A number of words (which are italicized) from the Kodava life are incorporated into it. All these contribute towards the depiction of their life and culture.

Most of the villages in India have their own local deities. These village goddesses are believed to look after the needs of a particular domain (like goddess Kenchamma in Kanthapura and the Kaleyanda belief in Lord Igguthappa who protects their clan). The religious minded and superstitious people of the villages have a strong faith in the local deity who is different from gods like Shiva and Vishnu who are concerned with larger issues. The village deities, like Kenchamma and Talasamma, are regarded as a more present help in trouble, and are more intimately concerned with the happiness and prosperity of the villagers. Being deeply religious, the villagers of Kanthapura have full faith in goddess Kenchamma, the presiding deity of the village. Like the puranic gods, Kenchamma too has her jurisdiction within which she operates. When cholera breaks out Ramappa and Subbanna die because "they got it in town and [the] goddess could do nothing. She is the goddess of Kanthapura, not of Talassana. They ought to have stayed in Talassana and gone to goddess Talassanamma to offer their prayers" (8-9). The people have a strong faith in the goddess's powers and look up to her in their hour of need. The novel describes at length the villagers' faith in their goddess:

> Kenchamma is our goddess. Great and bounteous is she. She killed a demon ages, ages ago, a demon that had come to ask our young sons as food and our young women as wives. Kenchamma came from the Heavens—it was the sage Tripura who had made penances to bring her down—and she waged such a battle and she fought so many a night that the blood soaked and soaked into the earth, and that is why the Kenchamma Hill is all red. (8)

The goddess colours every aspect of their life:

> [The] momentous battle becomes imbedded in the racial unconscious, providing an illuminating and clarifying focal point for every historical experience felt by the community. The villagers seek the aid of this munificent deity in all their trials and tribulations. (Rao, *The Fiction of Raja Rao* 51)

The villagers try to placate the goddess by making offerings of saris, gold trinkets, rice, flowers, fruits, sugar candy, and perfumed sweetmeats. They make vows to walk the holy fire. These are carried out either as a penance or as a way of thanking the goddess for her blessings. The people dance, sing, prostrate before the goddess, ring the temple bells, blow the conch and light camphor before her idol, be it a social or political occasion. This expresses their ardent faith in her. As M.K. Naik observes, "Kenchamma, indeed, represents an ubiquitous phenomenon—the Grama-devata (deity of the village) indispensable to a south Indian village" (Rao 66). The village deity is regarded as a more present help in trouble and more intimately concerned with the happiness and prosperity of the villagers. These gods, mostly feminine, are depicted as not related to the great world forces but to simple facts as cholera, small pox, and other sicknesses. According to the villagers in Kanthapura, Kenchamma saves them when there is cholera or small pox. The superstitious people make vows and offerings to please the goddess, who never fails them, and defend their own faith in her whenever she fails them (as when the old and those in town die due to cholera). Offerings are made to appease the deity and ward off curses. They even refuse to take medicine during sickness and many die due to this. To the people of Kanthapura, Kenchamma and Himavathy are living forces, capable of miracles, who actively participate in the destiny of the villagers. Their belief in Kenchamma saves them from injuries during the political struggle. Ratna, and the other villagers prostrate before the gods in the sanctum and vow to make offerings if Moorthy is released from jail thus merging the social and the political aspects of life in Kanthapura. Their firm belief in the goddess is depicted at the very opening of the novel:

> Thank heaven, not only did she slay the demon, but she even settled down among us [the people of Kanthapura], and...never has failed us in our grief. If rains come not [Kenchamma is also their agricultural goddess as evident from the ploughing ceremonies depicted in the novel], you fall at her feet and say 'Kenchamma, goddess, you are not kind to us. Our fields are full of younglings and you have given us no water. Tell us, Kenchamma, why do you seek to make our stomachs burn?' And Kenchamma...opens her eyes...and smiles on you.... (8)

Rains fall that very night strengthening their belief in the local deity's power. Kenchamma is their agricultural goddess as well as goddess of sickness. The goddess is prayed to during agricultural ceremonies in the village. The description of the ploughing ceremony throws light on their devotion:

> 'There, there the goddess is going to show her face,' and they [the villagers] tremble and press against each other, and when the legs itch they do not scratch, when the waters drip they do not shake, and then suddenly the curtain is drawn, and Mother Kenchamma is there straight, bright and benign, and the candelabras weave their lights around her,...the priest...lights the camphor and lifts it up to her jewelled face...and then flowers quietly roll down her face, and they all say, 'There, she has sent us her blessing. Oh, Kenchamma, give us a fine harvest and no sickness, Kenchamma, Kenchamma, goddess,' and even the bulls stand without waving their tails. (116)

The farmers send their prayers to the goddess for a good weather after they have ploughed, manured, and sowed. All the activities of their life are thus watched over by the deity. At the centre of the village (indicating the significance of the local deity) is a temple dedicated to the goddess, and this Kanthapurishwari's temple becomes the centre of their life. Even the people of the Skeffington Coffee Estate pray to goddess Kenchamma who sanctifies the neighbouring region. Marriage, sickness, death, plague, funeral, harvesting, arrests, release are all watched over by the goddess. Various offerings are made to thank the goddess who has blessed them with bounty, and also to propitiate her. Life in Kanthapura, as in most Indian villages, is rooted in customs, superstitions and rituals. The novel creates a *sthalapurana* (a legendary history to a specific locality). The entrenched orthodoxy and extreme conservatism prevalent in Kanthapura are seen in the evocative description of the village. The description of such a village will not "ring authentic unless the village life, with its tradition and superstition, its ritual and custom, is befittingly evoked" (Rao 118-19). Starting from an invocation to goddess Kenchamma to the end of the novel, religion sustains the spirit of the people of Kanthapura. The Kenchamma legend is used as a choric refrain to ritualize the pattern of events affecting the lives of the villagers. The novelist here tries to create a style which reflects the sensibility of the Indian psyche. The narrator being a garrulous old woman, it is natural for her to describe at length the various festivals and ceremonies she has witnessed during her life in the village. The novel is made up of the stream of her memory in which many events and characters have been blurred by the passage of time and others have been heightened by her imagination. The lengthy account of the Karthik festival and the coming of rains in Vaisakh, along with the conversational style add to the effect of the festivals mentioned in it. Many of the Indian words like *arati*, *puja*, *kumkum, tirtham* are italicized in the novel. The language used here in the description of festivals and ceremonies is different from the lingo of the ordinary folk.

Apart from agricultural festivals and the ceremonies related to them, creative works also contain reference to ceremonies like the fire-walking ceremony that are performed by the people in the country. *A Handful of Rice* refers to the fire-walkers who arrive soon after the festival of Deepavali. The novel describes the ceremony which Apu's family attends. The absence of Puttanna (Nalini's brother-in-law) raises suspicion. This is proved true for Puttanna steals Apu's money and leaves. For an eager Jayamma (Apu's wife), who had seen the ceremony a number of times, it is a respite from nursing her husband who is old and sick. The incident throws light on the character of Apu and his wife. While Apu (despite his weakness) seeing his wife's eagerness decides to go, Jayamma is irritated to have him attached "like a drag-weight to her" (167). Their reaction to the ceremony reveals this difference in temperament:

> He [Apu] had always done so [accompanied Jayamma silently], every single time, distrusting the extreme reactions of his wife which to the others passed for natural excitement, but which made him afraid for her

> safety, as if she might somehow come to harm through her emotions. (166)

A different attitude is found in Jayamma:

> Why did he [Apu] have to come, she thought with mounting irritation. In his condition the only sane thing was to stay at home.... She would not altogether withdraw from his side, but she stiffened her arm resentfully each time he reached for her. Apu was aware of the grudging help she gave him, but he said nothing.... (167)

A crowd gathers at the scene where a bed of coal had been laid for the fire-walkers. Apu is preoccupied with the thoughts of life and death. The acrid smell of burning reminds him of funeral pyres. The sound of drums and chanting fill the air. Jayamma's eyes reflect the "fire". The fire-walkers invoke the god and walk over the glowing fire-bed. Ravi does not show much interest in the fire-walking ceremony though he is moved seeing the ordinary people touched by the power of God. The religious frenzy Jayamma displays at the sight of the fire-walkers is not totally based on her faith but has something to do with the unsatisfactory relationship with her husband which culminates in her sexual relationship with Ravi. These ceremonies create a festive air and provide moments of respite from work. After the celebrations the family returns to its normal life. The novel also refers to a procession (the crosses held by the people in the procession indicate it to be a Christian festival) which the family watches from Ravi's little retreat. The intrusion of people (his family members) into his retreat on the terrace signifies the burden and problems that intrude Ravi's life after Apu's death. The fall and the ascension depicted (which refers to the divine cycle) turn Ravi nostalgic and remind him of a similar festival in his own village. He is "suddenly seized by a ravening desire to follow" (106) the procession, an interest he does not show during the fire-walking ceremony. Apart from the use of Indian words like kumkum and colam Kamala Markandaya explains the superstitions, rituals and traditions by way of authorial intrusion, or glossary. Most of the descriptions of marriages, festivals and other customs in Kamala Markandaya's novels serve to highlight her favourite themes.

Apart from the agricultural and other festivals celebrated annually, each temple has its own particular feast recurring at intervals during the course of the year. Feasts are held and festival days are given up to rejoicing. These festivals, which usually take place at fixed periods, are also referred to in literary works. A similar festival is found in *The Man-Eater of Malgudi* and *Samskara*. R.K. Narayan's novel revolves around Vasu, a taxidermist who enters the well-ordered life of Malgudi like a maelstrom disturbing its tranquility. His demonic activities culminate in his decision to kill the temple elephant. R.K. Narayan's characters are rooted in the local customs and traditions of Malgudi. His themes, characters, and dialogues carry the atmosphere of the south Indian society and present a traditional set-up. He refers to the various temples in Malgudi, like the Saraswati temple in *The Guide*, the small newly-constructed Srinivas temple in *The English Teacher*, and the Krishna Temple in *The Man-Eater of Malgudi*. The festival described in *The Man-Eater of Malgudi* fills the small town with excitement. The archetypal struggle between the forces of good (Nataraj) and that of evil (Vasu, the embodiment of evil) is perceivable here. The puranic mythical pattern is suggestively used and has ironic implications. The novel is a reworking of the ancient Hindu myth of Bhasmasura—the demon who was granted a boon by Shiva of reducing to ashes anyone he touched on the head, while nothing could destroy him. He is finally killed by Lord Vishnu (in the form of Mohini). She (Mohini) promises to yield to him only if he imitated all the gestures and movements of her own dancing. Bhasmasura is tricked into touching himself to death. A mythical dimension is kept alive throughout the plot. This opposition between good and evil, *sura* (good) and *asura* (demon), is an undercurrent theme in Hindu mythology. The novel illustrates a modern version of the Bhasmasura myth about the self-destruction of evil. An old myth is applied to a contemporary situation and finds a parallel in the modern story. R.K. Narayan "follows the familiar pattern of a tale from the Puranas where a demon gets too powerful, threatens the heavens with his elemental forces of disorder, but finally goes up in the air like a bubble in the sea, leaving the universe as calm as before" (Mukherjee 153). An explicit reference to the myth is found in the novel when Sastri an orthodox-minded semi-scholar puts forward the didactic point that "'[e]very rakshasa gets swollen with his ego. He thinks he is invincible, beyond every law. But sooner or later something or other will destroy him'" (76). Vasu accidentally kills himself while trying to kill a mosquito. Sastri cites the examples of Ravana, Mahisha, Daksha, and Bhasmasura to bring home his point:

> Every demon appears in the world with a special boon of indestructibility. Yet the universe has survived all the rakshasas that were ever born. Every demon carries within him, unknown to himself, a tiny seed of self-destruction, and goes up in thin air at the most unexpected moment. (185)

In the wake of Vasu's demonic activities the orthodox people of Malgudi tend to understand their situation in terms of myths and use them to validate or condemn their predicament (as in *Kanthapura*). Through an adaptation of the puranic story, R.K. Narayan presents an archetypal situation emerging from the collective unconscious of humanity. The Mohini-Bhasmasura episode is adopted as a structural parallel throughout the novel. Vasu the rakshasa is opposed to the benign aspect of life as represented by the festival where thousands of men, women and children reaffirm the positive values of life through their celebrations. It is significant that Vasu does not participate in the celebrations, but tries to kill the temple elephant. He interferes with the temple festival and hampers its celebration. He does not have the slightest intention of being answerable to anyone for the money collected in his self-appointed capacity of a treasurer of the festival accounts. Through Vasu the absurd pretensions of Nataraj and his friends is exposed. Vasu refers to melas as a way to keep the population "within manageable limits" (151), and ironically asks, "'If God is everywhere, why follow Him only in a procession?'" (151). He provides a rational explanation of the event. While the orthodox people of Malgudi consider it a "sacred function" (151) in which the "people are out...to be with their God...." (151), Vasu views it as a sheer waste of national income in a country where many go without food. The novelist mixes satire with gentle humour to present the ridiculous foibles and eccentricities of human nature and to expose the evils of society. The event exposes the hypocrisy of the rice-merchant who donates all the rice needed for the festival on condition that his shop is mentioned in any public speech made during the occasion. The two main centres that attract people are Nataraj's press and the Krishna temple in connection with the temple festival. The struggle between the forces of good and evil culminate in the festival described at the end of the novel. Disorder is at its height and soon after, with Vasu's death, things return to the normal routine. A lengthy description of the spring festival at the Krishna temple is provided in the novel. The festival brings out the unity of the people of Malgudi in the wake of danger. It tries to draw Vasu back into the human fold. The temple idols are decked and carried out in a procession at the festival. The temple is decorated and there are temple dancers, pipers, and drummers. Fireworks are displayed and food is organized for the public. The people come together to witness the festival:

> People I [Nataraj] had never seen in my life acted as a padding to my right and left and fore and aft. I had lived a circumscribed life and had never thought that our town contained such a variety of humanity.... (140)

While the people dressed in colourful clothes enjoy themselves, Vasu's demonic behaviour makes him an intruder in this world. To the villagers an aura of sanctity surrounds the temple elephant which to Vasu is more worth dead. The joy of the festival is marred by Vasu's vicious acts. The people come together to put an end to the asura who, fortunately brings about his own doom. The smell of incense, flowers, and the religious chants fill the atmosphere. The story makes way for its conclusion by bringing the elephant, which heads the procession, to Malgudi to be treated. Though its safety obsesses Nataraj, his passivity and inaction strikes one as odd.

Through Nataraj's firm faith in God R.K. Narayan weaves another Hindu legend into the story—the myth of the elephant Gajendra in mythology who had his leg caught in the jaws of a mighty crocodile and was saved by Lord Vishnu. Nataraj too waits for the elephant (and the people of Malgudi) to be saved from Vasu's atrocities by divine intervention, as Lord Krishna is an incarnation of Lord Vishnu. Evil ultimately destroys itself and the elephant is saved from the *asura*. The novel is an exposition of the novelist's own belief that "...the hold of religion and the conception of the gods ingrained in us must necessarily find a place in any accurate portrayal of life" (Walsh, *R.K. Narayan: A Critical Appreciation* 17). The life in Malgudi is restored to normalcy and the outsider is destroyed. Vasu represents the elemental forces of disorder (*asura*). The festival as a social event serves to reaffirm the integrity of the social group. R.K. Narayan, by using the two myths, states that in the struggle between good and evil, good however passive it be wins ultimately. The festival is like a fantasy full of colour, glitter, crowd, and song. Evil finally destroys itself.

A similar atmosphere of noise and bustle is created by U.R. Anantha Murthy in *Samskara* when he describes the temple festival at Melige. After his flight from the *agrahara* Praneshacharya wanders through a world of fairs and festivals experiencing the world of Naranappa. The transition is thus from an orthodox set-up to one full of excitement and activity at the festival. The new world presents a contrast to the arid and joyless life of the brahmins in the *agrahara*. The festival throws the Acharya into a demonic world (once inhabited by his counterpart) and exposes the conflicting attitudes in him—the tussle between the orthodox life of the brahmins and the unorthodox existence of Naranappa and his friends. This serves to highlight the impoverished life at the *agrahara*. A carnival like atmosphere, in which there is the flouting of authority, inversion of social hierarchies, and profaning what is ordinarily regarded as sacrosanct is presented. A period of indulgence and concentration on the material aspects of life follows. The carnival atmosphere is considered a release for the tensions that build up in any hierarchic, highly structured society (as in *Samskara*). It becomes a way of expressing resentment against authority (as rituals of rebellion) but do not change anything, and in fact strengthen the established social order (Praneshacharya like Naranappa is unable to shed his brahminism). The extravagant, illicit behaviour provides an emotional release. *Samskara* presents the topsy-turvy world of the carnival. Carnival images of food, sex, violence, and a world of fights, blows, confusion, curses and insults is found here. It is a world of energy and youthfulness in which the usual values of normal life are turned upside down. Ironically, Praneshacharya whose very name implies "life" practices a complete denial of life through renunciation, and finds it difficult to be a part of the lively world he encounters in Melige. The life at the festival presents a contrast to the monotonous life of the brahmins. It represents Naranappa's life. The Acharya finds himself involved in a human world of bustle and experience. His journey into the new world enables him to realize the importance of human interdependence. Accompanied by Putta he is exposed to the sordid world of lowcaste people and cock-fights. Praneshacharya is unable to identify himself completely with the demonic world. He realizes the inevitability of shedding his Brahminism to be a part of the "tigerish world of cock-fights" (130-31). The world of passion and pleasure makes him identify himself with Naranappa and Mahabala who had gone against the ways of brahminism. Among the brahmins in the *agrahara* the festivals are celebrated as a part of their routinized living. The opposition between the values of the *agrahara* and that of the libertine surfaces throughout. The festival highlights the two conflicting worlds. The notions of purity and pollution are so deeply and strongly embedded in their minds that Praneshacharya (as well as Naranappa) finds it difficult to escape. The Dionysian world of Naranappa threatens the repressed orderliness of the brahmin *agrahara*. Praneshacharya realizes that for a person like him, Naranappa's freedom is an unattainable ideal. The transformation of the protagonist culminates in the festival scene. Like Naranappa and his friends, Putta is a part of this world and moves with ease in his familiar surroundings. Putta (like Velan in *The Guide*) plays an important role in the hero's transformation. He initiates Praneshacharya into a world of reality (in contrast to the cloistered life at the agrahara) and leads him through the din and bustle of festival and cock-fight (the demonic world at the festival). Putta presents a contrast to the Acharya, and is not plagued by metaphysical dilemma. Even at the festival, the *agrahara* and its problems plague the Acharya's mind. The sight of the beggars' rotting bodies reminds him of the dead body yet to be disposed of. The novelist provides a description of the car-festival at Melige. The chariot is decorated and people make offerings while the priest conducts the rites. A huge crowd turns up to take part in the festival. There are children, balloon sellers, acrobats and people dressed in new clothes. The smell of burning camphor and joss-sticks permeate the air. Putta who is a part of this world enjoys himself while the Acharya feels "like a hovering demon, a rootless object in the hustle and noise" (114). Here the initiate is neither a part of the old world nor the new one. Praneshacharya stands outside the world of ordinary pleasures and observes the gathered crowd. This indicates his separate existence from the carnival like atmosphere. The protagonist is in the liminal phase. He is neither a part of the *agrahara* nor the world of cock-fights—"I am neither here, nor there" (115). Though he is transported to the demonic world of passion and sensation at the temple festival, Praneshacharya is unable to identify himself with it:

> In all [the] bustle and busyness...Praneshacharya walked as one entranced, following Putta. Purposeful eyes everywhere, engaged in things. His eyes, the only disengaged ones incapable of involvement in anything. (115)

The novelist portrays the psychological turmoil faced by the protagonist. Through the Acharya's experiences at the festival the novelist concentrates on his inability to shed his fear as well as brahminism. The spiritual leader becomes conscious that "[h]e would never have the courage to defy brahmin practice as Naranappa did" (116). The cock-fight turns out to be a traumatic experience. For him a total identification with this world is impossible. He may have rejected the brahminic world but cannot accept the demonic—"[I]t became clear that he did'nt have the skills to live in [the] world of sharp and cruel feelings" (117). Gradually the Acharya becomes involved in the life around him. By the time they leave the festival the Acharya (who had tried to get rid of him at first) is filled with a fatherly affection for Putta and longs for his company. At the festival is a world of liquor, greed, and revenge. Praneshacharya finally decides to take on the responsibility of carrying out Naranappa's last rites, and shed his respectability. In a way the Acharya's experience of this demonic world at the festival becomes his new *samskara*.

The change of seasons and festivals mark the progress of time as well as provide occasions for rejoicing. Each creative writer conveys the Indian life in his own inimitable manner. The Indian writer writing in English tries to present a clear and accurate picture of the traditions, customs and beliefs of the Indian people. There are references to Indian festivals and the ceremonies related to them in many of the novels in Indian English. They help in recreating the Indian culture and the Indian sensibility. Words like Karthik, Vaisakh, *kolu*, *arati*, and *puja* are used to conjure up the image of India's rich culture filled with festivals. Their descriptions help to create a local colour. People come together to perform the ceremonies and celebrate the festivals. These periodic celebrations help to refresh the numb spirits of the urban as well as the rural folk. Festivals and the ceremonies associated with them become a means by which the society acts upon its individual members and keeps alive in their minds a certain system of sentiments which contribute towards social cohesion. They facilitate a temporary liberation from the established order. Sometimes these ceremonies tend to get politicized. People cast aside their differences and enthusiastically celebrate the moments of mutual participation and rejoicing. Novelists depict these occasions in numerous ways. The festivals, in life as well as creative works, serve to strengthen social bonds and bring about social solidarity. Be it the rural or the urban life, they play an important role in bringing the people together. Similar customs and practices generate moments of happiness and enjoyment. The myths associated with some of these festivals give them a greater significance in the context in which they are used. The temporary suspension of order during the festivals is followed by the rejuvenation and renewal of life.

6

An Overview

Indian English fiction which struck deep roots in the Indian soil has had inextricable links with the socio-political milieu since its inception. One finds delineated in it the life, customs, practices, religious beliefs, and thus the very Indian ethos of the people living in the country. Religion, being an integral part of the Indian psyche, is a recurring motif in many creative works. It is a fictive world inhabited by the Tamilians of R.K. Narayan, the Kannada people of Raja Rao, the Punjabis of Mulk Raj Anand, and the Bengalis of Bhabani Bhattacharya. The deep rooted values of Indian culture find an echo in literary works. Novelists adopt different approaches to deal with the rituals and practices in Indian society—serious and philosophical in Raja Rao, satirical and cynical in Mulk Raj Anand, humorous and detached in R.K. Narayan. The novelist justifies, defies, or remains a passive chronicler of the life and society. Works like *Samskara*, *Kanthapura*, and *The Bachelor of Arts* reveal a world threaded with religious customs and rituals.

Rituals and ceremonies mark socially important occasions, define beginnings and endings, and social transitions. They influence almost every aspect of man's life and mark the transition in life from one phase to another. The relevance of the various rituals which mark the different phases of human life is seen in the works mentioned here. These rites vary not only from community to community but also on the basis of sex. This is evident in Vaikom Muhammad Basheer's *Childhood Friend* and *The Scent of Pepper*. With the passage of time most of these rituals and ceremonies are often reduced to a mere show of social status and wealth. This is also true of marriage ceremonies. The rituals associated with transition, as well as the transformation of the initiate are depicted in a number of Indian English fiction. The three phases in the rites of passage have been applied to literary works. The archetypal pattern of rejection, initiation, and reintegration is traceable. The transition and change involved in initiation rites are found in the works which deal with the process of initiation. They highlight the importance of these rites and rituals in human life. Most of the novelists concentrate on the transformation the neophyte undergoes, than on the rituals and ceremonies performed. Abhay, Gian Talwar, Subbu, Majid all go through the process of initiation. Only Majid's initiation rites are described in detail. These rites mark the beginning of a new life of responsibility as with Majid and Subbu. The various rites enable a smooth transition from one phase to another. It is possible to see how the various rites in the initial phase of a person's life enable him and the society to accept the change which takes place.

The works here also reveal the readjustment of social structure involved when a marriage takes place. The woman's relation with her family is greatly modified and she enters into a new relation with her husband. It involves a disjunction and conjunction. Novelists point out how the various marriage ceremonies, which "bind" the husband and the wife together, do not always ensure success in marriage. Ira, Uma, Gauri, all fail to make a good marriage in spite of their being married off with all the rituals and ceremonies. Most of the novels stress the importance of love and understanding in marriage. While Maya's (*Cry, the Peacock*) marriage fails, Rukmani and Nathan (*Nectar in a Sieve*) enjoy an ideal marriage. Marriages become an occasion for the people to join and celebrate. The various ceremonies contribute towards bringing the people together and ensuring social solidarity. The hold of astrology on the Indian mind gets full recognition in literary works. This is seen in the custom of consulting the horoscope. The economic considerations, which have become a part of the

Indian marriage, often relegate the rituals (which sanctify the union) to the background. It becomes a mere display of wealth. This aspect of marriage is hinted at in *The Scent of Pepper* and *The Princes*. Novelists like Mulk Raj Anand decry the corrupt rituals and practices in society. Through Majid, Vaikom Muhammad Basheer denounces the custom of dowry. Throwing light on the different forms of marriage in Indian society *Grandmother's Tale* portrays a child marriage, while *The Painter of Signs* depicts the Gandharva form of marriage. These ceremonies are different from those associated with marriage among the Kodavas (*The Scent of Pepper*). A glimpse of the varying customs and beliefs prevalent in India, and their significance in the particular culture, is got through these works. The marriage invitation, procession, music, and feast act as social signals which indicate that a marriage is taking place. The treatment meted out to widows in Indian society too differs from one community to another. Through the portrayal of characters like Ratna (*Kanthapura*) writers point to the necessity of change in the treatment extended to widows. They question the society's orthodoxies and articulate openly their dissent from accepted notions. The social changes in Indian society, the manner in which people respond to them, the encroachment of modernity and the resultant conflict between tradition and modernity are all found in Indian English fiction. Rituals, ceremonies, and practices have a tremendous influence on Indian women. In a traditional and convention bound society like Malgudi various rituals and taboos are clamped on them. It subjugates their position, and fosters a patriarchal set-up.

Rites associated with death ensure a proper disposal of the body, and a good afterlife for the dead. This Indian belief is also expressed in a number of creative works. Most of the social groups in the country perform elaborate death rites. Many of the works in Indian English fiction provide a detailed account (often gruesome as in *Lament*) of the rites associated with death. They reveal the human mind's fear of death, ghosts, and man's preoccupation with immortality. The strength of collective sympathy and communal grief is discernible. The fear of the dead haunting the living looms large in the human mind. This fear is clearly expressed through the brahmins and the outcasts in *Samskara*. Death also involves a readjustment of social roles and relations. The position of the dead is gradually filled by his successor. This is seen in *The English Teacher* and *The Scent of Pepper*. The various death rites help to make smooth the transition involved, and to accept the death that has taken place. The creation of the new is thus preceded by the destruction of the old.

The unity or solidarity of a country or community is strikingly expressed in the celebration of various festivals. The festivals, be it in *Kanthapura*, *Samskara*, *Nectar in a Sieve*, or *The Scent of Pepper*, are occasions of enjoyment and rejuvenation. They provide opportunities for celebration beyond religious barriers. Stress is laid on group solidarity. While Navaratri and Deepavali are celebrated by the people of Malgudi, the Kodavas have their own festivals like Puthari, Sankramana, and Kailpodh. The common pattern of birth-death-rebirth, found in the vegetative world, is also traceable in literary works. Various agricultural festivals mark the seasonal changes in Nature. They indicate the passage of time, as in *The Dark Room*, *The Guide*, or *The Scent of Pepper*. Rituals reveal a dialectic of desire and repugnance—desire for fertility, victory etc. and repugnance to drought, disaster and the like. The sway of rituals, ceremonies, and superstitious practices over the minds of the simple minded people of the villages is also perceptible. An aura of sanctity surrounds almost every activity in the village of Kanthapura. The tempo of Indian life can be created as much by the use of mythical parables, philosophical symbols, and metaphysical ideas as by the use of geographical settings, historical facts, and the evocation of Indian social, cultural, and religious life. Since myths have a universal significance and timelessness, creative writers have found in them a powerful medium for expressing man's subtle feelings or profound thoughts. Myths also have a psychological appeal. This is seen in R.K. Narayan's *Man-Eater of Malgudi*. The psycho-therapeutic value of rituals and myths in Indian culture find ample recognition in the literary works in Indian English.

Creative works often become a medium for exposing the pretentious piety and ignorance of religious practitioners. Novelists like Mulk Raj Anand, R.K. Narayan, and U.R. Anantha Murthy, through the portrayal of rites and rituals, lash out against the exploitation they indulge in. Rituals and ceremonies are often framed by man to suit his selfish ends. By exposing the hypocrisy and pretensions of the practitioners of religion, novelists give voice to the problems which beset common man. *Samskara*, *The Scent of Pepper*, and *Waiting for the Mahatma* reveal this. Sometimes rituals are not collective creations. They are fostered by those classes or strata of people within a society who have the power to define them, or to impose them on the group. Through their works, creative writers denounce and protest against the detrimental and obsolete customs and practices prevalent in Indian society. This helps in bringing about social changes. The rites and ceremonies described in Indian English fiction play a significant role in the life depicted in it. They cannot be overlooked as mere digressions.

Apart from the creative works found in regional languages, which reflect the life and culture of a particular region, those written in Indian English too give one a glimpse of the Indian rituals and beliefs. Diverse rituals and ceremonies are prevalent in Indian society. The ethnic Parsi culture is revealed in Rohinton Mistry. His work concentrates on his Parsi origin and gives expression to his ethnic community's rites and rituals. It portrays the way of life of his community which takes pride in living together, sharing collective memories, and perpetuating the values of its heritage. Works of expatriate writers like Kamala Markandaya and Rohinton Mistry reveal their diasporic consciousness. Through the depiction of different rites novelists also try to bring out the difference between the eastern and western cultures. This is seen in *The Scent of Pepper*, *The Coffer Dams*, and *The Nowhere Man*. In an alien land the native culture and practices sustain people. The rituals and ceremonies portrayed in a literary work even lend the reader an understanding of the life and culture presented therein. While Rohinton Mistry's portrayal of the Parsi life in *Such a Long Journey* gives one an understanding of their culture, Kavery Nambisan's *Scent of Pepper* provides one an insight into the Kodava life, and Vaikom Muhammad Basheer's *Childhood Friend* gives one a glimpse of the Muslim life and culture. The description of life in these works would have been incomplete without a reference to the customs and practices followed by the people inhabiting them. The translations of works, like *Childhood Friend*, in regional languages offer the reader an insight into the practices and ceremonies of different social groups. These works attain a wider audience. It enables the reader to get acquainted with the rituals, practices, and way of life of those living in other parts of the country.

The psychological and sociological relevance of rites and rituals is indisputable. The individual is fundamentally a member of his group, with its complex rules, rituals, and taboos. People feel themselves united to each other by the simple fact that they have a common faith. Rituals and ceremonies help to reaffirm and strengthen social solidarity. They are essential to the maintenance of society as they give collective expression to the sentiments which unite the society. That rituals contribute towards societal integration in the rural as well as the urban atmosphere is seen in their depiction in most of the works. Despite individual differences, the members of a particular society share common beliefs, values, and attitudes which constitute their culture. Both the religious activity and its meaning are shared by the members of a social group (as seen in Kanthapura, or among the Kodavas) by virtue of their acquisition from a shared cultural heritage. The public ceremonies and collective rituals contribute towards social unity and cohesion. By reinforcing human beings psychologically in times of tragedy and crisis, rituals and practices give security and meaning in a world which appears full of unpredictable things. They help one to endure situations of emotional stress by opening up escape routes from such situations, and offering a way out by rituals and beliefs into the domain of the supernatural. The psychological influence of rituals and customs is evident in *Gauri*, *Nectar in a Sieve*, and *The Guide*. While the superstitious beliefs psychologically have an effect on Panchi (Gauri), the villagers in *Nectar in a Sieve*, and *The Guide* resort to ritualistic practices in times of crisis. Rites and rituals provide reassurance, and help the individual to secure psychological stability.

Changes in the structure of societies necessitate change in its customs. The ideals of a receding generation often appear as superstitions and baseless convention to the later ones. The changes in customs and practices are a natural product of the environment. The shared beliefs and values are at times replaced or modified with time. This is seen in the transformation which some of the customs undergo in *The Scent of Pepper*. Here the custom of defeating nine suitors at a Kodava marriage is gradually replaced with the one in which nine banana trees are cut by the suitor. Rituals may undergo change with the passage of time. The elaborate ceremonies in an orthodox society hence appear irrational to a modern one. While Majid denounces some of the customs followed by the Muslim community, his parents passively accept them. Mali in *The Vendor of Sweets* too does not share his father's views regarding marriage and the ceremonies associated with it. Through their works, novelists depict the forces of change in society. This is seen in Subbu's dry wedding which creates much communal resentment among the Kodava community. Most of the instances in which the individual tries to break the tradition with the accepted beliefs and ways of living bring unhappiness to him. As with Moorthy, Naranappa, and Appachu, social ostracism is the punishment meted out for the breach of caste rules. They are considered outcasts by the community. While the characters conforming to time-honoured norms lead a contented life, the deviants head towards a frustrating, lonely existence. Novelists not only expose the need for reforms in a particular society, but also portray the changes that accompany them. The growing frustration makes people rebel against the traditional practices in society. But, the rebellion is mostly thwarted in a conventional social set-up.

They find themselves unable to go against the established social values. This is true of the society depicted in R.K. Narayan's works. The new values and approaches which find their way into this society are often unable to establish themselves because of the existing ones which have a firm hold on the people. Though novelists portray characters (like Savitri, Chandran, and Naranappa) that make an attempt to go against the prevailing practices in society, they also hint at the impossibility of a total break with the past. These rebels find it difficult to face the collective force of a traditional society. This is true of Indian life and society too. The tendency of social systems to resist or minimize the effects of disturbing outside influence, and a natural tendency to return to a prior steady state. But, as psychologists observe, whoever protects himself against what is new and strange and thereby regresses to the past, falls into the same neurotic condition as the man who identifies himself with the new and runs away from the past.

The depiction of Indian life and society is influenced by the novelist's life and background. Works of creative writers like R.K. Narayan, U.R. Anantha Murthy, and Raja Rao are conditioned by their traditional social set-up. In their orthodox milieu rituals and ceremonies form a central part of the life of the characters. Their characters are more or less conservative and move within a tradition-bound atmosphere which has its bearing on their mind. Naranappa reveals the hold of his orthodox community before his death. This is also conveyed through Moorthy in *Kanthapura*. The Hindu social backgrounds against which these novelists develop their stories throw light on some of the rituals and practices found in Indian society. R.K. Narayan himself has admitted his inability to write novels without Krishna, Ganesh, astrologers etc. The influence which is deeply ingrained in these creative writers finds expression in their works.

Various linguistic means are adopted by novelists to refer to Indian rituals and ceremonies in their works. The Indian English novelist finds it difficult to use a language equivalent to convey the unique flavour of Indian life. They try to reflect the rhythm and sensibility of the Indian psyche. Novelists like

Rohinton Mistry, Kavery Nambisan, and Mulk Raj Anand use words associated with rituals and ceremonies. This not only evokes the Indian atmosphere, but also contributes toward depicting the particular culture described. They help in conveying the Indian sensibility. Indian words are employed to convey ideas which are difficult to translate. These native words are sometimes used because they come spontaneously when the character is emotionally charged. The translations at times seem out of place and hence a native equivalent is preferred. Words pertaining to Indian rituals and ceremonies occur in works like *Samskara*, *Childhood Friend* (words pertaining to Muslim life), *Such a Long Journey* (words associated with Parsi life), and *The God of Small Things* (words from the Malayalam vocabulary). *The Scent of Pepper* is scattered with words from the Kodava life. The general tempo of Indian sensibility and the rhythm of Indian speech are conveyed through some of the Indian English works. Though the native words are often italicized, the absence of a glossary or other ways of description (as in *Such a Long Journey* and *The Scent of Pepper*) at times makes it difficult to understand them. The use of native words helps to create a local ambience.

A bewildering variety of beliefs and practices are prevalent in the country. The powerful hold of festivals, rituals, traditional values and attitudes on the Indian psyche is seen here. Rites and rituals differ from community to community (apart from regional variation), and society to society. Besides being significant sociologically and psychologically, they serve as literary devices too. The description of these rituals in Indian English literature serves different purpose in the context in which they are used. They become integral to the total pattern and enhance the atmosphere created therein. They have been dealt with in different ways in these works. Indian English fiction not only describes the rituals, but also focuses on their influence on Indian society and people.

The superstitions and taboos which characterized primitive thought linger in the human mind. Man finds himself unable to shed these age old superstitions and beliefs. Rituals and ceremonies hold a significant place in human life. But, religion is often confused with the mechanical participation in a rite or passive acquiescence to dogmas. The ceremony often becomes the essential thing and pushes aside the underlying spirit. The special conscientiousness with which it is carried out, and the anxiety which springs from its neglect stamp the ceremony as a sacred act. Religion, with its rituals and practices, gives man an assurance which permits him to bear courageously the burden of his present life, and face the uncertainties which surround him. In spite of rapid industrialization and scientific developments, people cling on to religious practices and ceremonies. Man has to adapt to these changes, while the society tries to maintain its *status quo* and attain stability in the midst of change. Various rituals and customs survive the advent of modernity, as is evident from their hold over human life and thought. The preceding chapters affirm this wholesome process to a remarkable extent. Indian English novels gain a lot of impetus and inspiration from the rites, rituals, and ceremonies in human life. In turn, Indian English novels do serve as a critique on Indian life and society. They form an essential layer of Indian culture and civilization.

Bibliography

Novels

Achebe, Chinua. *Things Fall Apart, The African Trilogy.* London: Picador, 1988.

Anand, Mulk Raj. *Coolie.* Delhi: Hind Pocket Books, 1972.

——. *Gauri.* New Delhi: Orient Paperback, 1976.

——. *Lament on the Death of a Master of Arts.* Delhi: Hind Pocket Books, 1967.

——. *Untouchable.* Delhi: Orient Paperbacks, 1970.

Antharjanam, Lalithambika. *Agnisaakshi.* Thrissur: Current Books, 1976.

Banerjee, Tarasankar. *Ganadevata.* Trans. Lila Ray. Mumbai: Pearl Publications Pvt. Ltd., 1969.

Basheer, Vaikom Muhammad. *Childhood Friend.* Trans. R.E. Asher and Achamma. *Me Grandad' Ad An Elephant!* Edinburgh: Edinburgh University Press, 1980.

Bhattacharya, Bhabani. *A Goddess Named Gold.* Delhi: Hind Pocket Books, 1960.

——. *He Who Rides A Tiger.* New Delhi: Arnold-Heinemann, 1977.

Desai, Anita. *Cry, the Peacock.* Delhi: Orient Paperback, 1980.

——. *Fasting, Feasting.* London: Vintage, 2000.

Krishnan, Rajam. *Lamps in the Whirlpool.* Trans. Uma Narayanan and Prema Seetharam. Madras: Macmillan Indian Ltd., 1995.

Malgonkar, Manohar. *A Bend in the Ganges.* New Delhi: Orient Paperback, 1964.

——. *The Princes.* New Delhi: Orient Paperback, 1970.

Markandaya, Kamala. *The Coffer Dams*. Delhi: Hind Pocket Books, 1969.

——. *The Golden Honeycomb*. London: Chatto and Windus, 1977.

——. *A Handful of Rice*. New Delhi: Orient Paperback, 1966.

——. *Nectar in a Sieve*. Mumbai: Jaico Publishing House, 1956.

——. *The Nowhere Man*. London: Allen Lane, 1973.

——. *Two Virgins*. New Delhi: Vikas Publishing House Pvt. Ltd., 1977.

Menon, O. Chandu. *Indulekha*. Trans. W. Dumergue. Calicut: Mathrubhumi Printing & Publishing, Co. Ltd., 1965.

Mistry, Rohinton. *A Fine Balance*. New York: Vintage Books, 1996.

——. *Such a Long Journey*. New Delhi: Penguin Books, 1998.

Murthy, U.R. Anantha. *Samskara*. Trans. A.K. Ramanujan. New Delhi: Oxford University Press, 1995.

Nambisan, Kavery. *The Scent of Pepper*. New Delhi: Penguin Books, 1996.

Narayan, R.K. *The Bachelor of Arts*. Madras: Indian Thought Publications, 1995.

——. *The Dark Room*. Mysore: Indian Thought Publications, 1996.

——. *The English Teacher*. Chennai: Indian Thought Publications, 1998.

——. *The Financial Expert*. London: Methuen, 1952.

——. *Grandmother's Tale*. Madras: Indian Thought Publications, 1992.

——. *The Guide*. Mysore: Indian Thought Publications, 1992.

——. *The Man-Eater of Malgudi*. London: Four Square, 1965.

——. *The Painter of Signs*. Mysore: Indian Thought Publications, 1993.

——. *Swami and Friends*. Mysore: Indian Thought Publications, 1944.

——. *The Vendor of Sweets*. Madras: Indian Thought Publications, 1994.

——. *Waiting for the Mahatma*. Mysore: Indian Thought Publications, 1997.

——. *The World of Nagaraj*. Mysore: Indian Thought Publications, 1993.

Rao, Raja. *Kanthapura*. Delhi: Orient Paperback, 1970.

——. *The Cat and Shakespeare*. Delhi: Orient Paperback, 1991.

——. *The Serpent and the Rope*. Delhi: Orient Paperback, 1995.

Roy, Arundhati. *The God of Small Things*. New Delhi: India Ink, 1997.

Sethumadhavan, A. *Pandavapuram*. Trans. Prema Jayakumar. Madras: Macmillan India Ltd., 1995.

Sreedevi, K.B. *Yajnam*. Thrissur: Life Books Pvt. Ltd., 1974.

Singh, Khushwant. *Train to Pakistan*. 1956. London: Four Square, 1961.

Subramanian, Vani. *Reminiscences*. Madras: Affiliated East-West Press Pvt. Ltd., 1995.

Towers, Robert. *The Necklace of Kali*. London: Transworld Publishers, 1963.

Tharoor, Shashi. *The Great Indian Novel*. New Delhi: Penguin Books, 1989.

Books

Amur, G.S. *Manohar Malgonkar*. New Delhi: Arnold-Heinemann, 1973.

Banton, Michael, ed. *Anthropological Approaches to the Study of Religion*. London: Tavistock Publication Ltd., 1966.

Bapat, Tara. *Rituals and Festivals of India*. Mumbai: Popular Prakashan Pvt. Ltd., 1998.

Benedict, Ruth. *Patterns of Culture*. London: Routledge and Kegan Paul Ltd., 1935.

Bharucha, Nilufer. E. and Vilas Sarang, eds. *Indian English Fiction: 1980-90: An Assessment*. Delhi: B.R. Publishing Corporation, 1994.

Bhatnagar, Manmohan. K., ed. *Commonwealth English Literature*. New Delhi: Atlantic Publishers and Distributors, 1999.

——. ed. *Indian Writings in English*. Vol. 1. New Delhi: Atlantic Publishers and Distributors, 1996.

Bhatnagar, Manmohan. K. and M. Rajeshwar, eds. *Indian Writings in English*, 8 vols. New Delhi: Atlantic Publishers and Distributors, 2000.

Bhattacharyya, Narendra Nath. *Ancient Indian Rituals and their Social Contents*. Delhi: Manohar Book Service, 1975.

Brown, A.R. Radcliffe. *Structure and Function in Primitive Society*. London: Cohen and West Ltd., 1969.

Cowasjee, Saros. *Studies in Indian and Anglo-Indian Fiction*. New Delhi: Harper Collins-Indus, 1993.

Crawley, Ernest. *Dimensions of Marriage in Primitive Society*. Vol. II. New Delhi: Caxton Publications, 1989.

Das, Bijay Kumar. *Critical Essays on Post-Colonial Literature*. New Delhi: Atlantic Publishers and Distributors, 1999.

Dayananda, James. Y. *Manohar Malgonkar*. Boston: Twayne Publishers, 1974.

Desai, S.K. and G.N. Devy. *Critical Thought: An Anthology of Twentieth Century Indian English Essays*. New Delhi: Sterling Publishers, 1987.

Dhawan, R.K. ed. *Commonwealth Fiction*. Vol. 1. New Delhi: Classical Publishing Company, 1988.

——. ed. *Post-Colonial Discourse: A Study of Contemporary Literature*. New Delhi: Prestige Books, 1997.

Dinesh, Kamini, ed. *Between Spaces of Silence: Women Creative Writers*. New Delhi: Sterling Publishers Pvt. Ltd., 1994.

Dodiya, Jaydipsinh, ed. *Contemporary Indian Writings in English*. New Delhi: Atlantic Publishers and Distributors, 1998.

Dodiya, Jaydipsinh and K.V. Surendran, eds. *Indian Women Writers: Critical Perspectives*. New Delhi: Sarup and Sons, 1999.

Drisen, Cynthia Vanden. *Centering the Margins: Perspectives on Literatures in English from India, Africa, Australia*. New Delhi: Prestige Books, 1995.

Eakambaram, N. and V. Saraswathi, eds. *Glimpses of World Literature: Essays presented to Prof. M.S. Nagarajan*. Delhi: Pencraft International, 1988.

Ember, Carol R. and Melvin Ember. *Anthropology*. 6th ed. New Jersey: Prentice Hall, 1973.

Frazer, James G. *The Golden Bough*. Abr. ed. London: Macmillan Press Ltd., 1922.

Freud, Sigmund. *The Psycho-Pathology of Everyday Life*. Trans. Alan Tyson. Ed. James Strachey. London: Ernest Benn Ltd., 1966.

Frye, Northrop. *The Anatomy of Criticism: Four Essays*. Princeton: Princeton University Press, 1971.

Gay, Peter, ed. *The Freud-Reader*. London: Vintage, 1995.

Gopal, N.R. and Suman Sachar, eds. *Indian English Poetry and Fiction: A Critical Evaluation*. New Delhi: Atlantic Publishers and Distributors, 2000.

Gupta, G.S. Balarama, ed. *Studies in Indian Fiction in English*. Gulbarga: Jiwe Publications, 1987.

Gupta, Santhosh, ed. *Contemporary Indian Literature: Positions and Expositions*. Jaipur: Rawat Publications, 2000.

Hammond, Peter B. *An Introduction to Cultural and Social Anthropology*. New York: Macmillan Publishing Co., Inc.; London: Collier Macmillan Publishers, 1971.

Hemenway, Stephen Ignatius. *The Novel of India*. 2 vols. Calcutta: Writers Workshop, 1975.

Herder, J.G. *On Social and Political Culture*. Trans. F.M. Barnard. London: Cambridge University Press, 1969.

Hume, Robert Ernest, Trans. *The Thirteen Principal Upanishads*. Rev. ed. Delhi: Oxford University Press, 1995.

Hutchinson, Walter, ed. *Customs of the World: A Popular Account of the Manners, Rites and Ceremonies of Men and Women in All Countries*. Vol. 1. New Delhi: Concept Publishing Company, 1984.

Iyengar, K.R. Srinivasa. *Indian Writing in English*, 5th ed. New Delhi: Sterling Publishers Pvt. Ltd., 1985.

Jain, Jasbir. *Writers of the Indian Diaspora*. Jaipur: Rawat Publications, 1998.

Joseph, Margaret P. *Kamala Markandaya*. New Delhi: Arnold-Heinemann, 1980.

Joseph, Mariamma. *Marriage Among Indian Christians*. Jaipur: Rawat Publications, 1994.

Juneja, O.M.P. *Post-Colonial Novel: Narratives of Colonial Consciousness*. New Delhi: Creative Books, 1995.

Jung, Carl. *Modern Man in Search of a Soul*. Trans. W.S. Dell, and Cary. F. Baynes. London: Routledge and Kegan Paul, 1933.

Kachru, Braj B. *The Indianization of English: The English Language in India*. New Delhi: Oxford University Press, 1983.

Kantak, V.Y. *Perspectives on Indian Literary Culture*. Delhi: Pencraft International, 1996.

Keesing, Roger M. *Cultural Anthropology: A Contemporary Perspective*. New York: Holt, Rinehart and Winston, 1976.

Khan, A.G. *Canadian Literature and Indian Literature: New Perspective*. New Delhi: Creative Books, 1995.

Khan, M.Q. and A.G. Khan, eds. *Changing Faces of Women in Indian Writing in English*. New Delhi: Creative Books, 1995.

Kirpal, Viney, ed. *The Post-Modern Indian English Novel: Interrogating the 1980's and 1990's*. Mumbai: Allied Publishers Ltd., 1996.

Krishnaswamy, Shantha. *The Woman in Indian Fiction in English*. New Delhi: Ashish Publishing House, 1984.

Kudchedkar, Shirin, ed. *Post-Modernism and Feminism: Canadian Contexts*. Delhi: Pencraft International, 1995.

Lal, Malashri, ed. *Feminist Spaces: Cultural Readings from India and Canada*. New Delhi: Allied Publishers Ltd., 1997.

Madan, T.N., ed. *Religion in India*. Delhi: Oxford University Press, 1991.

Malinowski, Bronislaw. *Crime and Custom in Savage Society*. ed. C.K. Ogden. London: Routledge and Kegan Paul Ltd., 1926.

Manuel. M. and K. Ayyappa Panicker, eds. *English and India: Essays Presented to Prof. Samuel Mathai on his Seventieth Birthday*. Madras: Macmillan India Ltd., 1998.

Marudanayagam, P. *Decolonisation and After: Studies in Indian and Canadian Writings*. New Delhi: Creative Books, 1999.

Mehta, P.P. *Indo-Anglian Fiction: An Assessment*. Bareilly: Prakash Book Depot, 1968.

Moore, Alexander. *Cultural Anthropology*. New York: Harper and Row Publishers, 1978.

Muir, Edward. *Ritual in Early Modern Europe*. Cambridge: Cambridge University Press, 1997.

Mukherjee, Meenakshi, ed. *Considerations: Twelve Studies of Indo-Anglian Writing*. New Delhi: Allied Publishers, 1977.

——. *Realism and Reality: The Novel and Society in India*. New Delhi: Oxford University Press, 1994.

——. *The Twice Born Fiction: Themes and Techniques of the Indian Novel in English*. New Delhi: Heinemann Educational Books Ltd., 1971.

Murphy, Robert F. *Cultural and Social Anthropology: An Overture*. New Jersey: Prentice-Hall, 1989.

Naik, M.K., ed. *Aspects of Indian Writing in English*. Madras: Macmillan India Ltd., 1979.

——. *A History of Indian English Literature*. New Delhi: Sahitya Akademi, 1982.

——. *Studies in Indian English Literature*. New Delhi: Sterling Publishers Pvt. Ltd., 1987.

Naipaul, V.S. *An Area of Darkness*. England: Penguin Books Ltd., 1964.

——. *The Wounded Civilization*. New Delhi: Penguin Books India (P) Ltd., 1979.

Narasimhaiah, C.D., ed. *Fiction and the Reading Public in India*. Mysore: University of Mysore, 1967.

Narasimhaiah, C.D. and C.N. Srinath, eds. *Indian Literature in English: Contemporary Assessments*. Mysore: Dhvanyaloka Publication, 1980.

——. *The Swan and the Eagle*. Simla: Indian Institute of Advanced Study, 1968.

Osmania University. Dept. of English. *Critical Responses: Commonwealth Literature*. Vol. 1. New Delhi: Sterling Publishers Pvt. Ltd., 1993.

Page, Norman, ed. *The Language of Literature*. London: Macmillan Press Ltd., 1994.

Panday, Birendra. *Indian Women Novelists in English*. New Delhi: Sarup and Sons, 2001.

Pandey, Raj Bali. *Hindu Samskaras: Socio-religious Study of the Hindu Sacraments*. Delhi: Motilal Banarsidass, 1969.

Pandey, Mithilesh. K., ed. *Recent Indian Literature in English: A Cultural Perspective*. New Delhi: Anmol Publications Pvt. Ltd., 1999.

Pandey, Sudhakar and R. Raj Rao, eds. *Image of India in the Indian Novel in English: 1960-85*. Hyderabad: Orient Longman Ltd., 1993.

Pandey, Surya Nath, ed. *Contemporary Indian Women Writers in English: A Feminist Perspective*. New Delhi: Atlantic Publishers and Distributors, 1999.

——. ed. *Writing in a Post-Colonial Space*. New Delhi: Atlantic Publishers and Distributors, 1999.

Parameswaran, Uma. *Kamala Markandaya*. Jaipur: Rawat Publications, 2000.

——. *A Study of Representative Indo-English Novelists*. New Delhi: Vikas Publishing House Pvt. Ltd., 1976.

Pathak, R.S. *Modern Indian Novel in English*. New Delhi: Creative Books, 1999.

Paul, Premila. *The Novel of Mulk Raj Anand: A Thematic Study*. New Delhi: Sterling Publishers Pvt. Ltd., 1983.

Prasad, Amar Nath, ed. *Critical Response to Indian Fiction in English*. New Delhi: Atlantic Publishers and Distributors, 2001.

——. *Studies in Indian English Fiction*. New Delhi: Sarup and Sons, 2001.

Prasad, Madhusudan. *Indian English Novelists: An Anthology of Critical Essays*. New Delhi: Sterling Publishers Pvt. Ltd., 1982.

——. *Perspectives on Kamala Markandaya*. Ghaziabad: Vimal Prakashan Publishers, 1984.

Raghavacharyulu, V.K. *The Critical Response: Selected Essays on the American, Commonwealth, Indian and British Traditions in Literature*. Madras: Macmillan Company India Ltd., 1980.

Rajan, P.K., et al. eds. *Commonwealth Literature: Themes and Techniques: Essays in Honour of Ayyappa Panicker*. Delhi: Ajanta Publishers, 1993.

Rao, Adapa Ramakrishnan, and M. Sivaram Krishna, eds. *When East Meets West: Indian Thought in Anglo-Indian and Indo-English Fiction*. New Delhi: Sterling Publishers Pvt. Ltd., 1994.

Rao, P. Mallikarjuna and M. Rajeshwar, eds. *Indian Fiction in English*. New Delhi: Atlantic Publishers and Distributors, 1999.

Reddy, V. Narayan Karan. *Marriages in India: A Psycho-Sociological Study*. Delhi: The Academic Press, 1978.

Reddy, K. Venkata, and P. Bayapa Reddy, eds. *The Indian Novel with a Social Purpose*. New Delhi: Atlantic Publishers and Distributors, 1999.

Righter, William. *Myth and Literature*. London: Routledge and Kegan Paul Ltd., 1975.

Rockwell, Joan. *Fact in Fiction: The Use of Literature in the Systematic Study of Society*. London: Routledge and Kegan Paul, 1974.

Rothenbuhler, Eric. W. *Ritual Communication: From Everyday Conversation to Mediated Ceremony*. New Delhi: Sage Publications, 1998.

Rushdie, Salman. *Imaginary Homelands*. London: Gramta Books, 1991.

Ruthevan, K.K. *Myth*. London: Methuen & Co. Ltd., 1976.

Sankari, Siva. *Knit India Through Literature*. Vol. 1. Chennai: East-West Books Pvt. Ltd., 1998.

Schusky, Ernest. L. *The Study of Cultural Anthropology*. New York: Holt, Rinehart and Winston, 1975.

Sharma, Ashok Kumar. *The Novels of Manohar Malgonkar: A Study*. Delhi: B.R. Publishing Corporation, 1995.

Sharma, Krishna. *Protest in Indian English Fiction*. Jaipur: Bohra Prakashan, 1995.

Sharma, R.S. *Anita Desai*. New Delhi: Arnold-Heinemann Publishers, 1981.

Shirwadkar, Meena. *Image of Woman in the Indo-Anglian Novel*. New Delhi: Sterling Publishers Pvt. Ltd., 1979.

Sinari, Ramakant A. *The Structure of Indian Thought*. New Delhi: Oxford Paperbacks, 1990.

Singh, Avadhesh K., ed. *Contemporary Indian Fiction in English*. New Delhi: Creative Books, 1993.

Singh, Nagendra K.R., ed. *Encyclopaedia of Hinduism: A Continuing Series*. 30 vols. New Delhi: Anmol Publications Pvt. Ltd., 1997.

Singh, P.K. *The Novels of R.K. Narayan: A Critical Evaluation*. New Delhi: Atlantic Publishers and Distributors, 1999.

Singh, Pramod Kumar. *Five Contemporary Indian Novelists: An Anthology of Critical Studies on Mulk Raj Anand, Raja Rao, R.K. Narayan, Kamala Markandaya, Bhabani Bhattacharya*. Jaipur: Book Enclave, 2001.

——. ed. *Indian Fiction in English*. New Delhi: Atlantic Publishers and Distributors, 2001.

Singh, Sunaina. *The Novels of Margaret Atwood and Anita Desai: A Comparative Study in Feminist Perspectives*. New Delhi: Creative Books, 1994.

Sinha, K.N. *Mulk Raj Anand*. New Delhi: Kalyani Publishers, 1989.

Sinha, Krishna Nandan, ed. *Indian Writing in English*. New Delhi: Heritage Publishers, 1979.

Sodhi, Meena. *The Indian English Writing: The Autobiographical Mode*. New Delhi: Creative Books, 1999.

Srivastava, Avadesh K., ed. *Alien Voice: Perspective on Commonwealth Literature*. Lucknow: Print House, 1981.

Srivastava, Sharad. *The New Woman in Indian English Fiction*. New Delhi: Creative Books, 1996.

Staal, Frits. *Ritual and Mantras: Rules without Meaning*. Delhi: Motilal Banarsidass Publishers Pvt. Ltd., 1996.

Sundaram, P.S. *R.K. Narayan*. New Delhi: Arnold-Heinemann Publishers Pvt. Ltd., 1973.

Surendran, K.V. *The God of Small Things: A Saga of Lost Dreams*. New Delhi: Atlantic Publishers and Distributors, 2000.

——. *Indian Writing: Critical Perspectives*. New Delhi: Sarup and Sons, 2000.

——. *New Perspectives on Indian and Western Fiction*. New Delhi: Sarup and Sons, 2000.

Symp, A., ed. *Indian Literature Since Independence*. New Delhi: Sahitya Akademi, 1973.

Tharu, Susie and K. Lalita, eds. *Women Writing in India*. Delhi: Oxford University Press, 1993.

Trumbell, H. Clay. *Oriental Customs Traditions and Social Life*. Delhi: Mittal Publications, 1986.

Uniyal, Ranu. *The Fiction of Margaret Drabble and Anita Desai: Women and Landscape*. New Delhi: Creative Books, 2000.

Verghese, C. Paul. *Essays on Indian Writings in English*. New Delhi: N.V. Publications, 1975.

Verma, C.D. *The Exile-Hero and the Reintegrating Vision in Indian English Fiction*. New Delhi: Sterling Publishers Pvt. Ltd., 1991.

Wali, S.K. *Kamala Markandaya's Nectar in a Sieve: A Stylistic Study*. Jaipur: Print Well Publishers, 1987.

Walsh, William. *Commonwealth Literature*. London: Oxford University Press, 1973.

——. *R.K. Narayan: A Critical Appreciation*. London: William Heinemann Ltd., 1982.

Wandrekar, Kalpana. *The Ailing Aliens: A Study of 'the Immigrant Psyche' in Six Indian English Novels*. Gulbarga: Jiwe Publications, 1996.

Whitman, R. Douglas. *Adjustment: The Development and Organization of Human Behaviour*. Oxford: Oxford University Press, 1980.

Wilkins, W.J. *Hindu Mythology*. 2nd ed. Calcutta: Rupa & Co., 1998.

Williams, Haydn Moore. *Studies in Modern Indian Fiction in English*. Vol. 2. Calcutta: A Writers Workshop Publication, 1973.

Young-Eisendrath, Polly and Terence Dawson, eds. *The Cambridge Companion to Jung*. Cambridge: Cambridge University Press, 1997.

Articles

Journals

Asher, R.E. "Basheer's Diversity." *Haritham* 4 (1994): 11-18.

Basheer, Vaikom Muhammad. "How I Became a Writer." *Haritham* 4 (1994): 20-25.

Deshpande, Shashi. "The Dilemma of the Woman Writer." *Literary Criterion* XX. 4 (1985): 31-34.

Devsen, Nabaneeta. "Man, Woman and Fiction." *Literary Criterion* XX. 4 (1985): 91-101.

Dey, Esha. "Woman as Object: The Feminine Condition in a Decadent Patriarchy." *Literary Criterion* XX. 4 (1985): 9-19.

Gowri, G. "Kamala Markandaya's Male Protagonists." *Literary Half-Yearly* XXXIII. 2 (1992): 56-61.

Gupta, R.K. "The 'Ghost' and the 'Demon': An Approach to U.R. Anantha Murthy's *Samskara*." *Journal of Commonwealth Literature* XVI. 1 (1981): 16-24.

Heilbrun, Carolyn. G. "Marriage and Contemporary Fiction." *Critical Inquiry* 5.2 (1978): 309-22.

Kirpal, Vineypal Kaur. "An Analysis of Narayan's Technique." *Ariel* 14. 4 (1983): 16-19.

Knippling, Alpana Sharma. "R.K. Narayan, Raja Rao and Modern English Discourse in Colonial India." *Modern Fiction Studies* 39.1 (1993): 169-86.

Korg, Jacob. "Ritual and Experiment in Modern Poetry." *Journal of Modern Literature* 7.1 (1979): 127-46.

Libert, Florence. "An Interview with Anita Desai. 1 August 1989. Cambridge. England." *World Literature Written in English* 30.1 (1990): 47-55.

Murthy, U.R. Anantha. "Is Indian Society Congenial to the Creation of a Classic? A Writer's View." *Literary Criterion* XV. 2 (1980): 54-61.

Narasimhaiah, C.D. "Women in Fiction and Fiction by Women." *Literary Criterion* XX. 4 (1985): 1-8.

Nayar, Pramod K. "The (B) Other of Borders: Kavery Nambisan's *The Scent of Pepper*." *Haritham* 10 (1998): 80-84.

Olinder, Britta. "Reality and Myth in R.K. Narayan's Novels." *Literary Criterion* XX.2 (1985): 8-22.

Paniker, K. Ayyappa. "Basheer." *Haritham* 4 (1994): 7-10.

Perera, Senath W. "Towards a Limited Emancipation: Women in Raja Rao's Kanthapura." *Ariel* 23.4 (1992): 99-110.

Poduval, Satish. "Region & Community: Questions for Modernity and Culture." *Haritham* 12 (2000): 11-37.

Radha, K. "The Hunger and Anger of Ravi in Kamala Markandaya's *A Handful of Rice*." *Indian Journal of English Studies* XXX (1991-92): 13-20.

Sengupta, Jayita. "East-West Encounter in the Novels of Kamala Markandaya." *Quest* X. 2 (1996): 21-28.

Magazines

Murthy, Sachidananda. "The Forbidden Fruits of Malgudi." *Week* 27 May 2001: 68-69.

Singh, Khushwant. "Ban Cremation of Hindus and Sikhs by Using Fire wood." *Mirror Today* Oct. 2000: 90-91.

——. "Modesty? Blase!" *Week* 27 May 2001: 67-68.

Newspaper

Chakravarthy, Chandrima. "Roots and Routes: A Search for India." *New Sunday Express Magazine* [Kozhikode] Nov. 2000: 24.

Dasgupta, Sayantan. "Weed Out the Colonial Hangover." *New Sunday Express Magazine* [Kozhikode] 8 July 2001: 25.

Electronic sources

Coorg-Online. 7 Jan. 2002 <http: //www.coorg-online.com>.

Landow, Shoshana M. "Changing Faces of Women in South Asian Fiction." 1991. 19 Oct. 2001 <http://65.107.211.208/india/literature/sml3.html>.

——. "The Value of Suffering in Kamala Markandaya's *Nectar in a Sieve*." 1991. 22 Feb. 2002 <http://65.107.211.208/india/literature/sml9.html>.

Index